# DEDICATION

## THIS BOOK IS DEDICATED TO LIDIA ZUBLER (20.8.1936 - 20.10.2012).

Lidia originally attended the group for support when her then husband came into conflict with the criminal law. Lidia, who worked in the self-governing, collectively run, politically engaged and organically focused Café Zähringer in Zurich, served as the National representative of the Group for Switzerland. She attended nearly all the group's conferences, travelling independently and staying at the cheapest accommodation in the most interesting parts of the host city. Lidia was a gentle, quiet and thoughtful person of great integrity who lived her life according to her values. At conferences she listened attentively to every speaker and enjoyed interesting and informative conversations. Although her contributions were few Lidia provided perceptive insights on a range of topics. Her presence and contribution to conferences will be missed. The values she taught us we hope will live on.

# ACKNOWLEDGEMENTS

The editors would like to thank the following for permission to reproduce copyright material.

**Chapter**

| | |
|---|---|
| 3 | Reprinted by permission of Maeve McMahon and Gail Kellough. 1987 |
| 4 | Reprinted by permission of the European Group for the Study of Deviancy and Social Control, 1974 |
| 5 | Reprinted by permission of the European Group for the Study of Deviancy and Social Control, 2013 |
| 6 | Reprinted by permission of the European Group for the Study of Deviancy and Social Control, 1991 |
| 7 | Reprinted by permission of Phil Scraton, 2006 |
| 8 | Reprinted by permission of Andrea Beckmann, 2009 |
| 9 | Reprinted by permission of Stanley Cohen, 2009 |
| 10 | Reprinted by permission of the European Group for the Study of Deviancy and Social Control, 2013 |
| 11 | Reprinted by permission of the European Group for the Study of Deviancy and Social Control, 2013 |
| 13 | Reprinted by permission of the European Group for the Study of Deviancy and Social Control, 1979 |
| 14 | Reprinted by permission of Lit Verlag, 2010 |
| 15 | Reprinted by permission of the European Group for the Study of Deviancy and Social Control, 1988 |
| 16 | Reprinted by permission of the European Group for the Study of Deviancy and Social Control, 1989 |
| 17 | Reprinted by permission of the European Group for the Study of Deviancy and Social Control, 1979 |
| 18 | Reprinted by permission of the European Group for the Study of Deviancy and Social Control, 2013 |

| 20 | Reprinted by permission of the European Group for the Study of Deviancy and Social Control, 1982 |
|----|---|
| 21 | Reprinted by permission of the European Group for the Study of Deviancy and Social Control, 1984 |
| 22 | Reprinted by permission of the European Group for the Study of Deviancy and Social Control, 1985 |
| 23 | Reprinted by permission of the European Group for the Study of Deviancy and Social Control, 1986 |
| 24 | Reprinted by permission of the European Group for the Study of Deviancy and Social Control, 1987 |
| 25 | Reprinted by permission of the estate of Karen Leander 2007 |

All possible care has been taken to trace ownership of the selections included and to make full acknowledgement for their use.

# CONTENTS

# CRITIQUE AND DISSENT

## AN INTRODUCTION

### Joanna Gilmore, J.M. Moore and David Scott

Since its first conference in 1973 the *European Group for the Study of Deviance and Social Control* (European Group) has been at the forefront of debates and creative developments in the emergence and consolidation of critical criminologies in Europe and beyond. 40 years on from its founding conference, the European Group remains a vibrant and relevant organisation. *Critique and Dissent* has been put together to help mark the 40th Anniversary of the first conference and brings together papers delivered at the annual conferences of the European Group from 1973–2012. In compiling this anthology we have sought to:

- bring together and explore the diversity and richness of some of the most innovative and exciting writings from European Group conferences;
- provide an anthology for academics, postgraduate and advanced undergraduate students wishing to explore the theoretical contribution of the European Group to the development of critical analysis;

- discuss detailed, critical and analytical accounts of the changing face of deviance and social control in Europe and beyond;
- illustrate the theoretical depth of critical analysis and critical criminologies through the different interpretive frameworks and understandings that have character-ised the development of the European Group.

In this opening chapter we provide a brief history of the European Group and highlight some of its key theoretical and political influences before explaining the rationale of the selection of the following chapters.

## THEORETICAL AND POLITICAL PRIORITIES

*Critique and Dissent* emphasises the theoretical and political priorities of the *European Group for the Study of Deviance and Social Control.* Its conferences have explored deviant behav-iour, harm, power, social control, punishment and regulation from various philosophical viewpoints. Indeed, European Group conferences have been characterised by the absence of a uniform dogma. State punishment's function as an instru-ment of dominance has been repeatedly emphasised together with explanations of 'crime' and criminality that perceives them as reflections of the societal structure. Within the group, there has been a desire to investigate how human/civil rights are being eroded through shifting political and State control. The European Group has over the last 40 years sought to promote critical and radical criminology as a legitimate field of research and to provide a forum through which critical academics can connect with those outside the academy who are actively working for social justice.

The development of the sociology of deviance and 'critical criminology' since the 1970s in Europe and elsewhere has thus been reflected in the publication of papers delivered at the 40 previous European Group conferences. Making connec-tions between everyday struggles, lived experiences and social structures - firstly around class, but later around 'race', sexuality, gender, age and disability - European Group papers have helped produce a new critical discourse for understanding conflicts, harms and troubles that are popularly referred to as 'crime'. Papers at European Group conferences have encouraged the embedding of a critical analysis exploring the relationship between the individual and the social through consideration of the boundaries placed upon everyday interactions, choices, meanings and motivations by determining structural contexts.[1] Constructions of 'crime', deviance and social control have been located within the power-knowledge axis and social structures pertaining in our given historical conjuncture. This has ultimately led to the centrality of questions concerning power, inequality and legitimacy. Yet the European Group has always encouraged a nuanced and sophisticated understanding of the role of social control. Rather than seeing the law as a crude instrument of capitalist oppressors, members have pointed to the contradictory nature of the law in capitalist societies: law enforcement and mechanisms of social control can both protect the general population, including vulnerable and/or impoverished individuals, whilst at the same time play a decisive role in maintaining structural divisions. Each conference has located the group's theoretical and political priorities to the study of deviance and social control within its localised/national context to encourage connections with grass roots activism and social movements.

The origins of the European Group lie in a range of projects that occurred in a number of European countries in the late 1960s and early 1970s. These included various patients' and prisoners' movements; radical and social lawyers; the *Arbeitsgruppe Junger Kriminologen* (AJK) in Germany; and the *National Deviancy Conference* (NDC) in Britain. In 1970 three visiting scholars at the *School of Criminology* in the University

---

[1]    For further discussion of political and theoretical priorities see Sim et al. "Crime, the state and critical analysis" 1987; Scraton & Chadwick, "Challenging new orthodoxies: the theoretical and political priorities of critical criminology", 1991; Barton et al, "Developing a criminological imagination", 2006.

of California at Berkeley - Stan Cohen, from Durham University, England; Mario Simondi, from the University of Florence, Italy; and Karl Schuman from Bielefeld University in Germany - were allocated the same office to share. As they exchanged ideas from their various parts of Europe, Cohen declared, 'it's crazy that we have to come to Berkeley to see each other. Let's do something when we go back to Europe?'[2] From this chance encounter plans developed and, together with Laurie Taylor and Margherita Ciacci, the three produced the first draft of the manifesto of the *European Group*. A later version of this manifesto, adopted by the Group at its second conference, is included as chapter three of this collection.

## OVERVIEW OF CONFERENCES

From its beginnings the European Group has been explicitly political. Although the original Manifesto stated that the group was 'Marxist' Stan Cohen has highlighted how, from its earliest days, the European Group had 'a strong anarchistic and libertarian ethos'.[3] It has always been willing to take sides - siding consistently with the powerless and progressive forces. The focus of the first conference - held in Florence, Italy - was on prisoners' struggles and part of this conference was suspended so that participants could join a demonstration of 15,000 people against the overthrow of the democratic Chilean government of Salvador Allende. Subsequent conferences have been characterised both by the involvement of local activists in the agendas of the group's conferences and the conference participants' involvement in local campaigns.

The conferences during the first few years focused on issues central to radical and critical criminology: 'crimes' of the powerful; the political economy of legal control; the political nature of criminal law; the role of prisoners' and patients' movements in penal and psychiatric reform; and the State's

---

[2]   Cited in McMahon and Kellough, chapter two of this book.
[3]   Cohen *personal correspondence with David Scott,* 2010.

use of violence. Towards the late 1970s, the concept of power and its manifestations were analysed both theoretically and in specific contexts such as terrorism and State violence. The 1979 Danish conference explored fluctuating forms of discipline in our societies in a series of papers that were strongly influenced by the work of Michel Foucault.

During the 1980s, the group focused on State social control policies and the response and counter strategies of the groups targeted by these policies. These considerations were often linked to ongoing local struggles. In 1981 the conference was held in Derry, Ireland during the Republican hunger strikes; in 1983 it was in Finland where an attempt by the government to outlaw 'any encouragement of homosexuality' was being resisted by the local lesbian and gay community; and in 1984 it took place in Wales during the coal miners' strike. Each conference was able to incorporate these events into its programme to both enable and enhance understanding of social control/resistance and to provide support for those engaged in the various struggles. An important conference took place in Hamburg in 1985, under the theme 'The Expansion of European Prison Systems'. This reviewed the carceral expansion setting out the major trends in European penality: harsher sentences for some crimes and some social groups; longer pre-trail detentions; increased use of both life imprisonment and short prison sentences; extended further sentences for those already imprisoned and the particularly rapid increase in the imprisonment of women and girls.

Issues relating to gender and the insights of feminism were central to the group's meetings in the late 1980s. In 1986 in Madrid meetings took place with the Spanish women's movement. In Vienna, under the theme of 'Justice and Ideology', abolitionist responses to violence against women were discussed and at the 1988 conference feminist research on justice and violence was the central theme. These discussions highlighted a continuing debate within the European Group between those who have argued that criminal justice's failure to address violence against women needs rectifying and those who question the desirability and usefulness of criminal justice and penal responses.

In the 1990s the Group responded to political changes taking place in Europe. On the one hand this involved moving away from a western European focus to incorporate the experiences/relevance of eastern European countries and on the other hand an engagement with the developing 'integration' of Europe through initiatives such as the Schengen agreement. Conferences at Potsdam (Germany) in 1991, Prague (Czech Republic) in 1993, Kazimierz Dolny (Poland) in 1997 and Palanga (Lithuania) in 1999 all took place in cities located in former communist countries. In Haarlem, in 1990, the conference explored the close relationship between penal policy and labour migration and how this was influencing a restructuring of legal systems, predating much of the contemporary analysis today on the scope and remit of 'crimmigration'. At the next conference in 1991 the implications of the changes taking place in Europe for social justice were examined. In particular the Potsdam conference explored the implications of 'Fortress Europe' for those countries and people excluded from it. This theme remained central to a number of other 1990s conferences. In 1992 in Padova, social control in the 'New' Europe was explored along with the inclusionary and exclusionary impacts of redefined citizenship. In Prague in 1993 social control strategies in Eastern and Western Europe were interrogated. The 1997 conference in Kazimierz Dolny (Poland) explored 'Europe in Transition' whilst in 1998 in Spetses (Greece) the conference focused on the control of the movement of people.

The 1990s were also characterised by the European Group's critical engagement with the concept of 'Human Rights'. In 1992 the Padova conference focused on the politics of 'rights'. Whilst human rights offered potential for progressive social transformation they also risked being deployed to support the status quo or reinforce the position of the powerful. The relationship between State crimes and human rights were

CRITIQUE AND DISSENT 19

explored in the 1996 Bangor conference. Central to the discussions of a number of conferences was the manner in which the discourse of 'rights' was being deployed to support the exclusion of the non-citizen 'other'. The manner in which migrants and refugees, minorities, deviants and prisoners were seen to be outside the scope of these 'rights' was consistently exposed.

By the end of the twentieth century the European Group had held twenty-seven annual conferences and many of the key themes explored were to be revisited in the following thirteen conferences in the current century. State punishment was analysed at the 2000 conference in Nyneshamn (Sweden) and in Padova (Italy) in 2008. In 2006 and 2011, in Corinth (Greece) and Chambery (France) respectively the politics and policing of migration were central themes. Once again these conferences engaged with the pertinent issues of the day and provided an opportunity for critical thinkers across Europe and beyond to come together and think about the problem posed and strategies of resistance. The major theme of the 2001 conference in Venice was social change, whilst Utrecht (Netherlands) in 2007 explored power. The conference held in Belfast in 2005 focused on transition whilst the 2012 conference in Nicosia explored the theme of 'Beyond the Wire'. In 2002 at Krakow (Poland) social control was explored in the context of its relationship with violence and in 2009 in Preston (England) the implications of the (then new) recession for both social control and justice was explored.

Throughout its history the European Group has questioned the role of criminologists and the control of research and knowledge within the field of criminal justice and social control. The discipline of criminology was a major themes in 2003 (Helsinki, Finland), in 2004 (Bristol, England) and in 2010 (Lesvos, Greece). It will also be the theme of the 41st Conference in Oslo, Norway in 2013. These discussions have questioned the type of research project that received State funding; which groups of researchers were granted [and which were denied] access to institutions and data, and the value placed on State commissioned research over independent research. Many in the European Group have argued that the role of the criminologist is to be a critical observer with no obligation to offer alternative/improved criminal policies. Others have argued for the direct participation in policy formation and for critical criminology's direct engagement with the various components of the criminal justice system.

# THE EUROPEAN GROUP TODAY[4]

Despite the troubling economic and political times and widespread attacks on intellectual autonomy across Universities in Europe and beyond, the European Group continues to be an essential forum for students of deviance and social control. The European Group continues to attract membership from a broad range of people - local advocacy and activist groups, academics, researchers, students, practitioners – with an array of different philosophies - Anarchism, Marxism, Feminism, Anti-racism and Penal Abolitionism. European Group conferences continue to highlight the importance of understanding the political nature of private troubles and public issues; the essentially contested nature of 'crime'; and how deviancy, normality and disorder must be located within the structural contexts of a given society. Further, by critically scrutinising the 'organised ways in which society responds to behaviour and people it regards as deviant, problematic, worrying, threatening, troublesome or undesirable in some way or another',[5] manifestations of social control, such as migration and border controls, policing, the judiciary and detention, are placed firmly in the spotlight.

The European Group continues a critical tradition that challenges privilege, power and social and economic inequalities; exposes human suffering in its many different manifestations; provides a platform for those people whose voice is elsewhere denied; and work towards profound social transformations that can promote the genuine freedom and fulfilment of *humanity*

---

[4]   See Scott, 'Opening Address of 40th Annual Conference of the European Group.'
[5]   Cohen, *Visions of Social Control* 1985: 1.

*for all.* Whilst the critique and transformation of class hierarchies remains important to the European Group, its conferences also address a myriad of wider concerns regarding nationalism, heterophobia, racism, ability, ageism, hetero-normativity and sexual divisions.[6] The European Group therefore aims to foster 'emancipatory knowledge'[7] which has the explicit political and theoretical intention of not just understanding individual and social problems, but also challenging and transforming existing power relations.

The European Group remains rooted in a philosophy of anti-elitism and non-hierarchy – at conferences it makes no difference whether someone is a first year PhD Student or highly distinguished Professor, *all* are students of deviancy and social control who meet as equals. This non-hierarchical ethos continues to be central to the democratic and participatory workings of the European Group itself with conferences deliberately organised in an informal manner which emphasises a sense of camaraderie and friendship. The European Group offers a radical alternative to the values and politics underscoring capitalist, patriarchal and neo-colonial social relations and the managerial ethos that seems to characterise many universities today. In terms of the core values of the European Group:

- rather than individualised competition, *the European Group looks to foster mutual support, cooperation and sisterly and brotherly warmth;*
- rather than false hierarchies and elitism, *the European Group aims to nurture comradeship, collegiality and solidarity with sufferers and the oppressed;*
- rather than become politically sterile through claims to scientific objectivity, neutrality and value freedom, *the European Group emphasises political commitments, direct engagement in struggle and compassion for fellow human beings in need;*

---

[6]    van Swaanigen, *Critical Criminology* 1997.
[7]    Wright, *Envisioning a real utopia* 2010.

- rather than determining research agendas simply by 'where the money is' or where the source and size of a research grant becomes more significant than the research undertaken itself, *the European Group promotes craftsmanship, intellectual autonomy and integrity;*
- And, rather than providing knowledge that can be used by the powerful to maintain the status quo, *the European Group endeavours to facilitate emancipatory knowledge that can be used to challenge existing power relations.*

The collegiality and solidarity offered by European Group conferences and the visions of social justice that they promote are undoubtedly even more important under neoliberal capitalism and its collateral consequences. Active participation in the European Group is perhaps higher today than at any other time in its history and with the development of new social media – *YouTube, Facebook, Twitter* and so on – the reach and presence of the European Group in lives of academics, students and activists can now be a daily experience.[8] The European Group coordinator and secretary also compile a detailed monthly newsletter delivered to over 1,200 subscribers which includes updates on activism and articles from members. Despite a proliferation of international conferences on the topics of 'crime, deviance and social control', most notably the now well established meetings by the *European Society of Criminology,* the distinct radical and emancipatory values and message of the Europe Group is today reaching an ever widening audience.

## RATIONALE FOR THE SELECTION OF PAPERS AND OVERVIEW OF BOOK

*Critique and Dissent* brings together and showcases some of the most exciting and theoretically innovative contributions delivered at the last 40 conferences. The edited book draws largely upon papers previously published by the European Group in

---

[8]   See for example the European Group Facebook page https://www.Facebook.com/groups/105017501664/.

the 1980s and 1990s in the series 'Working papers in European Criminology'. In addition we have included a small number of the papers published elsewhere and one paper, by Paddy Hillyard, not previously published. Choosing which papers to include was a difficult task. In doing so we rejected any attempt to determine which were the 'best' papers presented at the conferences. Such attempts are doomed to fail - a quick glance at Appendix 2 which lists the detailed content of the fourteen books of European Group papers previously published will show the difficulty of this task. Further, it must be remembered that though papers are generally written and presented in the English language, this is not the first language of many authors/presenters. This means that gems can sometimes be mistaken for stones, and what was required was a careful reading exploring ideas and arguments – a recognition of substance over style.

What immediately struck us was the quality of the papers. These included many important contributions to critical criminology which were no longer generally available. They needed rescuing from the shadows where they have remained hidden for many years and made available to scholars, activists and others. Whilst individually we were familiar with two or three of the editions of the working papers none of us had had previous access to the complete sets. Fortunately Bill Rolston, who edited many of the editions of the working papers, was able to provide us with nine of the ten published editions. Volume 4, *Disputing Deviance: Experience of Youth in the* 80s proved difficult to track down and although we now have a copy it was not available when we selected the papers for inclusion in this edition. In addition to the working papers Bill had kindly supplied us with a number of the *Bulletins* published by the Group which included a number of important papers. All of the material was initially read by at least two of us and a (very) long list of papers for inclusion drawn up. We then met up for a weekend in Manchester to agree some general principles for selection and then to apply these to choosing the papers.

The selection principles we agreed on were that:
- the papers selected for inclusion should be representative of the papers as a whole;
- we actively sought to avoid giving preference to the 'biggest' names;
- we should avoid publishing papers that had subsequently been published elsewhere and were, as a consequence, readily available;
- we should include papers from founders, former co-ordinators of the group and a number of editors of the 'working papers';
- the papers selected should be drawn from across Europe and maintain a gender balance;
- papers published elsewhere that made important contributions to the history of the European Group should be included;
- contributions that were original, introduced new theoretical insights or pre-empted developments in the discipline of criminology should be prioritised;

These criteria enabled us to move from our long list of papers to the selection contained in this anthology. We were however acutely aware of two deficiencies, an absence of contributions on the development of zemiology and the absence of any papers on 'race'. Zemiology, an important theoretical development that emerged from the group, has argued for rejecting the paradigms of 'crime' and the sociology of deviancy and called instead for a focus on the harms of (legal and illegal) acts. Its introduction is one of the most important contributions of the group and to reflect this we approached Paddy Hillyard to ask if he could write up the paper he delivered to the Chambery conference in 2011. Paddy kindly agreed and this paper is included in chapter eighteen of this collection.

The reasons for the absence of any papers directly discussing 'race' and racism is more complex and requires some explanation. First it should be made clear that this is not because the European Group has failed to engage with the issues of 'race', racism or neo-colonialism at its conference. There is considerable evidence of the commitment of members of the European Group to tackle these issues head on: even the most cursory of glances at the publications of prominent members, previous conference programmes or the calls of papers indicate the depth of engagement. There have also been elements of previous conferences which have engaged with the issues of institutional, structural and State racism directly. One example is the 1989 Annual Conference (Ormskirk), where not only did the conference itself move for one of day to the Irish Centre and Liverpool 8, but the organisers brought together activists and campaigners from L8 whom Group members had worked with during the uprisings in the community in 1980 and 1985.[9] Indeed many other examples of engagement with issues of 'race' and racism could be given from other previous conferences, and some of these are highlighted in the papers selected for the book. On numerous occasions then the European Group has been involved in the heart of struggles around 'race' and racism, providing a platform for subjugated knowledges and the 'view from below', and therefore the omission of a specific chapter on 'race' and racism in this collection is ultimately the consequence of our decision to ensure the papers included in this book were representative of those published in the original ten *Working Papers in European Criminology* and that we should not publish papers from European Group conferences that have been published elsewhere and are currently widely available. Rather than commission a new unpublished paper to fill this gap,[10] we have decided to highlight it for the European Group to address in the agendas of, and publications of proceedings from, future annual conferences.

---

[9] Scraton, P. 'Personal correspondence with the editors' 2013.

[10] There have been a significant number of papers on the issues of 'race' and racism delivered at European Group conferences and some of these papers have been subsequently published as influential book chapters and journal articles. The extent of discussion of 'race' and racism will become more obvious when all of the conference programmes of the European Group have been collated and digitalised. Given the absence from this volume, it is important to highlight that discussions on 'race' and racism derived from papers of European Group annual conferences have entered the public domain and influenced the development of critical criminologies, but this is not reflected in the *Working Papers in European Criminology* / other publications based exclusively on conference proceedings, from which contributions to this anthology are primarily derived. See the 'call for papers' of 42nd Annual Conference of the European Group for the Study of Deviance and Social Control, Liverpool John Moores University, to be held 3rd - 6th September, 2014 at www.europeangroup.org/conferences.

As indicated above, the majority of the papers in this anthology were previously published in one of the European Group's *Working Papers in European Criminology*. These were published for ten years by the European Group based entirely on the efforts of volunteers. They are an impressive achievement. Throughout the decade of their publication they were all published within a year of the conference at which they were delivered. Written by scholars from across the world, many of whose first language was not English, the papers often required considerable editing and the technological challenges faced by the editors are well illustrated by Bill Rolston's introduction to *Working Paper Number 6* in 1985.

> I typed all the edited papers onto a mainframe computer (a VAX 780) with the intention of transferring the files on-line to a computer at Oxford capable of laser typesetting (Lasercomp). However, time ran out, and an alternative plan had to be activated. The main frame computer did not have a word processing facility, so the files were transferred to floppy disc and word processed on a micro-computer (a Gemini Galaxy 1); each floppy has an amazing 800K capacity. Finally, the files were printed out on a daisy wheel printer, pasted down on lay-out sheets and presented to the printer photo-ready.[11]

Given that the contributions were 'working papers' and the challenges faced by their editors many of the papers included in this collection required further editing. We have also tried to be more consistent in referencing style and to, where possible, provide further or fuller references. Many of the authors have cited sources written in languages other than English. These references have been retained in the language of the source. Whilst we have made every effort to remain true to the meaning of the original we have had to rewrite sections of the papers and substantially edit a number of the papers.

---

[11]    Rolston, 'Introduction' in *Working Paper Number 6* 1985 p.7.

The compilation of this anthology is one part of a bigger project to share the work of the European Group with a wider audience and plans are underway to digitally republish all ten of the working papers in their original format. It is also hoped to digitalise other European Group material, including its Bulletins and Conference Programmes, and make these available through the Group's website (http://www.europeangroup.org/).

We have organised this selection of papers into three sections: (1) Theoretical Priorities of the European Group; (2) Critique and (3) Dissent. Each section has a dedicated introduction which provides a brief outline of the themes which the papers collectively engage. This is then followed by a brief overview of the following chapters. The anthology concludes with three appendices: Appendix 1 provides details of the 41 conferences of the European Group (1973-2013) whilst Appendix 2 (as explained above) provides details of all the books published based on conference proceedings. Appendix 3 details all the coordinators of the group.

## Bibliography

Barton, A., Corteen, K., Scott, D. and Whyte, D. "Developing a criminological imagination" pp 1- 25 in Barton, A., Corteen, K., Scott, D. and Whyte, D. (eds) *Expanding the criminological imagination: critical readings on criminology* Devon: Willan. 2006

Cohen, S. *Visions of Social Control* Cambridge: Polity, 1985

Cohen, S. *Personal correspondence with David Scott,* September 20th 2010

Rolston, B. *The State of Information in 1984: Working Papers in European Criminology No. 6.* Belfast: EGSDSC 1985

Scott, D. *Opening Address of the 40th Annual European Group Conference.* 2012 http://www.YouTube.com/watch?v=YOBsQjQ5xus

Scraton, P. *Personal correspondence with editors,* 18th June, 2013

Scraton, P. & Chadwick, K. "Challenging new orthodoxies: the theoretical and political priorities of critical criminology" pp 161-187 in Stenson, K. & Cowell, D. (eds) *The Politics Of Crime Control* London: Sage. 1991

Sim, J., Scraton, P. & Gordon, P. "Crime, the state and critical analysis" pp 1-70 in Scraton, P. (ed) *Law, Order & The Authoritarian State: Readings In Critical Criminology* Milton Keynes: Open University Press. 1987

Van Swaaningen, R. *Critical Criminology: Visions from Europe* London: Sage. 1996

Wright, E.O. *Envisioning a real utopia* London: Verso 2010

# SECTION A

THE THEORETICAL PRIORITIES OF THE
EUROPEAN GROUP FOR THE STUDY OF
DEVIANCE AND SOCIAL CONTROL

# TOWARDS A CRITICAL, EMANCIPATORY AND INNOVATIVE CRIMINOLOGY [1]

## AN INTRODUCTION TO SECTION A

### Joanna Gilmore, J.M. Moore and David Scott

The first section of this anthology focuses on the history and politics of the European Group for the Study of Deviance and Social Control. The selected papers, written between 1974 and 2013, highlight key continuities in the European Group's history: its independence, both politically and financially, from State agencies; its willingness to answer clearly the question of whose side it is on, consistently aligning itself with the weak and oppressed; a clear understanding of the relationship of theory to practice/action; and a commitment to resist hierarchies and elitism. The values and aspirations of the European Group's founders are shown

---

[1]    Scraton, P. chapter six of this book.

throughout this section to have remained central to the group throughout its 40 years of operation.

The European Group for the Study of Deviance and Social Control held its first conference in 1973. Its origins lie in intellectual and political developments that occurred in the 1960s and these are explored in the opening chapter of this section; an interview of Stan Cohen, the European Group's founder, by Maeve McMahon and Gail Kellough. In this chapter, an abridged version of an interview previously published in 1987, Cohen talks at length about the emergence of radical criminology placing it in the context of political and cultural developments and the influence of writers such as Laing, Marcuse, Fanon, Illich and Foucault. Cohen's ambivalent relationship with abolitionism, an important influence throughout the European Group's history, is also explored in this interview. Whilst Cohen is clearly attracted to the ideals and morality of abolitionism he fears that it 'doesn't sound politically relevant'. This leads him towards the left realist position; however he then concedes that the realists 'have lost their visionary edge' and discarded, at least in part, 'theoretical integrity.' This conflict in Cohen's thinking is explored in more depth by David Scott in chapter eight of this section.

The interview concludes with a discussion of criminology's neglected areas. This is particularly important as the motivation for both developing a radical criminology and for forming the European Group for the Study of Deviance and Social Control was, at least in part, to address these absences from the criminological endeavour. In 1987 Cohen identified three neglected areas: white-collar/corporate crime, social control, and comparative criminology. Cohen's call for a refocusing of attention away from 'young male working-class property offenders' towards the 'crimes of the powerful' has been responded to by the European Group in both the agendas of its conferences and the scholarly outputs of its members. In particular it is from the European Group that a fundamental critique of criminology and the sociology of deviancy, zemiology, has emerged. By arguing for a focus on

'harm' rather than 'crime' or 'deviancy', zemiology facilitates a movement away from the often petty and relatively
insignificant harms of street crime to the far more harmful
acts of States and corporations.[2] Cohen's selection of social
control as his second neglected area is a little more surprising.
However, his critique is directed specifically at the tendency
of studies of social control to focus on 'the State organized
criminal justice system' and he argues for a broader exploration of social control that encompasses the whole range of
social organisations that exert control including 'families,
schools, the media, consumer culture.' This critique remains
relevant and a possible challenge to the European Group in
coming years will be to broaden its focus on social control,
punishment and the penal system to incorporate fully the
mechanisms for regulating (or not) individuals, corporations
and States. Cohen's final neglected area is comparative criminology which he dismisses as 'what happens when Western
criminologists get on a plane and land in some place and come
back and write about it.' The European Group for the Study
of Deviance and Social Control has been in a unique place
to address this defect but whilst its conferences have often
provided the opportunity to explore areas from different
national perspectives there remains a failure to engage with
the task of developing work which is truly comparative.

At the group's second conference in Colchester in England
in 1974 those attending agreed its first manifesto which is
reproduced here as chapter four. Building on the ideas behind
the emergence of Radical Criminology articulated by Cohen
in the previous chapter, the manifesto opens with a critique
of the state of criminology which largely, it argues, 'consists
of variants of positivism'. These locate 'crime' and deviancy
in 'abnormal' personalities and State agencies responsible
for social control were viewed in a supportive and uncritical
manner. In response, the European Group was committed

---

[2]   Hillyard, P. and Tombs, S. *Beyond criminology?* in Hillyard, P., Pantazis, C., Tombs, S. and
Gordon, D. *Beyond Criminology: Taking harm Seriously,* London, Pluto Press 2004.

to developing a theory which both granted 'deviant' actors agency and recognised that their acts took place in a social setting not of their own making. Although initially this approach was avowed Marxist, the European Group recognised 'the problematic nature of that framework' and sought to avoid 'a dogmatic stance within that debate.'

The Manifesto makes clear the internationalist nature of the European Group and establishes its independence from State agencies and funding. It sets out the method by which it hoped to achieve these aims, by regular annual meetings of members and its working groups; publishing regular newsletters; maintaining a register of members' research interests; and encouraging co-operation. Looking back 40 years after its formation, this approach remains largely intact. The *European Group for the Study of Deviance and Social Control* remains both political and financially independent. It has held annual conferences in every year, although there have been times when the working groups have not function a number are currently active and with the introduction of social media the scale of collaboration and communication between group members has never been greater. The relevance and aspirations of the 1975 Manifesto remain in 2013

The early theoretical significance of the *European Group for the Study of Deviance and Social Control* to understandings of criminological knowledge is explored by Margherita Ciacci and Mario Simondi in chapter five. Their paper, originally published in 1977 in French has been translated by Emma Bell and is published in English in this volume for the first time. The chapter locates the emergences of new ideas in criminology and the sociology of deviance in the political economy of the 1960s and early 1970s. Ciacci and Simondi argue that Western European capitalism in that period had generated on the one hand surplus labour and on the other hand developed the Welfare State. The structural unemployment they highlight disproportionately impacted on 'a young qualified workforce in possession of an average higher education diploma.' Ciacci and Simondi show how the Welfare State was deployed as the mechanism to manage this problem and enable the 'continua-tion of a set political order'. Where the Welfare State appeared to be unable to achieve this the State resorted to repressive measures, by 'widen(ing) the field of action punishable by law'. This analysis makes fascinating reading in 2013. Firstly following the 2008 banking crisis unemployment in Europe has doubled with current levels of unemployment among young people averaging 24.4% in the euro area with rates of 40.5% in Italy, 42.5% in Portugal, 56.4% in Spain and 62.5% in Greece.[3] The neo-liberal response has not been to extend the Welfare State but instead, under the banner of austerity, to subject it to substantial and severe contraction and cuts. The deployment of criminal processes and penal sanctions has in recent years been more extensively deployed. What has remained consistent is, as Ciacci and Simondi argue, the need to place both the State and political economy at the centre of any attempt to understand social control.

This spotlight on the State and contemporary political economy by Ciacci and Simondi has led members of the European Group from its foundation to reject the focus on the individual deviant actor which had previously dominated criminology and instead see 'the exercise of social control as being its principal reference point.' The impact of this approach is highlighted by the approach of European Group members to white collar crime, which Ciacci and Simondi see as a radical departure from the tradition started by Sutherland. Whereas previously work had seen crimes of the powerful 'as a (rectifiable) incidence of the dysfunction of the social system', European Group members have instead highlighted how they are 'the inevitable corollary of the management of power in a capitalist society.'

Chapter six is a history of the *European Group for the Study of Deviance and Social Control* from its foundation until 1991. In this chapter René van Swaaningen identifies four distinct periods in the group's early history. From 1973 to 1976 the focus was on

---

[3]    Eurostat News release 2013.

filling gaps in criminological knowledge by thematic conferences on radical themes such as prisoners' actions, white collar crime and the relationship between the economy and crime. In the second phase, between 1977 and 1981, the central theme of conferences was the role of the State. In this second phase, van Swaaningen argues, the European Group 'had slowly deteriorated into a slightly blindfolded political instrument'. However in the period between 1982 and 1986 he sees an attempt to create a more even balance between scientific and political commitment with in particular a stronger emphasis on the 'original agenda of critical criminology and its relation with social movements.' His final period, from 1987 until the article was drafted in 1991, is characterised by a movement away from the 'strongly Anglo-centric Marxist analyses of the generation of 68' towards 'thoughts which had their roots in abolitionist insights or deconstructivist philosophies of the post 68 generation.' In particular he highlights the growing influence of both feminism and Foucaultian thought on the European Group.

Looking forward (from 1991) van Swaaningen makes a number of suggestions which echo those of Cohen in chapter three. Firstly he also argues for the development of analysis of social control that are much wider than the State and its agencies. Secondly he argues for a 'more explicit international orientation' (and far less time spent focusing on 'typically British hobby horses') that would allow a genuinely comparative criminology to emerge. He concludes that whilst it is important to retain the European Group's commitment to social justice this must be complemented by a far greater appreciation of diversity. An international critical criminology cannot be based on 'uniform paradigms and strategies which are supposed to be applicable in every country' but needs to be able 'to do justice to (the) diversities' of different countries political, economic and legal structures.

Throughout its history the *European Group for the Study of Deviance and Social Control* has remained critical of much of the criminological enterprise, critiquing the way it generates knowledge to serve the interests of the powerful. In turn this has led to those operating at the centre of State-sponsored criminology to dismiss the European Group and its members' contributions as unimportant, idealistic and irrelevant. Writing in response to a reference that the European Group was 'marginal', Phil Scraton in chapter seven provides a powerful defence of the value and importance of the European Group. Scraton draws heavily on his personal experiences both of attending conferences and of wider relationships made possible through his membership of the European Group. His account of the Belfast conference in 2005 demonstrates the unique qualities of European Group conferences: how they connect with what is happening politically in the host city/country; the range of topics and speakers; the inclusive and non-hierarchical organisation and activities which take participants out from the conference venue and into the local community. Scraton shows that the European Group is far from marginal to much that is important and suggests that if it is in fact marginal to mainstream administrative and the priorities of government agencies then this should be seen as a strength.

In recent years the European Group has sadly experienced the deaths of a number of members who have made important contributions. Andrea Beckmann's moving tribute to Louk Hulsman following his death in 2009 is included as chapter eight of this collection. Although Hulsman published sparingly he was a hugely inspirational thinker and teacher whose contribution to the life of the European Group was immense. Beckmann's paper captures this and places it in the context of his life and career. A member of the resistance to the occupation of the Netherlands by Nazi Germany he was captured and held in a concentration camp before escaping and re-engaging in resistance activity. Beckmann charts his career as a civil servant, his role as one of the main architects of the tolerant Dutch drug policy, as Chair of the Dutch Probation Service as well as his contribution as a professor of penal law and criminology. But central to this appreciation is Hulsman the human being. For Beckmann Hulsman 'embodied and lived the humanistic, open and eclectic core of abolitionist thought that takes care to be sensitive to the contextual, situational and personal interpretations of 'lived experiences' as they are defined by people'. Later in 2009, shortly after the successful Preston conference which had celebrated Louk's life and contribution to the group the longstanding co-ordinator of the Group, Karen Leander died. Karen's immense contribution to the group is recognised by the inclusion of her paper 'The Decade of Rape' in chapter twenty-five of this collection.

One of the speakers at the 2009 conference was Stan Cohen, who had played a central role in the birth of the European Group. It was to be his last European Group conference and the paper he delivered is included as chapter nine of this anthology. The paper starts out by highlighting how the values promoted by a 'decent university' such as 'care for learning in itself; scepticism about accepted knowledge; the personal qualities of tolerance and friendship; the political values of fairness and social justice' are often, incorrectly, deemed as not belonging to the real world. Cohen moves on to review his own contribution to our understanding of the concepts of 'moral panics' and 'denial' and the inherent conflict between the two concepts. Central to the exposure of moral panics was an understanding of labelling theory which determined that whatever it was that was being panicked about was being over reacted to; that in reality 'there's no need to panic, calm down, it's not that serious, it's not the end of the world'. The logical conclusion was that the appropriate response to a moral panic was denial. In his later work Cohen's focus was on the reactions to atrocities such as torture and genocide and how these were routinely denied. Whereas earlier he had warned about 'moral panics' as over responses he was subsequently challenging 'denial' as a failure to respond adequately. Are these concepts therefore just political tools, labels to be given to situations to reflect your own individual beliefs? To further explore these two concepts and to determine if they can be deployed objectively Cohen uses the example of climate change, reaching some quite surprising conclusions.

Sadly, whilst we were working on this anthology, Stan Cohen died after a long illness. In chapter ten David Scott pays tribute to his contribution to criminology over the past four decades. Scott uses Cohen's major work to demonstrate the development of his ideas and the way they underpinned the development of the discipline of criminology. Highlighting Cohen's scholarship and moral purpose Scott shows how so much of the language of contemporary criminology was shaped by Cohen's work. He concludes by highlighting the continued relevance of Cohen's values to criminologist working and writing in the contemporary managerial university.

This section concludes with another European Group Manifesto. Chapter eleven is the manifesto of the group's recently re-established working group on prison, detention and punishment. Re-launched at the *Sites of Confinement* conference in Liverpool in March 2013 the working group provides a network for radical scholars and campaigners.[4] The manifesto illustrates the continued link between theory and practice which has characterised the European Group since its formation. The working group sets out its aspiration to promote both 'intellectual interventions and direct activism' aimed at exposing 'the brutal realities of detention, penal confinement and community punishments'. Drawing on a long tradition of engaging critically with the rationale of social control interventions that has characterised the European Group, the manifesto argues that they should be evaluated within 'wider moral and political contexts'. It is the weakest and most vulnerable who are targeted by penal interventions which are carried out in institutions that 'fail to uphold human rights' or 'meet the demands of social justice'. The working group is distinct from other research groups, inter-governmental agencies or alliances of penal reform groups in that it is not concerned with the more effective functioning of penal institutions. It sets out to be unashamedly 'marginal' to that enterprise

---

[4]    For a report of this conference see Jefferson 2013 and Hayes 2013.

instead arguing for 'the utilisation of strategies drawing upon direct action and abolitionist praxis to facilitate radical penal and social transformations'. The *European Group for the Study of Deviance and Social Control* maybe 40 years old but this Manifesto demonstrates it has not lost its radicalism or moved from its mission to challenge the orthodoxy of mainstream criminology.

## Bibliography

European Union, *Euro area unemployment rate at 12.2%'* Eurostat News release 82/2013 31 May 2013. Online at: http://epp.eurostat.ec.europa.eu/cache/ITY_PUBLIC/3-31052013-BP/EN/3-31052013-BP-EN.PDF

Hayes, M. 'European Group/ Centre for the Study of Crime, Criminalisation and Social Exclusion Conference ' *European Group Spring Newsletter.* April 2013. Online at: http://www.europeangroup.org/links/April%202013/SpringInewsletter.pdf

Hillyard, P and Tombs, S. 'Beyond criminology?' in Hillyard, P., Pantazis, C., Tombs, S. and Gordon, D. *Beyond Criminology: Taking harm Seriously,* London, Pluto Press 2004

Jefferson, A. 'Conference Report – Sites of Confinement', *Dignity Danish Institute Against Torture website,* 2013 Online at: http://www.dignityinstitute.org/servicenavigation/news-and-activities/news/2013/3/conference-report-sites-of-confinement.aspx

# AN INTERVIEW WITH STANLEY COHEN

**Maeve McMahon and Gail Kellough**

*This is an abridged version of Maeve McMahon (MM) and Gail Kellough's (GK) interview of European Group founder Stan Cohen (SC) which originally appeared in Canadian Criminology Forum, Volume 8 in 1987. The subheadings have been added by the editors of this anthology.*

## ON MORAL VALUES

(SC) […] The stress on moral values is something which has always been a constant for me. If I look back on everything I've written, I'm always insisting that some connection be made between the theory and the practice - and peoples' stated or implied values (whether you call them moral or not).

That doesn't mean I'm advocating this for everybody. I'm not a preacher. I'm not saying every sociologist should be willing to do that and you're a 'moral imbecile' if you don't. That's just how I prefer doing it. I think that in criminology, or sociology of deviance, or justice studies - as opposed to many other branches of the social sciences and many branches of history and many abstract areas of political science itself - those questions keep coming up. That's our subject matter. Without moral choices, and without values, we wouldn't have a subject. Where the connections come out, is when you're writing about ways of dealing with deviance or trying to look at the policy implications of causal theories. So I don't think it's an artificial exercise for us to talk about values. It might be artificial for historians of the nineteenth century to do so; it might be artificial perhaps for even somebody talking about the sociology of industry or the modern family. But I think our area is so impregnated with values that we can't avoid them. [...]

# DRIFTING INTO CRIMINOLOGY

(SC) [...] I was in London and the London School of Economics was a supposedly great sociology department - so I drifted into sociology and criminology. I started doing my thesis on the mods and rockers; this turned into *Folk Devils and Moral Panics*.[1] I think that was about the time labelling theory 'hit'. You know, I still remember reading Becker's *Outsiders* and being quite knocked out by it, even though it's so simple.[2] It is absolutely simple, any idiot can understand it. And yet it still has all sorts of very fascinating implications if you take it seriously. That, I think was the first theory that hit me, and I was more influenced by that than much of the stuff that I learned at LSE (London School of Economics). I learned orthodox criminology and the sociological type of criminology. I wasn't too influenced by that, nor was I by what was happening academically around me. [...]

I guess though, that I was influenced more by the kind of cultural politics of London at that time. The 1966-67 'Dialectics of Liberation' conferences, Laing, then the Student Movement, the anti Vietnam activities. I think that all this

---

[1]   Cohen, S. (1972) *Folk Devils and Moral Panics: The Creation of the Mods and Rockers.* London: MacGibbon and Kee.

[2]   Becker, H. (1963) *Outsiders: Studies in the Sociology of Deviance.* New York: Glencoe Free Press.

was culturally an enormous influence on me as well as all the generation of people I was with at the time, Jock Young was a student with me and Ian Taylor was a student of mine. We were all part of that circle. I suppose my influence came very much from the type of communal activity which began building around the National Deviancy Conference. It was something of my idea at the start. I'd moved up from London to Durham, and I was isolated from my buddies in London. I thought, let's find some kinds of opportunities to get together. So I contacted Jock - Ian was already in Durham as a student when I was there - and we rounded up others for a meeting.

Unlike North American academic life the emerging group had two distinct features: for one, it was intensely political, and this is, I think, a difference which people don't quite appreciate when they see leftist radical English academic writing. Because it was always engaged - not just in an abstract sense - with the world. Most people were members of various political groups, or they saw their academic work in sociology and deviance as connected with their politics. I've written about this in a paper on the evolution of the NDC, and Geoff Pearson's book *The Deviant Imagination* describes that atmosphere very well.[3] So, the atmosphere was very political and very engaged, and that influenced me. I was fascinated and caught up in it. Second, unlike a lot of North American academic life, it was collective, it was very non-competitive. I really don't think people were competing with each other to get publications.

## ON THE ESTABLISHMENT OF THE EUROPEAN GROUP

(MM): Did that branch out into the European Group (for the Study of Deviance and Control)?

(SC) Yes, the European Group was also a chance idea of mine because I was at Berkeley in 1970 and met an Italian, Mario

---

[3]    Pearson, G. (1975) *The Deviant imagination: Psychiatry, Social Work and Social Change.* London: Macmillan.

Simondi and Karl Schuman from Germany. We just happened to be sharing an office, and I said – 'Well it's crazy that we have to come to Berkeley to see each other. Let's do something when we go back to Europe'. That's how the European Group started.

## ON THE ORIGINS OF RADICAL CRIMINOLOGY

To go back to those biographical, cultural influences. It was England - London at the end of the sixties - and that kind of cultural and New Left politics … reading Marcuse, Fanon, Illich, and Laing, the cultural heroes of the sixties, who (perhaps we'll get onto this later) are now being denounced. To me, they have always remained people of importance. I've always had a secret project - which I'll never do - which is to go back to 1960's left idealist cultural heroes and to try to see what one could make of them now.

I think I kept up all along my old worry about the personal. I think the NDC in its early years retained that. So it didn't worry me so much, because I think everybody there - again quite unlike North American academic sociologists or criminologists - was pretty much in touch with social work. People knew probation officers and youth workers, they came to the conferences. Few North American social scientists - radicals or not - would have had these contacts.

So I didn't sense the tension so much. And I think the early publications of the NDC (*Images of Deviance*, or *Politics and Deviance*, early stuff by Jock Young on drugs, my own stuff on mods and rockers) weren't immediately so macro and structural that they ruled out the personal.[4] They were really a political version of Becker. That's really what the early years of the NDC were. We were mixing together the kind of 'low level' truths of labelling theory (and the excitement provoked by

---

[4]   Cohen, S. (ed) *Images of Deviance*, Harmondsworth: Penguin. Taylor, I & Taylor, L (1973) *Politics and Deviance,* Harmondsworth: Penguin.

Laing's notion of decategorization) with our political commitments and our sense that all these fixed categories of social life were actually more fluid than they appeared. 'Storm the bastions of reality'. That's the way I'm now writing something (again!) about the evolution of those theories.

I think that it's very parallel to what happened in literary theory, the direction that led to deconstructionism. The group was saying 'Look: crime is not really crime … what we call crime, street crime, is not really as important as it appears … it's all mystification. There's other crime, there's crimes of the powerful.' And so on - for drugs, violence, mental illness, homosexuality. In other words, things aren't what you think they are. Crime isn't crime, mental illness isn't illness.

So everything we said was deconstructionist. This was the political version of labelling theory which emerged - and a version of labelling theory more influenced by European thinking which Americans (then particularly) were just hopeless at. They really didn't know much about the type of European Marxist and anarchist thinking of the time. […]

## A SHORT READING LIST FOR CRIMINOLOGY STUDENTS

(SC) […] If I had to choose two books to give criminology students to read on a desert island, I'd say *Becoming Deviant* and *Discipline and Punish*.[5] For me, at the moment, if I had to choose two it would be those two!

(MM) Which would you make them read first?!

(SC) *Becoming Deviant* first! That's an exercise in the sociology of knowledge, and the sociology of knowledge does interest me. I think many of the things I've written about criminology … are really exercises in the sociology of knowledge. I'm interested in ideas, and how ideas change: this fascinates more than any other intellectual problem.

---

[5]    Matza, D. (1969) *Becoming Deviant.* Englewood Cliffs, N.J.: Prentice-Hall. Foucault, M. (1977) *Discipline and Punish: The Birth of the Prison.* New York: Pantheon.

I don't think I write very original stuff, but I think I'm good at picking up what ideas are around, and putting them in boxes and saying, 'well, that leads there, and that led to that, and this was similar to that.' So that's why I like Matza, because I thought he did this superbly; charting the limits and relationships between various forms of thinking in the last century about crime, delinquency and deviance. When he talks about affinity, affiliation, and signification, those are the boxes in which all theories can be categorized. When he talks about correction versus appreciation, well that's exactly the problem that remains. He put his finger on it. I remained sympathetic to labelling theory, and stayed worried about the split between the personal and the political [...]

## ON THE INFLUENCE (AND LIMITATIONS) OF ABOLITIONISM

(SC) I met Nils Christie and I was influenced by his kind of thinking, which is now called 'abolitionism'. I was very impressed by his combination of deep personal commitment to the society he lives in, and his posing of theory in terms of that commitment. It's not the way I would actually do it, but I was always impressed by that. Writers who influenced me afterwards were people like Ivan Illich. I was a great fan of Illich - again a sixties figure, much discredited now - whom I think is important in making a humanist statement against bureaucracy, the professions, and technology. That's a deep personal value for me.

I think out of all this mixture, we're left with not just a split between the personal and political, we're left with a three-fold split; one direction is, the practice of macro-social change, revolutionary politics if you like. Another is dealing with people at a personal level - social work values. The third, which I think has become more important to me recently, is a commitment to knowledge in itself. An old-fashioned liberal commitment, that is: the way you talk about knowledge should allow some room for you to be able to do so without worrying about whose interests it's going to serve or whether it's going to be useful. Not exclusively so, but of the three, I've become much more sensitive to this last direction. [...]

(GK) [...] How would you describe differences between your approach and Nils Christie's and Thomas Mathiesen's in relation to theory/experience/practice?

(SC) I find the whole abolitionist package very attractive. For *Contemporary Crises* (which I now edit) I collected articles by all those people, to try to force them a bit to put their position down. I think that their problem is they take too literally the theoretical truths of labelling theory and deconstructionism. In other words, they convert what seems to me correct theoretical insights about the relativity of crime (that criminal justice is only one way of dealing with troubles, etc.) into immediate policy. They take those theoretical insights in their very naive way (not really naive, because they're not naive people, but in what appears a naive way) and they say, 'well if that's true, why can't we do this?! That's why everyone is amazed. When I hear them talk, people say, 'how can you actually do something like that?', and Nils Christie answers 'Why not?!' Because that's his approach, and there is something appealingly attractive, very romantic about that.

The critique of the penal law seems to me to make a lot of sense; their critique of the penal law model, their notion of alternative forms of dispute mediation, their continued attack on the prison ... when everyone else has dropped the idea of prison abolition or prison reform as a hopeless business and looked elsewhere. Those are all appealing.

Where I part company with them slightly, is that what they're saying doesn't sound politically relevant, and that's where I'm more sympathetic to the left realist position. I find myself in between. I always do, I always find I never quite agree with the people on 'my side'. Although they seem to be so practical, they (the abolitionists) are dreamers and thinkers, and that's great and I think it's important to have that, and I'm critical of the realists because they've jettisoned that. I think the realists, in order to be so realistic, have lost their visionary edge and have thrown aside some theoretical integrity.

(GK) But sometimes the abolitionists 'define themselves out' ...

(SC) Right, they do 'define themselves out' and I think Mathiesen's extreme position on abolitionism as a value in itself is a problem. Again I must say I was attracted to it, but now I do think that it is carrying the abolitionist argument too far. There are all sorts of ways in which you do have to look relevant to others. And I think that they're wrong in thinking that what we call crime can all be called 'disputes', or 'conflicts', or 'troubles'. Much of what we call crime is not a dispute or a conflict or a trouble - an armed robber steals something from a gas station - where's the conflict? What's the dispute? Where's the trouble? When a woman is raped, is that 'trouble'?

(GK) It involves a much broader thing – more than just eliminating or abolishing ...

(SC) Right, it involves more than just simply saying the words, and I think that's what Louk Hulsman and Nils Christie are implying. You can't just substitute the words. I don't think you can because much of crime is not like this. I don't think it can deal with crimes of the powerful very well. I think if one is concerned with ecological issues, and corporate crime, and State crime - government organized exploitation of the poor and the powerless I don't think the abolitionist programme answers very much.

(GK) Also there are instances in which exploitation of people occurs outside the entire formal system. To me, that's where the experience of women is relevant. There is an awful lot occurring outside the formal system so abolishing it doesn't help.

(SC) Yes. So, temperamentally, I find myself very sympathetic to what they're doing and I think it's important to keep that tradition alive. I also think the split today between the left realist position and the abolitionist one is very healthy. I think we've now got to a healthy point in critical criminology ... they both seem to me, to offer, in their own ways, viable alternatives to administrative criminology.

I think that while these paradigms have been emerging from the cocoon in the last five years, administrative criminology has declined even further. In this assessment I think the left realists are absolutely correct. By refusing to deal with aetiology, by insisting that we work only with what they define as 'manageable' policy matters, today's technicist criminologists have retreated from any serious intellectual pretence. Curiously, this is where anti-positivism has triumphed. I very much agree with Jock Young's recent argument (in Confronting Crime) that we need to return to the traditional agenda of sociological positivism.[6] Go back, he says to Cloward and Ohlin, to Albert Cohen, to Merton, and see what they were saying about the generation of working-class crime, inequality, social pressures; be clear about things like race, and gender, and see how they structure the world. In other words, go back to being decent sociologists. By opting out of that altogether, managerial criminology has moved to the side: a correctionalism without any theory at all. Those of us who are interested in developing alternatives have now got in realism and abolitionism two fine positions. There are all sorts of unfinished ideas and objectionable bits to either, but put together, they are an alternative. […]

## CRIMINOLOGY S NEGLECTED AREAS

(SC) […] I think that criminology is always very programmatic. Every couple of years, you know, somebody says 'this is what we should do'. The new criminology was initially very programmatic saying what should be done, more than doing it. Certainly if we're looking at mainstream criminology the topics which have long been alleged to have been neglected are still neglected. So for example, despite the growth of literature on white-collar crime and corporate crime, this still remains one area that's neglected. But I'm not saying anything

---

6   Young, J. (1986) "The Failure of Criminology: The Need for a Radical Realism." In R Matthews and J. Young (eds.) *Confronting Crime*. London: Sage.

original here; Sutherland said this forty years ago. I still think white-collar crime, crimes of corporations, crimes of the powerful in general, State crime, multi-nationals' dumping of bad drugs in the third world, I think these are absolutely important areas and have to be more seriously discussed. If you look at a recent book such as Pepinsky and Jesilow's *Myths That Cause Crime* - they do make a very good case for switching attention away from the traditional objects of criminology like young male working-class property offenders to moving more seriously than ever before to looking at crimes of the power-ful.[7] That seems to me one area.

The second one relates to our discussion about the clutches of criminology. I think we must, if we are talking seriously about social control, rules, norms and justice, get away from the setting of criminal justice - and move towards studying forms of social control outside the State organized system. We don't want to do this because there's the ghost of Parsons and all other such theories that lead us to the vague idea that social control is everything. But I think we must follow this through. I'm as guilty here as anyone else. To carry on talking about social control as if all we were talking about was the State organized criminal justice system is absurd. We must return to looking at what happens in families, schools, the media, consumer culture. The whole question of the market, the commodification of desire, the ways in which advertising shapes our needs and our tastes and our desires ... you know, the old preoccupations of the Frankfurt school. We mustn't be scared of this direction. It does lead everywhere ... and it becomes everything; it becomes all sociology. But I think unless we work in those areas (and on utopian communes and forms of regulation such as private justice internal disciplinary systems) then, it seems to me, social control still qualifies as a 'neglected area'. [...]

Up to now 'comparative criminology' has been a joke; 'comparative criminology' is what happens when Western

---

[7]   Pepinsky, H.E. and Jesilow, P. (1984) *Myths That Cause Crime*. Washington, Seven Locks.

criminologists get on a plane and land in some place and come back and write about it. It really is a joke. There's no serious text which examines as sociologists do in other areas: what is the effect of different political ideologies, political economies or social structures on the way crime emerges?

Certainly the communication of ideas in the direction of a genuine comparative and historical criminology is very important. It can be facilitated by international meetings which are not just professional circuses. The European Group for the Study of Deviance is one forum which emerged where different national preoccupations became evident. I remember how at one point the Germans were totally preoccupied with political prisoners, and with new laws which were affecting academic freedom and criminalizing forms of political dissent; the Italians were all interested in terrorism and the Red Brigades; people in Britain would focus on Northern Ireland. Now, conventional non-political crime has returned to this forum.

In Britain for example, policing has now become a common subject because it connects with the left realist strand, and it connects with particular strands of British political life. You can't understand the left realist theory unless you understand what has happened to the Labour Party in England, and why a cohort of English academics (not just criminologists) have moved to the Labour Party and are developing a criminology for the Labour Party. I think that's what left realism is: it's a socialist version of law and order. They've campaigned on local councils. Some of them are standing to be elected as local councillors. They're working on democratization of the police or police accountability practices. All these are genuine issues - but ones which would be remote to some committed intellectual criminologists working elsewhere, perhaps in Latin America. That's not saying that one is right and the other is wrong. That's not what I'm saying, There are some common viable theories and I think that the left realist/abolitionist debate is at some point sufficiently abstract to make it a common focus point for debate among committed critical criminologists everywhere.

But the preoccupations change. Take the example of the 'liberal' system of delinquency control in a country like Israel. In my book *Visions of Social Control* and in most critical theory, we criticize (or we used to criticize ten years ago) the rehabilitation ideal and the whole stress on psychiatry.[8] But historically the treatment orientation served as a counter to the most brutal excesses of classical criminology. Nils Christie's *Limits to Pain* explains this.[9] For example, in order to argue against the death penalty you might have had to produce the positivist image of the less-responsible deviant. Or, in order to argue for humanizing the prison, you had to bring in the baggage of the treatment ideology. And only afterwards could you reject it. You know, you had to go through this phase.

I wrote about this in a paper about the Third World. It is a terrible thought that some other countries might have to go through these mistakes first.[10] That is, to fight against brutalizing prison conditions and forms of social control which rest entirely on the worst excesses of classical or neo-classical ideas, it becomes 'progressive' to support the treatment ideology. Only a genuine comparative and historical sense can lead to these fascinating debates. [...]

## FINAL THOUGHT

(MM) We have many more questions to ask but we've run out of time! Would you like to add a concluding statement which summarizes your position?

(SC) Well, I think that people in our line of business - besides making a living and seeing the world - have to appease three voracious gods. The first is knowledge (in the traditional, liberal academic sense of a commitment to tell the truth);

---

8   Cohen, S. (1985) *Visions of Social control: Crime, Punishment and Classification*. Cambridge: Polity Press.

9   Christie, N. (1982) *Limits to Pain*. Oxford: Martin Robertson.

10  Cohen, S (1982) "Western Crime Control models in the Third world: Benign or Malignant?" In Spitzer, S. and Simon, R.J. (eds.) *Research in law Deviance and Social control, Vol. 4*. Greenwich, Conn.: JAI Press.

the second is politics (in the sense of trying to do something about the master structures of injustice and suffering); the third is personal action (in the sense of touching the lives of those we can actually know). At any time, one of these gods is more demanding and devouring than the others.

## Bibliography

Becker, H. *Outsiders: Studies in the Sociology of Deviance.* New York: Glencoe Free Press 1963

Christie, N. *Limits to Pain.* Oxford: Martin Robertson, 1982

Cohen, S. (ed.) *Images of Deviance,* Harmondsworth: Penguin, 1971

Cohen, S. *Folk Devils and Moral Panics: The Creation of the Mods and Rockers.* London: MacGibbon and Kee, 1972

Cohen, S 'Western Crime Control models in the Third world: Benign or Malignant?' In Spitzer, S. and Simon, R.J. (eds.) *Research in law Deviance and Social control, Vol. 4.* Greenwich, Conn.: JAI Press, 1982

Cohen, S. *Visions of Social control: Crime, Punishment and Classification.* Cambridge: Polity Press, 1985

Foucault, M. *Discipline and Punish: The Birth of the Prison.* New York: Pantheon, 1977

Matza, D. *Becoming Deviant.* Englewood Cliffs, N.J.: Prentice-Hall, 1969

Pearson, G. *The Deviant imagination: Psychiatry, Social Work and Social Change.* London: Macmillan, 1975

Pepinsky, H.E. and Jesilow, P. *Myths That Cause Crime.* Washington, Seven Locks, 1984

Taylor, I & Taylor, L (1973) *Politics and Deviance,* Harmondsworth: Penguin, 1973

Young, J. 'The Failure of Criminology: The Need for a Radical Realism.' In R Matthews and J. Young (eds.) *Confronting Crime.* London: Sage, 1986

# MANIFESTO 1974

## EUROPEAN GROUP FOR THE STUDY
## OF DEVIANCE & SOCIAL CONTROL

*This Manifesto was adopted at the European Group's second conference held in Colchester in 1974 and published in Crime and Social Justice, No. 4, 1975.*

1.  The dominant mode of analysis of crime, deviance and social control, as represented in research literature and policy practice, consists of variants of positivism: a concentration on the collection of criminal statistics and the attempt to characterise criminal and deviant acts as the products of psychologically defective and 'abnormal' personalities. Agencies of social control are studied in an uncritical way or from the point of view of how to make them more effective. The control perspective dominates comparative criminological research: in individual countries and in international organisations such as the Council of Europe, official and governmental agencies are funding research and expecting academics to provide findings which will help to improve methods and techniques of social control.

2.  In recent years, however, such analytical frameworks are being challenged by a growing number of academics in

their teaching, their research and their publications, and by social workers and by students. An increasing number of organisations and associations of the 'clients' and 'victims' of such frameworks and indeed of the political economy that conditions those frameworks, such as Women Liberation, Gay Liberation, Prisoners Organisations, Tenants Associations and many others, is further evidence of the challenge to that dominant perspective and practice.

3.  It is within the context of this challenge that the *European Group for the Study of Deviance and Social Control* is located. The European Group is an attempt to contribute to the development of a critical academic and political framework, to criticise social theory and political practice. It is committed to a theoretical approach that grants 'deviant' actors a conscious past, a present perceived problem and a future praxis. At the same time, an approach that recognizes that action takes place within a world of circumstances not of an individual's own making. It is, therefore, committed to develop theory that delineates the nature of the whole society which engenders such problems. In general the framework to which the Group, as an organisation, is committed is Marxist. Yet recognising the problematic nature of that framework, avoids a dogmatic stance within that debate.

    Commitment is to a theoretical and practical programme that generally is concerned to relate systems of domination and control to the structures of production and the division of labour.

4.  At another level the European Group is intended to facilitate communication between social scientists across national boundaries. Such communication is all the more necessary given the contemporary development of a variety of cross-national economic, political and social control enterprises. There is a need to exchange information about current developments in

research and theory, to encourage research in to crime, deviance and social control in a socially and politically relevant context, to relate individual research to less parochial interests and to foster joint research projects. The Group facilitates these objectives:

i. through regular meetings, not only of the Group as a whole but through the formation of working groups, e.g. Social Control of Women, Schools as Institutions of Social Control, Politics and Deviance, a Social Work Group, and a European Prisons Group.

ii. by publishing a Newsletter and a Register of Members Research Interests and

iii. by encouraging co-operation in social and political reform and policy with and between specific organisations and pressure groups with whom we share general theoretical and political perspectives.

iv. The European Group is independent of any official agencies and is financially self-supporting.

v. The initial formation of the Group took place in Florence, Italy in 1972 and has subsequently held two conferences, one in Florence, another at Colchester, England. Papers and discussions have been wide ranging and include Penal Institutions and Prisoners Movements, Psychiatric Control, Police Practice and Procedures, Politics and Deviance, and the Changing Nature of Legal Repression.

vi. The organisation of the European Group is undertaken by an annually elected Steering Committee and a permanent secretary, from whom further information and details can be obtained.

# A NEW TREND IN CRIMINOLOGICAL KNOWLEDGE

## THE EXPERIENCE OF THE EUROPEAN GROUP FOR THE STUDY OF DEVIANCE AND SOCIAL CONTROL

**Margherita Ciacci and Mario Simondi**

*This paper was originally written in French and published in Déviance et société (1977) Vol. 1(1):109-117 and has been translated for this collection by Emma Bell.*

Those seeking to understand the way in which new research trends in the field of criminology and the sociology of deviance came to assert themselves in Europe over the last ten years ought to rethink the structural origins of this 'new direction' as well as some of the key analyses proposed by it.[1]

---

[1]  Here, we will attempt to outline the political and social framework within which the development of this new current of 'criminological knowledge' can be understood. This particular framework will also allow us to situate the analyses offered by the European Group for the Study of Deviance and Social Control.

We will attempt to provide a synthesis of the elements of structural change inherent in European capitalist societies in the course of the 1960s and to evaluate the weight of these same factors in terms of changing values.

The aim here is not to return to an analysis of the concept of monopolistic capitalism. Moreover, we have little to add to what has already been said concerning its characteristics and working mechanisms. It will thus be suffice to observe the significant consequences of the phenomenon on the labour market and on the Welfare State. With regard to the labour market, it seems to us that the organisation of monopolistic capitalism tends to result in growing contradictions with relation to 'relative overpopulation' (above all concerning employment opportunities for a young qualified workforce in possession of an average higher education diploma). With regard to the Welfare State, it seems to us that the interventionist role of the State – which is constantly increasing – in the economies of all European countries constitutes an active attempt to gain the consensus of the masses without which the public management of the economy and the continuation of a set political order would be extremely difficult. The State thus guarantees the legitimation of its growing intervention in the economy via a process which has been described as 'building the loyalty of the masses'. One of the principal agents of this process seems to be represented by the machinery of the Welfare State which has been obliged to neutralise – or at least to relativise – the social costs of capitalist accumulation.

It would thus appear to us that it is not by chance that, beyond the crisis of values cited by many people as being the sole source of all evils, it is possible to identify a series of elements which seem to be the source of the generalised contestation of the prevailing order which has characterised advanced capitalist societies over the last ten years and more. It is undeniable that certain social institutions have experienced – and are still experiencing – a functional crisis which has in turn led to a crisis of legitimacy. We could cite for example the role played by institutions charged with transmitting society's values (the family and the school) or of that played by institutions charged with the guardianship of the collectivity and of social defence (the machinery of justice and segregation). Yet, to understand this crisis, it is necessary to determine the structural forces which accompanied its emergence. Amongst these, the increasing role of the State in the process of the incorporation of the masses (something which, as we have mentioned, was rendered essential by the crisis of State institutions themselves) has played a key role. Without going too far, it would seem that the State has responded by a strategy different in form – but the same in substance – which has reinforced the social security role of State bureaucracy.

With the eclipse of the traditional ideological supports for this machinery, a permissive strategy has developed which also plays an ideological function, dissimulating the growing obstacles to the resolution of the inherent contradictions of capitalist systems. For instance, we are referring to this process of formal decriminalisation or the informal non-application of laws relating to certain aspects of sexual deviance or the use of drugs. Taking another example in the same vein, the Melkweg, the famous cultural centre for young people in Amsterdam, constitutes a kind of controlled space in which the quest for self-expression by youth is rendered inoffensive precisely because it is managed, thanks to public funding, according to the principle of 'repressive tolerance'. These examples represent what may be called 'victimless crime' or manifestations of 'expressive' deviance. Alongside these phenomena, collective action has recently emerged (acts of vandalism, 'workers' expropriations' etc.) which, whilst apparently belonging to the same category of behaviour just described, raise the question of the more or less conscious political aim of collective deviance. Now that the traditional barriers which existed between these two different kinds of behaviour have broken down, it has become increasingly difficult to distinguish the deviant from the political act.

If these are the key (and in some sense, new) trends, the repressive machinery of the State, which takes the form of openly coercive measures and resorts increasingly to 'exceptional' or emergency legislation, remains intact. We may take the examples of the 1970 'anti-vandals' law in France, the 1974 public order laws in Italy, the 'Berufsverbot' law of 1973 in West Germany,[2] or the British anti-terrorist legislation of 1974. These laws may be understood as an expression of a desire to widen the field of actions punishable by law. Above all, they represent a restriction on political non-conformism. It is no coincidence if this process of the widening of the repressive machinery of the law goes hand-in-hand with legal permissiveness (referred to above) and focuses increasingly on particular forms of behaviour. Formerly considered as the object of a system of specific criminal sanctions, the punishment of 'victimless crimes' is today no longer thought of as being essential to maintaining the prevailing social order. Instead, the decriminalisation of such behaviour is regarded as a safety valve which allows the State to reinforce its control over political acts of deviance.

It follows that the State – via its institutions and in its practice – is at the centre of attention of those seeking to study the mechanisms intended to exercise social control in advanced capitalist societies. Public opinion itself seems to have recently understood the role played by State institutions in the management of private affairs. It is not by chance that we are currently witnessing the progressive erosion of the barrier which traditionally separated the State from its subjects (we might take the example of the demystifying function of events such as Watergate). The political and the private are no longer entirely separate. Hence the entanglement of political deviance and collective deviance on the one hand, and the mass media which, on the other hand, contributes increasingly to the amplification of such deviance by presenting it to public opinion in very ambiguous terms. This serves the ultimate aim of neutralising the subversive potential of political deviance. The strategy seems all the more 'successful' when interpreted as one which aims to obliterate all efforts to bring about a change in the established order.

---

[2] This law constituted a 'professional ban', forbidding those subject to it from practicing certain professions on the grounds of his or her criminal record, political convictions or membership of a particular group.

* * *

Together with the trend briefly analysed above has emerged a 'new trend' in 'criminological knowledge' in Western Europe. Traditionally, criminology had developed a vision of the individual which represented him as a passive carrier of a bio-psychic diversity which is open to detailed scientific analysis in the aim of setting aside all possible social causes of this diversity. A new perspective has now been added to, and even come to supplant, this viewpoint. It still considers the deviant as a passive entity, excusing him for being the product of a 'sick society'. In both cases, the universe of values, whether codified by laws or not, was conceived of as a homogeneous system based on what was thought to be a widespread consensus. This vision of normative homogeneity has been questioned as social transformations have seen the emergence of minority groups previously stripped of political weight and raised the issue of the plurality of values.

So, what are the essential characteristics of this 'new trend' which gradually gained ground in the second half of the 1960s? For us, there are two main ones which have critically opposed the criminological schools of both positivist and correctional inspiration as well as sociological analyses of deviance, carried out according to ecological parameters or according to a model of defective socialisation. Adding to a research trend focusing on the redefinition of labelling theory[3] imported from the United States, the new research trend adopted a critical approach to institutions of segregation (psychiatric hospitals, prisons etc.) and official agents of social control (the police, the judicial system, social workers etc.).

With regard to the development of labelling theory, we should not forget the contribution of groups formed around the

---

[3]    This term is used to refer to a whole range of theoretical propositions (some argue that it is not even really a theory) which result from an analysis of the negative consequences implicit in the attribution of a stigmatising label. The key labelling theorists are Erving Goffman, David Matza, Howard Becker and Edwin Lemert.

'National Deviancy Conference'[4] and the 'Arbeitskreis Junger Kriminologen'[5] which existed respectively in Britain and in West Germany. The English studies, starting from a position of cultural relativism implicit in labelling theory itself, succeeded in overturning the traditional image of crime and in creating a 'romantic' image of the deviant – a fully conscious agent, capable of making his own choices and creating his own moral universe, always in critical opposition to the status quo. As an extension of this hypothesis, the *animus* of the offender is seen as a political manifestation although in reality this analysis confines itself to individualising his resistance which – more often than not – is only generically libertarian. This analysis thus seems to be imprisoned in the field of a subjectivity from which the question of class is excluded.[6] Furthermore, for the German group, labelling theory was the starting point for a whole series of analyses which essentially developed the dynamic implicit in the 'process of definition' and of 'criminalisation' in linking itself, in part, but this time from a critical perspective, to the legal conjecture common to German criminology[7]. This body of research aimed to reveal the processes of selection implicit in the 'definitions' imposed by judges and the police, for example, using empirical data and 'field' studies. They showed that these processes can all be understood as a way of enforcing class-biased justice.

---

[4]   The National Deviancy Conference, first held in 1968, initially brought together a limited group of English sociologists 'united by a common sense of dissatisfaction with the declaration of value neutrality – considered as hypocritical – on the part of representatives of the theory'.

[5]   The 'Arbeitskreis Junger Kriminologen' was founded in 1969, in opposition to the conservative trend – widespread in Germany at that time – which was fundamentally centred on technical-judicial studies, focused on the professional training of judges. The aim of the group was to stimulate the development of a whole series of research projects aimed at providing empirical date on deviance, on crime and on the official agents of social control.

[6]   See, for example, the analyses published in *Images of Deviance* edited by Stan Cohen (Penguin, 1971) ; in *Politics and Deviance* edited by Ian Taylor and Laurie Taylor (Penguin 1973); in *The Drugtakes* by Jock Young (Paladin 1971).

[7]   See, for example, Manfred Brusten and K. Hurrelmann, *Abweichendes Verhalten in der Schule* (Munchen Juventa Verlag, 1973); Johannes Feest and Erhard Blankenburg, *Die Definitionsmacht der Polizei* (Giitersloh, Bertelsmann, 1972); Stephan Quensel, 'Soziale Fehlanpassung und Stigmati-Sierung', in *Jahrbuch fur Rechtssoziologie und Rechtstheorie*, Band 3 (Giitersloh, Bertelsmann, 1972); Rudiger Lautmann *Justiz: die stille Gewalt* (Frankfurt, Fischer Athenaum Taschenbuch); Karl Schumann, 'Ungleichheit, Stigmatisierung und Abweichendes Verhalten' in *Kriminologisches Journal*, 5 : 81-96.

A more or less deliberate attempt to correct the romantic vision of crime and deviance (and thus to confer political weight to their own analyses) is evident in a number of contemporary studies. Almost everywhere in Europe after 1968 – following certain developments which emerged out of the student and counterculture movements in different European countries – criminologists, social workers and others sought to discover what was common to all those subject to institutional segregation. The 'deviant actors' themselves became organised and formulated political objectives outside traditional political parties. It was at this time that KRUM in Scandinavia, the GIP in France, the PROP and the MPU in Britain and the SPK in Germany[8] represented for many a moment of militant participation which should have constituted the basis of an effort to remodel their theoretical positions.

Despite the remarkable differences on a theoretical level, these new trends in the 1970s constituted the *humus* which allowed groups of criminologists and sociologists from across Western Europe to get together in a group and form the European Group for the Study of Deviance and Social Control[9]. This practically self-financing group – independent vis-à-vis official international organisations such as the Council of Europe – was organised in an informal way from the very beginning. The members of the group, despite the inevitable differences between them in terms of the different disciplines they come from and their differences in methodological approach, all share an alternative view to that put forward by numerous positivist theorists. They aim to adopt

---

[8]    KRUM, Scandinavian Association for Penal Reform; GIP, Groupe d'Information sur les Prisons; PROP, Preservation of the Rights of the Prisoners; MPU, Mental Patients Union, SPK, Socialist Collective of Patients.

[9]    The European Group for the Study of Deviance and Social Control was founded in September 1972. At the time of writing, it has organised four conferences: in Florence in 1973; at the University of Essex in Colchester in 1974; at the Free University of Amsterdam in 1975; and at the University of Vienna in 1976. The next conference will be organised in Barcelona. Papers from the first conference were published in an edited collection entitled *Deviance and Control in Europe* (London, Wiley, 1975) by Herbert Bianchi, Mario Simondi and Ian Taylor. Papers delivered at subsequent conferences are also in the process of being published. Parallel to more general themes discussed during each conference, working groups have been formed since the Colchester conference on specific issues such as the state of prisons in Europe, the social control of female deviance, social welfare and deviance and the mass media, for instance.

a perspective capable of exposing the existing relations between systems of domination and control on the one hand and the relations of production and the division of labour on the other. In one of its earliest phases of activity, the work of the group seems to have redirected attention from the universe of the deviant and the different forms which deviance can take in contemporary societies towards a problematic which sees the exercise of social control as being its principal reference point. The criticism of totalitarian institutions thus seems to constitute a first step towards an analysis which seeks to take a broader approach, looking at all the official agents which have historically aimed at social control.

Such an analysis of institutions necessarily led to an analysis of the relationship which links these to the machinery of the State. This is a relationship which can be identified in all its complexity from the historical moment which marked the decline of absolutist régimes and the advent of the bourgeois State. Awareness of these relations stimulated a series of studies[10] on the rise of the Welfare State and its institutions. In these studies, these latter are considered to be means of exercising social control within societies in which overt repression had become unacceptable in favour of measures which seek to neutralise social conflict and create a widespread consensus. Leading on from these studies are those, currently very popular, which have taken a historical approach to a number of different disciplines (*cf.* the work of M. Foucault, E.P. Thompson and R. Castel, for instance). A number of contributions of this nature were presented at the last two European Group conferences.[11]

---

[10]   See, for example, several papers presented at Colchester : Tove Stang Dahl ('State Intervention and social control in nineteenth-century Europe'); Risto Erasaari ('On the Essence of German bourgeois-classical State-socialism'); Paul Corrigan and Simon Fright ('Education and Control: How the English Bourgeoisie tried to win the Hearts and Minds of the Working Class').

[11]   See, for example, the papers presented in Amsterdam, notably those by Dario Melossi ('Democracy and Public Order'); Frank Daniel, David Knights, Jeff Simm and Hugh Willmott ('Repressive Law or Lawful repression : The Problematics of Power'); Kevin Boyle ('The Changing Nature of Legal Repression in Europe : Report on Northern Ireland'); Jorgen Jepsen ('The Changing Nature of Legal Repression'); Mikko Kônkkola ('Emergency Legislation'); J. Feest, K. Huchting, W. Lange ('The Changing Nature of Legal.
Repression — A National Report'). See also the following papers from Vienna: D. Melossi and M. Pavarini ('Criminal Policies and Economic Change in the Italian Crisis of the past few years: the various positions of the left'); Boaventura de Sousa Santos, ('The experiences of popular justice after the 25th of April 1974 in Portugal'); Hilde von Balluseck ('State strategies Dealing with Deviant Behavior').

Radically distancing itself from a tradition launched in the wake of Sutherland on white collar crime, the European Group has recently chosen the criminality of the powerful as a key topic of discussion. The differences between the two may seem insignificant or even absent. Yet, whilst the Sutherland school sees white collar crime as a (rectifiable) incidence of the dysfunction of the social system, the study of the 'criminality of the powerful' sees such deviance as the inevitable corollary of the management of power in a capitalist society. Moreover, this management of power leads the State to have recourse to emergency legislation aimed at calming the anxieties created more or less artificially at the level of public opinion with regard to the problem of rising crime rates. It also allows the State to confront the new problems posed by economic recession in societies which have largely sought to manage social problems via welfare systems.

Thus, if we wish to understand the development of 'criminological knowledge' within the European Group, we could say that, after a first attempt at redefining deviance – often interpreted as a manifestation of subjective expressivity – the Group then dedicated itself to developing an analysis capable of highlighting the role played by the agents of social control in creating deviancy. This is something that labelling theory (in its European guise) had begun to shed light upon. The Group formed part of the 'New Left', standing in opposition to the traditional Left which had neglected to look at problems linked to deviance, social control and crime policy in general. Today, the analysis of crime policy has been enriched by the interest shown for the questions raised by political economy. The aim is to 'explain the permanency, the innovation or the abolition of legal and social norms and the interests that they defend, as well as of the functions they fulfil with regard to specific relations of production within societies founded upon private property, thus underlining how these are inextricably linked to the development of social contradictions'.[12]

If that is the definitive path that the most recent research carried out by the Group seems to have traced, it is nonetheless necessary to add that specific studies, carried out in the light of this research reorientation, do not yet seem to have reached the maturity we might expect owing to their adoption of a materialist methodology.

## Bibliography

Bianchi, H., Simondi, M. and Taylor, I. *Deviance and control in Europe: papers from the European Group for the Study of Deviance and Social Control*, London, Wiley, 1975

Brusten, M .and Hurrelmann, K. *Abweichendes Verhalten in der Schule*, Munchen Juventa Verlag, 1973

Cohen, S. (ed) *Images of Deviance*, Harmondsworth: Penguin, 1971

Feest, J. and Blankenburg, E. *Die Definitionsmacht der Polizei*, Giitersloh, Bertelsmann, 1972

Lautmann, R. *Justiz: die stille Gewalt* (Frankfurt, Fischer Athenaum Taschenbuch); 1972

Quensel, S. 'Soziale Fehlanpassung und Stigmati-Sierung', in *Jahrbuch fur Rechtssoziologie und Rechtstheorie*, Band 3,Giitersloh, Bertelsmann, 1972;

Schumann, K. 'Ungleichheit, Stigmatisierung und Abweichendes Verhalten' in *Kriminologisches Journal*, 5: 81-96, 1973

Taylor, I & Taylor, L (1973) *Politics and Deviance*, Harmondsworth: Penguin, 1973

Taylor, I., Walton, P. and Young, J. *The New Criminology: For a Social Theory of Deviance*, London, Routledge & Kegan Paul,1973

Taylor, I., Walton, P. and Young, J. (Editors) *Critical Criminology*, London, Routledge & Kegan Paul, 1975

Young, J. *The Drugtakers: the social meaning of drug use*, London, Paladin 1971

[12]   See 'Critical Criminology in Britain: Review and Prospects' by Ian Taylor, Paul Walton and Jock Young in *Critical Criminology* edited by Ian Taylor, Paul Walton and Jock Young (London, Routledge & Kegan Paul, 1975). This collection of essays from different English and American authors followed up on *New Criminology*, written by the same authors (London, Routledge & Kegan Paul,1973) which represented a first attempt to clear the field of criminological reflection by shedding all positivist theory. These two texts are, in part, the result of a series of debates which developed within the European Group.

# INSPIRATIONS AND ASPIRATIONS OF A CRITICAL CRIMINOLOGY?[1]

**René van Swaaningen**

*This paper was originally published in The Bulletin of the European Group for the Study of Deviance and Social Control, Issue No. 3, Summer 1991 pp. 34-45*

## INTRODUCTION

During its now eighteen years of existence, the European Group for the Study of Deviance and Social Control has set itself the task to 1) highlight social problems on the field of deviance and social control which are under-exposed by so-called 'establishment', 'administrative', or, 'governmental' criminology, 2) form an international network

---

[1]    This paper's a revised version of the introductory article to the Dutch-lingual special EGSDSC/Coornhert Liga conference issue of *Proces,* vol 69 (1990) no 9, pp 230-242. Thanks must go to Herman Bianchi, Stan Cohen and Karl Schumann for their remarks on this paper, they gave me a little confidence that my history of the European Group is at least not contradictory to that of people who were 'in' from the outset.

for academics, practitioners and activists working towards social justice, and 3) build links between intellectual and political activity, i.e. inter-relate academic enterprises with the needs and demands of social movements.

The European Group conducts an annual conference, each year in a different country, on a different theme, at which participants try to connect with left-wing politics in the host country. Thereby the European Group tries to be an impetus for overcoming the inertia produced by sub-group, class, ethnic, sexual and national boundaries. In this respect, it has already been a quite important contribution of the European Group that themes like feminism, crimes of the powerful, de-masking the political character of criminal law, the role of prisoners' and patients' movements in penal and penal-psychiatrical reform, or police-violence have been introduced into criminology. Stanley Cohen has character-ised the European Group as 'the most notable institutional achievement' of critical criminology and 'an influential force in bringing together like-minded sociologists and activists in Western Europe.'[2]

The political spectrum of Europe has changed quite a bit, from the days of the group's emergence in the 1970s, to the 1990s. It seems interesting enough to take a look at the way in which this 'spirit of time' has influenced the internal development of an explicitly political forum as the European Group, and, maybe even more important, which *basso continuo* has remained. These questions will be the topic of this paper

# ONCE UPON A TIME IN THE WEST

In 1970 Stanley Cohen, then living in England, the Italian Mario Simondi and the German Karl Schumann 'coinci-dentally' shared an office in the renowned critical *School of*

---

[2] Stanley Cohen, *Against Criminology*, Oxford. Transaction 1988, p 87. Later, Cohen depicted the concept 'social control', because of its rather flexible interpretation in critical criminology and its subsequent conceptual vagueness as a 'Mickey Mouse' or a 'hammer' concept.

*Criminology* in the University of California at Berkeley. They did not know each other previously. In their own countries, all three of them had had their experiences with the establishment of an alternative criminology, which should offer a counter-weight to the dominant Parsonian functionalism, and by doing so break the hegemony of the administrative criminology based on this paradigm. It can be called a little paradoxical that Europeans had to come to the United States to get their inspiration for the development of an alternative paradigm for functionalism - being itself the example par excellence of the North American imperialism within social sciences. Europe's specific history, and its large cultural and linguistic diversity, had prevented such a concerted action to grow, however, within the old continent itself. Now the time had come to break this situation of splendid isolation.[3]

Back in Europe, the three met in Florence and wrote together with the Englishman Laurie Taylor and the Italian Margherita Ciacci a preliminary draft of a manifesto which they circulated amongst critical minded colleagues all over Europe. The purpose was to organise a first Europe-wide conference. Amongst the invited speakers were the Dutchman Herman Bianchi, the Norwegians Thomas Mathiesen and Tove Stang Dahl, and further more various patients'- and prisoners' movements, radical or social lawyers, and, above all, the already united German and English young interactionist and (neo-) Marxist criminologists from the *Arbeitsgruppe Junger Krimlnologen* (AJK) and the National Deviancy Conference and their foreign

---

3   Stan Cohen in an interview with Maeve McMahon and Gail Kellough in the Canadian Criminology Forum vol 8 (1987) no 2, p 134 [*An abridged version of this interview is included in this anthology* Chapter 2.].

colleagues.[4]

In 1973 the time was right for this plenary international meeting. In the Italian town of Impruneta, close to Florence, the conference took place under the theme of *Deviance and Control in Europe Scope and Prospects for a Radical Criminology*. The establishment of the *European Group for the Study of Deviance and Social Control* was a fact. Herman Bianchi characterises this new criminology which had hereby emerged, in his imaginative introduction to criminology *Basismodellen*, as a 'blue jeans criminology' and gives an account of 'sleeping-bag and sit-in conferences', which were according to him a 'true relief' in comparison to the official world conferences of criminology, with 'frumpy ladies programmes', taking place in 'posh hotels', where one, 'before the second world-war in Hitler-Germany and Mussolini-Italy', generally speaks about 'problems of the level of bicycle theft', and later 'in Franco-Spain, in close harmony with Latin American participants in fine military uniforms', about virtually the same. By giving these examples, Bianchi explains how sinister it is not to be explicit about the political dimension of criminology.[5]

---

[4]   The AJK is still the mouthpiece of German-lingual critical criminologists. Next to its half-yearly conferences, the AJK forms the editorial board of the *Kriminologisches Journal*. The NDC was founded in 1968 and is, also due to both being English-lingual, merged into the European Group. See about the relationship between NDC and European Group Herman Bianchi, York en Florence, op weg naar een meuwe criminologie, in Nederlands *Tijdschrift voor Criminologie*, 1974, no 2, pp 3-17. In the Netherlands a strong macro-political oriented radical criminology has never been in strong evidence. First, the problem of the dominance of administrative criminology in the 1950s, early 60s, has been solved differently. After the democratisation of Dutch universities, governmental forces had less and less control over the independent, well blossoming institutes of criminology all over the country, i.e. in the 1970s an administrative approach of criminology was certainly not main-stream anymore. Next to this fact that at the time radical perspectives really came into being, the force to fight against was, in the Netherlands, rather absent, it was secondly, a o the pillarised Dutch society structure itself, with its less evident class-contradictions, which has just as well prevented Marxism in the more dogmatic sense to become a favourable option. It is therefore quite understandable that the resolution, which was notably voted upon during the 1975 conference at the Free University Amsterdam, to adopt Marxism as a guiding principle for the group, was rejected as a para-religious oath on Capital by the libertarian Dutch progressives - and in fact estranged quite a lot of them from the group The word 'abolitionism', which has no literal meaning in Dutch language, is in the Netherlands often used as an alternative label which indicates various radical perspectives on criminal policy.

[5]   Herman Bianchi, *Basismodellen in de Kriminologie*. Deventer Van Loghum Slaterus 1980, personal (RvS) paraphrase, to be found at pp 302-307.

Just prior to the first conference of the European Group in 1973, the military coup against the democratic Chilean government of Salvador Allende took place. The conference participants joined 15.000 people, when the Italian Communist Party (PCI, now PDS) organised a demonstration in Florence against this act of terror and to express solidarity with the Chilean workers' resistance. This spontaneous decision of the participants was more than a joined action; it embodied the outspoken unanimity about the necessity of a political commitment on the criminological subject-matter. Criminal policy was seen to be a clear battle-field for political interests. Denying these with positivist arguments implies a conservative position.[6]

Ever since, the European Group has tried to fulfil a forum-function for progressives (who have little possibilities to get their themes published and often have to speak from defensive positions) where scientific and social themes can be discussed in a co-operative and supportive atmosphere - as opposed to the classical competitive congress-atmosphere where arguments are often made for the sake of the argument. Another key-issue of the group has been the solidarity with left-wing social movements and the commitment to social justice as a starting-point for criminal policy. In this respect, it has been felt an important issue to match the theme, the conference venue and commitment to local political action.[7]

## DEVELOPMENTS WITHIN THE GROUP

The developments within the European Group could be divided in the following periods: 1) till 1977, 2) from 1977 to 1981, 3) from 1982 to 1986, and 4) after 1987.[8]

---

[6] The papers and national reports presented at this conference are, together with an elaborate history of the group, published in: Herman Bianchi, Mario Simondi & Ian Taylor (eds), *Deviance and Control in Europe*, London John Wiley & Sons 1975 A first conference-review is Drew Humphries, Report on the conference of the EGSDSC, in *Crime & Social Justice* 1974, no. 1, pp.11-17.

[7] Cf the first manifesto of the group (chapter 3 of this collection).

[8] A slightly different temporisation is given by Karen Leander in the Bulletin of the EGSDSC, no 1, winter 1989-90, pp.1-4 From her *Introducing the European Group* in this and previous EG Newsletters, several phrases are taken over by me without quotations, thank you Karen.

We can say that the first period, after having set out the direction in Florence, is characterised by filling in the radical agenda with study-themes: prisoners' actions and penal reform (University of Essex 1974), white collar crime (Free University Amsterdam 1975) and economy and crime (Vienna 1976).[9]

In the second period the role of the State becomes the central topic. In this way the tradition is started to link the conference-theme to issues which are central in the national setting of the host-country, which are to be expressed in resolutions adopted by the conference. It can therefore hardly come as a surprise that in Catalonia, which had just entered the period of transition after the Franco-dictatorship, the discussions were about State-security (Barcelona 1977), in Germany on terrorism and political violence (Bremen 1978) and in Ulster on the combination of both these themes in the specific North Irish situation - where during the conference a hunger-strike of IRA-prisoners took place (Derry 1981).[10]

In between of these quite heavily political conferences, one discussed in politically more quiet countries as Denmark or Belgium (no-one had still heard of any corrupted gendarmerie, gang of Nivel or CCC yet) on a more theoretical level about the Foucaultian inspired 'disciplined society' (Copenhagen 1979) and the use and misuse of criminological research-findings (Louvain 1980).

Maybe it goes a little far to say that many people from countries with relatively strong social-democrat traditions had become a little tired of a group which had slowly deteriorated into a slightly blindfolded political instrument, but I think it is a fair criticism to the group to say that in these days the balance between scientific and political commitment had tipped to the latter. In the third period I distinguished, we can

---

9   This period has been described by Margherita Ciacci 4 Mario Simondi, Un courant novateur de savoir criminologique l'experience de l'EGSDSC, in *Deviance et Societé,* 1977, vol 1, no 1, biz 109-117 Next to *Deviance et Societé,* other Journals indirectly linked to (the criminology of) the European Group, like (*Crime &) Social Justice, Contemporary Crises*, and the *Kriminologisches* Journal have been established in this time as well.

10  Han Janse de Jonge, Kort verslag van jaarlojkse conferentie van de EGSDSC, in *Tijdschrift voor Criminologie* 1982, no 2.

see a tendency of trying to re-find this balance by reverting the original agenda of critical criminology and its relation with social movements. After a conference which specifically dealt with youth-cultures (Bologna 1982), one conference has been fully dedicated to the variety of social movements. Here it were not in first instance the prisoners' movements which presented themselves, but rather those groups which are more indirectly confronted with the law. Papers were presented on the Basque youth-movement, North Irish republican groups, Dutch protest-groups like 'provo' (exploring the borders of the mythical Dutch tolerance in the 1960s), 'kabouters' (pre-ecologists of '68-'75) and squatters (post '75), the Norwegian women's movement, and, as a national topical political issue, the politics of sexuality and the Finnish homo-movement. (Hyytiala 1983).[11]

At later conferences of this era, on more classical themes as information technology (Cardiff 1984), prisons (Hamburg 1985)[12] and civil liberties (Madrid 1986), the social movements and political action kept playing an important role as well as the Welsh peace-groups and miners-strike, the German female and political prisoner, and the position of Andalusian day-labourers, the Spanish women's movement and other protest groups under the Franco-dictatorship and at present.

## VORWARTS, NICHT VERGESSEN[13]

In 1963 it might still have been possible to answer, in rather plain terms, Howard Becker's classical question for critical criminologists, whose side are you on? Socio-political developments

---

[11]  Whether or not the conference had to integrally support the demo against coming Finnish anti-homosexual legislation caused again a fight about the character of the group as an intolerant, dogmatic political instrument. The title of the conference-review of Reiner Kaulitzki speaks for itself: When intellectuals want to mingle on the problematic relation with social movements, in *Kriminologisches* Journal 1984, no 3, pp 232-236.

[12]  Willem de Haan, Criminologen waarschuwen tegen expansie van het strafrecht, in KRI 1985, nr 10, pp 29.

[13]  Title of a poem by Bertold Brecht, meaning 'forward, do not forget', which still is a classic song within German, and Dutch, socialist groups.

in the 1980s have made this increasingly difficult. Critical analyses with macro-scopic orientations became depicted as being irrelevant for criminal policy, and irresponsible with regards to the crime-problem. Budget-cuts at universities, increasing dependency of external contract-research, with an often strongly micro- and empiricist orientation, aiming at immediate application in criminal policy, have in fact facilitated a silent swing back to administrative criminology.[14]

All in all, there were reasons enough to dedicate a conference to some of the theoretical fundamentals of critical criminology again, at which the changed spirit of times had to be faced, the shape of justice and ideology and of the political commitment had re-evaluated; i.e. strategies for the 1990s had to be set out (Vienna 1987). Although one has to admit that the group never really formed one uniform strand within criminology, the variety of topics discussed at this particular conference was remarkable. It is also noteworthy that those critical criminologists who currently present themselves as left realists – the expression *par excellence* of the new matter-of-factness of social democrats of the 1980s - were absent. In a number of papers their work was discussed in content, but the general bantering attitude with which these 'renegades' were, point blank, placed outside of the left-wing spectrum, did not really witness good taste.[15]

At this *Wiener Kongre*, however, attempts were made to set out an alternative critical agenda, at which victimology, women's studies and informal justice studies were given an important place. And, in a certain way, one could also spot how, bit-by-bit, strongly Anglo-centristic Marxist analyses of 'the generation of '68', made way for thoughts which had their roots in abolitionist

---

[14]  Cf John Blad, Reimer van Loon & René van Swaaningen, *A decade of research on norm-production and penal control in the Netherlands*, the 1980s *confinement to utilitarianism*. Unpublished document of the Groupe Européen de Recherche sur les Normativités Paris CESDIP 1990.

[15]  Neither did the early writings of self-styled realists by, the way, in which a mere caricature of reality - i.e. labelling every previous critical criminological enterprise as 'left idealist' - was created as a background against which, obviously, the realist position turned out to be the more nuanced, serious and responsible.

insights or deconstructivist philosophies of a 'post-68 genera-tion'. In both directions feminism was remarkably placed on the foreground as a prominent source of inspiration. Within the group, women's workshops had been established, and these had an increasing input. The gender-question became an inte-gral part of every subject of discussion.

Seeing these recent developments, it was high time that the next annual conference was dedicated specifically to this theme (Jotunheimen 1988) Here, walking on Per Gynt's paths high in the rough Norwegian mountain-landscape, in complete isolation from any urban civilisation, the latent ideological and political controversies came to the surface in full intensity. Gender, sexuality and social control turned out to be an ideal 'battlefield' for opening up smouldering discontent. Put in ideal-typical terms, a strongly emotional and moralistic English-Norwegian contingent (for whom sexual violence looked not in the first place a political problem, but rather seemed to function as a new symbol of absolute evil) fought a heavy fight with a German-Dutch abolitionist group, which predominantly claimed that it is not an emancipatory move in the political sense to portray women solely as dependent, powerless victims, and that expectations of (patriarchal) criminal laws as contrib-uting to solving these problems are empirically unwarranted.[16] In theoretical abstraction we see two different models of power which are now confronted within the group 1) power as one-dimensional repression (Marxist), and 2) power as a relational dynamic process (Foucaultian).

Now this contradiction was there, it seemed useful to do something with it – can we call this scientific progress? A number of steering committee members felt, that slightly less attention should be given to the - so far - almost exclusive focus on negatively following 'the system'. This was undeniably a task critical criminology set itself, but it had really become so dominant that this other task, positively establishing an

---

[16]    It will be clear that the working-papers of this conference are extra exciting Bill Rolston & Mike Tomlinson, Gender, Sexuality and Social Control, working papers in European criminology no 10, Belfast EGSDSC 1990.

alternative approach, had been under-exposed. By following critically, we axiomatically remain one step behind, was the thesis of some dissident youngsters. For the next conference the proposal therefore was, to have a look at the resistance, the actions taken by social movements, as well as mechanisms of social control within the life-worlds at grassroots level, thereby turning around the strategic scope from *top-down* to *bottom-up* (Liverpool/Ormskirk 1989). It is clear that not all actions of black, Irish or women' groups are necessarily matching with all neo-Marxist, or indeed abolitionist, beliefs, but wasn't already the *Internationale* inviting us - at least the Dutch lyrics do so – to overcome old forms and thoughts.[17]

An attempt to transform the European Group really into an international platform - instead of a sum of various North-West European national interests — was made at the next annual conference where the still quite nationally oriented penal reformers were confronted with very up to date problems concerning east-west and south-north migration (Haarlem 1990).[18]

Anno 1990 it seemed to many that, at least in the West-European context, firstly it is a nineteenth century anachronism to speak in monolithic terms about 'The State' as a centralistic power-block with which, as an ally as well as 'as the enemy (this ambiguous relation to authorities has always existed amongst the left), society can be steered effectively. Secondly that the current character of the working-class, as well as the relations between capitalism and communism in general, have changed more rapidly than neo-Marxist analyses could explain with some sophistication; and thirdly that it cannot

---

[17] In Dutch "sterft gij oude vormen en gedachten" Unfortunately, only few people understood that the congress-title *Beyond Domination* indicated such an (attempt to) shifting the paradigm. Many contributions therefore stuckto the classical analyses. In January 1990 the 'battle of the branches' was re-fought amongst steering committee-members in Amsterdam, at which one of the members allowed himself the Freudian slip of labelling the steering committee as Central Committee.

[18] Hugo Durieux, Race and crime, what is the relation? On the, the 18th annual conference of the EGSDSC and Coornhert Liga, Haarlem (Netherlands), September 1990, in *The Bulletin of the EGSDSC*, no 2, 1990-91, pp 28-30.

be taken for granted that social movements draw one line with penal reformers, but that there are currently quite some a-typical moral entrepreneurs in favour for punitive answers amongst them.[19] In other words, old concepts are in need of a fundamental revision. We can see the European Group in this fourth period moving into a direction of a decreasing dogmatism, greater pluriformity, with a more international and, to a less evident extent, a slightly greater juridical awareness.

Personally I feel that recent social changes could well turn out to be a positive impetus to critical criminology, now it is, so to say, forced to some theoretical reorientation and political re-evaluation. It could well have been the necessary push for overcoming the repeatedly described 'crisis in critical criminology', with its impossiblisms (Jock Young), and its analytic despair and adversarial nihilism (Stan Cohen). Now being 'on the left' is no longer a 'fashionable mark of distinction, and certain proverbial leftist solidarities cannot be treated as self-evident (anymore), political commitment could well be a more fundamental choice than in those glorious 1960s and 70s, after which many 'hippies' turned quite quickly into 'yuppies'.

It is to be hoped that the balance now does not tip to the other side, that old heroes as Marx and Gramsci are not simply replaced by new ones like Lyotard and Baudrillard, and that a sort of post-modern positivism does not take the place of a commitment to social justice. Because, also in a micro-physics of power between different social relations and life-worlds, and in many ways de-centralised and often powerless State, power differences, and selective labelling of crime remain a fact. The bankruptcy of real existing socialism should, according to me, not lead us to leaving socialist traditions behind us, the idea as such has only gained topical value. As

---

[19] Scheerer explicitly points at tendencies within the German environmental, anti-fascist and women's movements to claim for penal repression of the problems they aim to tackle. He calls these 'a-typical' because the, 'typical moral entrepreneurs' are found amongst conservative law-and-order abiding citizens, whereas the new social movements have a progressive background. Sebastian Scheerer, Atypische Moralunternehmer, in *Kriminologisches Journal*, 1. Beiheft 1986, pp 133-155.

always, not everybody has equal opportunities to realise his or her ideas, income-differences increase all over Europe, and even in social-democratic strongholds such as the Netherlands the tolerance towards marginalised groups (notably ethnic minorities, refugees etc.) decreases rapidly, the word solidarity has almost become an abuse, a modern poverty can be seen growing, and the new left (nieuw links) has faded away to a 'new square' (nieuw flinks). And furthermore, can it, looking at all the empirical evidence gathered in criminology, ever be called 'outdated' to stress the relationship between economic factors and crime, and subsequently between socio-economic and criminal policy? With a new-styled critical criminology we should be wary not to throw away the baby with the bath-water. Or, as Stanley Cohen has put it, we should 'not use intellectual scepticism as an alibi for political inaction.'[20]

# UNITY IN DIVERSITY

At present, the European Group counts some four hundred members, divided over twenty-five countries. Of the 'hard-core' of participants who come to nearly every conference, the vast majority are, however, from North-West European countries. The group always tries to organise conferences on a low-budget basis, and reserves some money for serious participants who are unable to pay fees, in order to minimise financial obstacles for participation. Nonetheless, the lower participation from Eastern and Southern Europe has, next to the lingual (and cultural) dominance of the English, also financial reasons.[21]

---

[20] Stanley Cohen, *Intellectual scepticism and political commitment, the case of radical criminology*, University of Amsterdam 1990, p 32.

[21] Membership-fees and the sale of working papers form the main sources of income of the group. These can be used, after deducting the costs of the secretariat and the production of working papers, to subsidise participants. These funds are, however, increasingly insufficient. If it were possible anyway for the group to get it, the European Group is, up till now, reluctant to apply for structural subsidy, being afraid of losing some of its autonomy. Incidental subsidies for conferences have been accepted though. Thanks to a quite generous, and unconditional, subsidy of the city of Haarlem, and of the Netherlands Probation service and Ministry of Justice, it was possible to invite people from nearly all East European countries to the 1990 conference on migration and penal reform.

The continuity of this group, which is functioning on a voluntary basis, is safeguarded by one central secretariat [co-ordinator] and a so-called steering committee consisting of one representative of every country, who is annually elected by the national groups during the conference.[22] Together, these people take care that (paying) members receive two newsletters a year, in which a report of the previous conference, an announcement for the next, reports of national situations, and commentaries on relevant issues are inserted. In 1979 the group decided to take the publication of the conference-papers, in a series of *Working Papers in European Criminology*, in its own hands.[23] In 1990, open research-proposals and results of members are introduced; not only to inform other members, but also inviting them to make a more active contribution, and facilitating international comparative research. By this expansion of the newsletter to a true bulletin, the forum-function of the group has been improved.

With its eighteenth anniversary, the European Group has, in 1990, quite literary come of age. With labels like 'radical', 'critical' or 'new', criminologists in the 1970s have distinguished themselves from colleagues more loyal to the statal authorities, who saw little problems in taking over criminal definitions of certain social problems, and who, either silently or outspoken, accept the idea that criminologists should contribute to the fight against crime. In this sense, an adjective as 'critical' still seems a sensible borderline.

From the specific contextual point of departure it is understandable that an alternative forum as the European

---

[22] The secretariat was established by Mario Simondi in Florence, than continued by Didi Gipser and Sabine Klein-Schonnefeld in respectively Hamburg and Bremen, and has since and during the difficult period of the second half of the 1980s been run by Karen Leander in Stockholm. In order to prevent stagnation or clique formation, steering committee members are supposed to circulate every three years, but it has become quite difficult to find people willing to do the 'Job', so that this ideal-typical rule cannot always be upheld.

[23] Working papers bear the title of the respective conference at which the inserted papers are presented. No real selection of them is being made, but the whole volume is edited by Bill Rolston and Mike Tomlinson in Belfast. After having put a lot of time and energy in producing ten volumes, the motivation to continue the work had decreased below the minimum, merely because the selling and distribution of the Working papers to others than members turned out to be quite hard.

Group emerged; one simply cannot establish a competing paradigm in an established surrounding where the general level of discussions remains at attacking the most basic (political and scientific), assumptions of critical criminology. In retrospect, we have to admit, however, that a predominantly internal orientation of critical criminologists has also driven it into an isolated position. The cliché accusation that present critical criminology very much looks like an esoteric sect, where the 'believers' only convince each other of the 'true' knowledge, cannot be completely denied. And, when in a struggle between branches, pointing at differences becomes the dominant focus, the fact that there are important basic similarities is easily lost out of sight. In the political sense, I feel, this is also laming for a necessary alertness. The Netherlands' League for Penal Reform, the Coornhert Liga, is according to me, a good example how, with perspectives of both due process and abolitionism, people can quite successfully politically operate together, by taking the first option for short-term action and the latter as longer term point of orientation.[24]

A first necessity for a relevant critical criminology in the 1990s needs, according to me, to imply that on the balance of abstract, theoretical debates on the one scale, and of attempts to practical criminal political action on the other, some more weight should be placed on the latter.[25] In this more pragmatic and less dogmatic approach, more thorough empirical studies

---

[24]   Cf. about the Liga in English, the Netherlands' national report of the Haarlem conference of 1990.

[25]   For criminology in general it could seem as if I have come to slightly contradictory recommendations. In our research-inventory (Blad, Van Loon & Van Swaaningen op cit, p 60), we concluded that "empiricism has been shown to be an effective means to neutralise a possible critical input of science ( ) policy-subordinated studies are used as post hoc-legitimations." This analysis, however, should be seen in the light of the earlier described silent swing back to administrative criminology in the Netherlands. The case of critical criminology is radically different though, it has alienated itself too much from reality. I am sorry to sound so middle of the road, but in this case I frankly feel that the balance between theory-formation and empirical research should really in the middle if one wants to offer any serious political counter-weight. And, besides a strictly pragmatically oriented research-project is not what I mean with getting practical in the political sense. As in the Liga, lawyers, in my opinion, could play a more important role in 'translating' criminological aims into political claims.

of the whole subject-matter in the broader sense, which do no longer, take penal intervention as the sole starting-point, are of crucial importance. The shift indicated at the Vienna conference of 1987, and enforced by the theme chosen for the Liverpool [Ormskirk] conference of 1989, in which critically following of 'The State' and its agencies of social control should make some way for analyses of regulatory mechanisms and counter-strategies on meso- and life-world levels, still seems a fruitful starting-point. At the 1990 conference in Haarlem the spectrum has been opened up in another sense as well; a large percentage of non-typical European Group conference visitors participated i.e. East Europeans, lawyers and left realists.

It is also worth noting that the idea of the Haarlem conference of 1990 - the aim of bringing together various European penal reform movements in order to put some more emphasis on the forum-function of the European Group, and to facilitate international politics at grassroots level - comes also quite close to the origins of the group. Looking at, for example, the very first book of the group, the prominent place of analyses of penal reform in general and descriptions of prisoners' movements in particular - from Scandinavia (Thomas Mathiesen/ Wiggo Røine), England (Mike Fitzgerald), France (Jacques Donzelot) and Italy (Raffaele Rauty, Guido Neppi Modona & Irene Invernizzi) - is striking. At the Haarlem conference we were given a good picture of how these groups have developed over the 1980s - or why they have disappeared.[26]

Raising a plea for a more explicit international orientation within the European Group may seem slightly ridiculous.

---

[26] For 1973, in Bianchi, Simondi & Taylor op cit, in particular pp 85-143. For 1990 Rene van Swaaningen, The Penal Lobby in Europe, in The Bulletin of the EGSDSC, no 2, Winter 1990/91, pp 21-27. The idea of devoting a conference to finding out how some of these pilot movements of the European Group have developed over the 1980s, was launched by Stanley Cohen at the Jotunheimen conference of 1988 and was picked up by the need the Coornhert Liga felt to get into contact with some of its European sister-movements. According to me, this 'new' approach and the re-finding of some 'roots' remains in fact closer to the individual development of some non-English 'founders' of the group, like Karl Schumann, Johannes Feest, Manfred Brusten, Hemz Steinert, Stan Cohen, Herman Bianchi, Thomas Mathiesen or Nils Christie.

Nonetheless, I am completely serious about this. So far, the word 'international' has not implied much more than the sum of various national analyses. Real (empirical) comparative studies were rather exception than rule at European Group conferences. Taking this attempt seriously should now really be a number one priority for the group. But even on the more basic level of simply taking notice of cultural differences, and thereby hopefully de-constructing some national self-evidences and relativating national certainties, the European Group is not reaching what it could establish. The often ideological and globalising, generalising discussions within the group have in fact prevented cultural differences coming to the surface. Moreover, the European Group has for a long time predominantly debated upon typical British hobbyhorses, which were de-contextualised and then theoretically abstracted as universal problems. In this way the comical (or politically problematic?) situation emerged, that for example Spanish people were seriously speaking about net-widening effects and co-optation of alternatives, without any alternative sanctions being in evidence in some far horizon of their country. Could this not be one other reason why the European Group has largely remained a North-Western affair? Or what about the Dutch or Scandinavians discussing the authoritarian State? Obviously the English as a lingua franca goes a little further than just being a working-language. With the internationalisation of the European Group I therefore mean, secondly, breaking the Anglo-American imperialism on the discussion themes, by mapping out some clear national differences.

At the Haarlem conference of 1990 this has already got some dimension, because with the chosen topic of migration, on the abstract level, concepts of 'otherness' and 'diversity' play a role *par excellence*.[27] Here attempts have been made also to

---

[27]   Cf Frank Bovenkerk, Misdaad en de multi-etnische samenleving, in Justitiele Verkenningen, vol 16 (1990), no 5, pp 8-29, presented in English as Crime and the Multi-Ethnic Society at the Haarlem conference, and Willem de Haan, Allochtones and autochtones, equality and difference in culture and crime, *id*.

outline some already visible effects of the proposed (economic) West-European unification in both the typical immigration and the typical emigration countries, and some effects which are still to be expected - growing co-operation in police- and judicial actions; increasing exchange of data - (technology); *de facto* closure of so-called 'exterior borders'; introduction of identity-cards in countries without obligation to identify oneself (i.e. to the police); weakening social positions of migrants from so-called third countries; increasing collisions between cultural values of autochtone and allochtone groups etc. Next to signalling these problems, an attempt has been made as well to concentrate forces for social justice on a European level.

Attempts to 'opening up', true, internationalisation, and remaining committed to the group's basic principle of social justice, will be proceeded at the 1991 conference, which is taking place at a border-line of Eastern and Western cultures in Potsdam. May the nineteenth annual conference on *Processes of Marginalisation and Integration* provide the city with another image as it historically has got. By now critically analysing possible social consequences of increasingly internationally oriented criminal policies on bottlenecks like policing, social security, or labour-law, the European Group continues its maybe most important tradition; introducing under-exposed social problems into criminology.

## SOME CONCLUDING REMARKS

In fact, many of the points raised in the preceding para-graph on the future of the group, come down to re-affirming some, and *de facto* fulfilling some other, original expectations of critical criminology - commitment to social justice and to social movements, left wing pluriformity, the unmasking of the political implications of criminal politics, developing positive scenarios for a competing paradigm etc. Especially in the light of all current social configurations, political commitment will still imply that the claim of justice should always be followed by the question 'whose justice?', just as well as the choice of answering this question will still be made from a position of the marginal groups in society. The specific, informal and non-competitive, character of the group's conferences also deserves to be upheld - as long as this does not prevent people from being critical towards their 'own people', and leave 'true, critical positions' unreflected. The starting point that the group is a forum for both academics and activists, can certainly contribute to increasing the practical relevance of critical criminology, as well as for the development of an action-oriented theory.

Similar remarks could be made with regards to the establishment of a competing paradigm as such. After having 'liberated' social sciences from a North American-styled functionalism, now the specific *British* socio-political constellation styles general concepts of critical criminology to a large extent. Acknowledging the wide diversity between political climates and histories of the various European countries, I think we would do better not to strive any longer for uniform paradigms and strategies which are supposed to be applicable in every country. The establishment of the proposed, more open, structure, based on an international left pluralism, starts with the acknowledgement that certainly not all (critical) people working on the criminological subject-matter are sociologists. In some countries, such as Spain, social sciences are even in the stadium of infancy, but very interesting and relevant Marxian interpretations of State and law are to found within legal history or philosophy. And in some Northern European countries we will also find a majority of criminal lawyers, and (social) psychologists, amongst academic criminologists. These differences should be mirrored in a truly *European* Group.

Exact comparisons between the dogmatic legal cultures of Germany and Spain, with those of more case-law oriented cultures as Britain or the Netherlands; or the legitimations and functions of criminal law in the  transitory process towards democracy, by comparing countries with long democratic traditions, with those coming from dictatorships, or with States which have been blessed with the authoritarian structures of the real existing socialism, or *idem* in relation with the respective absence, emergence, long establishment or decline of the Welfare-State etc. are just some of the many issues which could offer interesting enough impulses for a critical criminology where unity is primarily expressed in the level in which it is able to do justice to these diversities.

## Bibliography

Bianchi, H. 'York en Florence, op weg naar een meuwe criminology', in *Nederlands Tijdschrift voor Criminologie*, 1974, no 2, pp. 3-17.

Bianchi, H., Simondi, M. and Taylor, I. *Deviance and control in Europe: papers from the European Group for the Study of Deviance and Social Control*, London, Wiley, 1975.

Bianchi, H. *Basismodellen in de Kriminologie*. Deventer Van Loghum Slaterus 1980.

Bovenkerk,F. 'Misdaad en de multi-etnische samenleving', in *Justitiele Verkenningen*, vol 16, no 5, pp. 8-29, 1990.

Blad, J., van Loon, R. and van Swaaningen, R. *A decade of research on norm-production and penal control in the Netherlands, the 1980s confinement to utilitarianism*. Unpublished document of the Groupe Européen de Recherche sur les Normativités Paris CESDIP 1990.

Cohen, S. *Intellectual scepticism and political commitment, the case of radical criminology*, University of Amsterdam, 1990 de Haan, W. 'Criminologen waarschuwen tegen expansie van het strafrecht', in *KRI*, no. 10, pp. 29, 1985.

Durieux, H. 'Race and crime, what is the relation? On the, the 18th annual conference of the EGSDSC and Coornhert Liga, Haarlem (Netherlands), September 1990', in *The Bulletin of the EGSDSC*, no 2, 1990-91, pp. 28-30.

Humphries, D. 'Report on the conference of the EGSDSC', in *Crime & Social Justice* 1974, no. 1, pp. 11-17.

Kaulitzki, R. 'When intellectuals want to mingle on the problematic relation with social movements', in *Kriminologisches Journal*, no 3, pp. 232-236, 1984.

Rolston, B. and Tomlinson, M. *Gender, Sexuality and Social Control, working papers in European Criminology no 10*, Belfast EGSDSC 1990.

Scheerer, S. 'Atypische Moralunternehmer', in *Kriminologisches Journal*, 1. pp. 133-155, 1986.

van Swaaningen, R. 'The Penal Lobby in Europe', in The Bulletin of the EGSDSC, no 2, Winter 1990/91, pp. 21-27.

# MARGINAL TO WHAT?

**Phil Scraton**

*This article was original published in the Socio-Legal Newsletter, No. 49, Summer 2006 as a response to David Nelken's paper 'Towards a European Sociology of Law' (Newsletter 47) in which he referred to the 'somewhat marginalised European Group for the Study of Deviance and Social Control'.*

It is a beautiful May Saturday in Padova 2006. The patio doors along the length of the recently refurbished lecture theatre are open, the scent of early summer flowers occasionally wafts across the room. I teach four sessions over eight hours to postgraduates drawn mainly from Northern Italy although there are also students from Greece, Argentina and Colombia. Each year I come to Italy's second oldest university to give seminars on critical criminological theory derived in my primary research. However intense the discussions, however punctuated by Ilaria's unhesitating translation and however exhausted at the day's end, it is always an exciting and privileged experience. It encapsulates precisely why I was first drawn to academic work. And like so many other opportunities it began with the European Group.

Its full title, the somewhat curious and long-winded *European Group for the Study of Deviance and Social Control,* masks its radical edge. As a young lecturer at the Open University I was intrigued by the stacks of bound European Group Working Papers occupying every inch of floor space in Martin Loney's study. He enthused relentlessly about the Group to anyone who would listen. Finally, in 1984 I went to Cardiff, now occasionally referred to as the 'left realist' conference. While British members disputed the appropriateness or otherwise of the 'left idealist' label, those outside the debate – geographically and politically – looked on in astonishment. The sometimes acrimonious exchanges seemed a sideshow. For this was the height of the 1984-85 Coal Dispute and Thatcher's all-out attack on the unions, having orchestrated the sinking of the Belgrano and the deaths of 10 hunger strikers in the H Blocks. The New Right's authoritarian grip was exemplified by the continuing increase in the powers of the police and security services and the expansion of European prisons accompanied by a parallel diminution in political accountability.

Never before had I attended an academic conference alongside striking workers and their families. Sessions were packed, the atmosphere electric and much of the broader European analysis has since proved prophetic. Yet the most moving moment came on the final evening. We were guests of the miners at a welfare club high in the South Wales valleys. Following passionate speeches from miners' leaders and Women Against Pit Closures and the full emotion of a male voice choir, Beppe Mosconi and Bill Rolston sang songs of struggle from Italy and Ireland. I have not missed a conference since.

It was with a wry smile that I read David Nelken's brief reference to the European Group in his important article on the possible agenda for a European sociology of law. There is no 'split' between the Group and the relatively recent European Society for Criminology. From the outset it was clear that the Society had a different agenda and so it has progressed. Unfortunately, our conferences have occasionally clashed in time and place. David's comment that the European Group is 'somewhat marginalised' is not particularly controversial but raises the question: 'marginal' to what? To administrative criminology? To mainstream academic discourses? To the British Society of Criminology or the European Society for Criminology? To the priorities of government departments, funding agencies or publishers? To the UK Research Assessment Exercise? If the answers are affirmative then perhaps all is well. For it is precisely to challenge the 'mainstream' that the European Group was established. Fast approaching its 34th Annual Conference it remains true to its roots. While some might caricature the Group as 'old-fashioned', as 'reductionist', as representing the 'State' and its institutions as monolithic rather than multi-layered and complex, three decades of conferences and a mass of publications reveal the naiveté of such comments.

Back in Padova the postgraduates are engaged in a sharp discussion around the complexity of political institutions and the overarching reach of structural relations. With contributions from Latin America and Southern Europe the exchange focuses on Sivanandan's conceptualisation of globalism. It is clear that while accepting the inherent diversity of power in interpersonal, social and societal relations, power relations - within international structures of production, within contemporary patriarchies and within the internalised dynamics of neo-colonialism - remain central to contextual, critical analysis. Later that evening conversations range from the political and economic marginalisation of the diverse immigrant communities in Via Anelli, on the edge of affluent Padova, to the expansive scandals in Italian soccer now enveloping politicians and the Vatican. It is inconceivable to attempt to make sense of these issues without foregrounding analysis of structural relations.

The Padovans' primary research in communities and prisons on difficult and contentious issues is carried out on a shoestring yet it provides an essential alternative to the State-sponsored evaluation studies passing as research. It demonstrates commitment to alternative discourses, yet not without personal risk or professional consequences. It typifies the marginalisation of critical analysis by established academic interests that serve and service advanced democratic states and their institutions. If such work is to be categorised marginal, it should be with regard to the politics of marginalisation directed against its critical priorities and its political implications. For it is from such challenging research that 'troubling recognitions', so well identified by Stan Cohen in *States of Denial*, emerge.[1]

In his account of the evolution of the National Deviancy Conference, Stan Cohen comments that the NDC's 'most notable institutional achievement' was its role in the creation of the European Group which had 'become a force in bringing together like-minded sociologists and activists in Western Europe'.[2]

The Group's founders were committed to connecting academic research and community-based activism, resisting the pre-eminence of 'conservative, positivist and functionalist orientations within criminology' and their translation into State policy and institutional practice. It was resistance to what Nils Christie, himself a founding member, later named 'useful knowledge': useful only to State institutions and their managers.[3] Utility, in this context, erodes the capacity and opportunity for 'critical thinking'. The European Group, initially focusing on the structural relations of class, political economy and State power, expanded its reach to 'overcome other national, linguistic, ethnic, sexual and gender barriers in an effort to develop a critical, emancipatory and innovative criminology' particularly in research and dissemination'.

In September 2005 the 33rd Annual Conference came to Queen's University, Belfast. It was the Group's third visit to Ireland, each typifying a direct connection to local events. The 1981 Derry Conference, *The Politics of Internal Security*, was held in the context of the ongoing hunger strikes. The 1995 Crossmaglen Conference reflected the moment of the ceasefires and the optimism of the Peace Process despite presentations constantly being interrupted by military helicopters coming

---

[1]  Cohen *States of Denial*, 2000.
[2]  Cohen, 'Footprints on the sand' 1981 pp. 240-241.
[3]  Christie, *Crime Control as Industry*, 1994 p.58.

and going to the adjacent army barracks. Ten years on the 2005 Belfast Conference, *Crime, Justice and Transition*, explored the significance of transition in understanding definitions of 'crime' and 'justice', political constructions of criminalization and ideologies of 'other'. It provided an opportunity to consider the theoretical and political imperatives of transition focusing particularly on crime and criminalisation, criminal justice and punishment, and social justice and human rights. While the timing had particular significance for Ireland, the aim was to broaden the debate, theoretically and politically, around 'transition'.

The Conference was gripped by a powerful and dignified opening address from Geraldine Finucane. Her husband, Pat Finucane, was murdered in their home on the 12th February 1989 by two Loyalist gunmen operating in collusion with the British State. He was shot 14 times in front of Geraldine and their three children. Pat Finucane was a prominent and principled lawyer who had worked to challenge the injustices suffered by many Republicans, including representation of those on hunger strike. A month before he was murdered a Home Office Minister in the Thatcher Government, Douglas Hogg, stated in Parliament that there was 'a number of solicitors who are unduly sympathetic to the cause of the IRA'. The Loyalist organisation that claimed responsibility for the murder alleged that Pat Finucane was an officer in the Provisional IRA - an allegation denied by the police.

What eventually emerged was the involvement by police, military and security services in Pat Finucane's murder, in protecting the killers, in initiating a cover-up and in undermining investigations. Persistent demands and campaigns for a full independent inquiry into State collusion in several killings, including that of Pat Finucane and of human rights lawyer Rosemary Nelson in March 1999, led to Canadian Judge Peter Cory recommending public inquiries in each case. In September 2004 the Secretary of State for Northern Ireland stated that the 'Government is determined that where there are allegations of collusion the truth should emerge'.

The Finucane family expressed profound concern regarding proposed restrictions on the 'public' nature of an inquiry. A UK Government official told the Human Rights Commission in Geneva that a 'large proportion' of the inquiry 'would probably have to be held in private'. Geraldine Finucane has remained at the forefront of the campaign to access the truth of her husband's murder and the cover-up that followed. Her talk covered the long sequence of events and argued there should be no hierarchy of death, that her family's case is not one in isolation.

Other plenary sessions were also significant. They included comparative analyses of 'societies in transition' and the 'implications of transition for criminology'. Returning to the local theme, Bill Rolston introduced the 'current political situation' in the North of Ireland. The panel included Danny Morrison, former Sinn Fein publicity director, David Ervine of the Progressive Unionist Party with close links to the Ulster Volunteer Force and Margaret Ward, author of *Unmanageable Revolutionaries: Women and Irish Nationalism*. Again, this proved to be a momentous and moving session. It was followed by an afternoon visit to the Loyalist Shankill community and to Republican West Belfast where Laurence McKeown's film on the hunger strikes, *H3*, was shown. (For full conference papers, including Geraldine Finucane's opening address, see EG web-site).[4]

The 2006 Conference, *The Regulation of Migration, Asylum and Movement in the 'New Europe'*, will be held at the University of the Peloponnese, Corinth (31st August to 3rd September). It will consider the regulatory responses to the movement and surveillance of people throughout Europe in the context of the 'war on terror'. As the European Union is going through unprecedented expansion other key events, such as the assassination of the film director Van Gogh in the Netherlands and the uprisings in Paris suburbs, have reignited controversies over immigration policies and models of integration within

---

[4]    http://www.europeangroup.org/conferences/2005/.

Europe. This expansion has revived theoretical and political debates about immigration, State borders and sovereignty.

It promises to be another engaging conference, a forum where established academics, community activists and new researchers present alongside each other, where reputations are irrelevant and where postgraduates and others developing new work have space and opportunity to meet and share ideas. On numerous occasions we have been virtually bankrupt yet the European Group has survived and the British/Irish section now holds an annual Easter conference. Whatever the frustrations we share over the Group's somewhat erratic communication, precarious finances and uncertain future venues the collaborations, support, exchanges and friendships have had a lasting significance for the many participants, occasional or regular. In terms of research, publication, teaching and campaigns the European Group has made a marked and lasting contribution.

## Bibliography

Christie, N *Crime Control as Industry* Routledge, London, 2nd Edn. 1994

Cohen, S 'Footprints on the sand: a further report on criminology and the sociology of deviance' in M. Fitzgerald et al. [eds] *Crime and Society: Readings in History and Theory* Routledge & Kegan Paul, London. 1981.

Cohen, S. *States of Denial: Knowing about suffering and atrocities* Cambridge: Polity Press 2000.

# 8

# LOUK HULSMAN

## Andrea Beckmann

*This paper was originally published in the journal 'Criminal Justice Matters' Volume 76, Issue 1, 2009 and a version is available also on the Louk Hulsman website.[1]*

The Rotterdam penal law and criminology professor emeritus Louk Hulsman died on the 28th of January 2009 at the age of 85. He was, along with Nils Christie and Thomas Mathiesen, one of the most important penal abolitionists worldwide.

Louk was further the director of the Rasphuys Institute and was, amongst other commitments, a leading member of the *European Group for the Study of Deviance and Social Control*, the Netherlands representative of ICOPA [International Conference on Penal Abolitionism] as well as Chair of The Coornhert League for the Reformation of the Criminal Law.

In the Netherlands, Louk is regarded as the founder of liberal drugs policy as his influential work and stance contributed significantly to the alteration of the Opium Act in 1976. His most influential publications include the *Report on Decriminalisation* (Council of Europe, 1980) and (with Jacqueline

---
[1] http://www.loukhulsman.org/.

Bernat de Celis) *Peines perdues. Le systeme penal en question.*[2] He is perhaps best well known for 'Critical criminology and the concept of crime' which was first published in 1986 and has been widely reproduced since.[3]

Louk was born in Kerkrade in 1923 and, after attending boarding school and the St. Bernadis Gymnasium, he became active in the resistance to Nazi Germany's occupation of his country. In return for his brave activism he was interned in the concentration camp in Amersfoort. He managed to escape and continued to work in the resistance. It is perhaps these early experiences that made Louk profoundly question the legitimacy of penal law, of State authority as well as the meaningfulness of the category of 'crime' as he kept reminding us that an awful lot of things were and are categorised as 'criminal' but that this does not say anything about their wrongness or indeed their harmfulness.

Louk worked as a civil servant in Dutch defence and justice administrations during the 1950s. In 1964 he became the first professor of Criminal Law at the Erasmus University, Rotterdam. Louk Hulsman always engaged in a critical manner with the State, for example by serving as a Councillor in the Dutch Ministry of Justice, as Chair of the Dutch Probation Service, Chair of the Dutch Association for Penal Reform and as a member of the advisory boards of the Dutch Police Academy and of the first Dutch Committee on Drug Policy. He continued his important work with worldwide lectures, workshops and seminar engagements that stimulated critical reflections and further developed alternative ideas to the hegemonic belief systems that govern much of the fields of law, criminology, the media and often strongly impact on public opinion.

He also acted as the Netherland's representative on the European Committee on Crime Problems of the Council of Europe in the 1980s and was once again an important and outspoken influence at last year's Cannabis Tribunal in

---

[2]    European Committee on Crime Problems, *Report on Decriminalisation,* 1980; Hulsman. and Bernat de Celis, *Peines perdues.* 1982.

[3]    Hulsman 'Critical criminology and the concept of crime', 1986.

The Hague (1.12.2008). He contributed to the development of European common study programs on drug policy and critical criminology (with Frederick McClintock and Stephan Quensel), preparing the ground for the Erasmus and Sokrates programs within the EU. He thus facilitated the development of new generations of critical criminological scholarship within Europe and world-wide.

Louk's important contribution was fundamentally interdependent with his extraordinary personality. He embodied and lived the humanistic, open and eclectic core of abolitionist thought that takes care to be sensitive to the contextual, situational and personal interpretations of 'lived experiences' as they are defined by people. In the current context of 'penal overkill' that characterises so many societies, it is important to re-appreciate the anascopic stance and associated practices that lie at the heart of Louk's life-work.

Louk was also a close friend who is now sadly missed by many, who was a genuinely cosmopolitan and warm-hearted person, who enjoyed being with people, in nature and to be in the midst of life itself. Louk continues to be an inspiration for the on-going struggle of challenging the very foundations of legitimizing systems of coercion that generate harm and suffering and to value and practice solidarity. His legacy as a pedagogue lies certainly within the tradition of critical pedagogy as: 'Pedagogy in the critical sense illuminates the relationship among knowledge, authority, and power.' Louk fulfilled this task as a critical criminologist.

## Bibliography

European Committee on Crime Problems, *Report on Decriminalisation,* Council of Europe, 1980

Giroux, H. A. *Disturbing pleasures: Learning popular culture.* New York: Routledge, 1994

Hulsman, L.H.C. and Bernat de Celis, J. *Peines perdues. Le systeme penal en question*, Ed. du Centurion, 1982

Hulsman, L.H.C. 'Critical criminology and the concept of crime', in *Contemporary Crisis,* Vol. 10, No. 1, pp. 63-80 1986

# 9

# PANIC OR DENIAL

## ON WHETHER TO TAKE CRIME SERIOUSLY

### Stanley Cohen

*This paper was delivered to the 37th Annual Conference of the European Group for the Study of Deviance and Social Control held in Preston in 2009. A similar paper was delivered to the British Society of Criminology conference in that year and a version of this paper was subsequently published in their Newsletter, No. 64, Special Edition, Autumn 2009 pp 1-10*

Last year, I gave a graduation day address to sociology students at Middlesex University. I talked about the clichéd advice that dominated these occasions: 'Put your three years at university behind you; it's time to enter the real world.' I told the students to please pay no attention to this advice. It's just another form of social control to stop you from continuing to appreciate the values that you should have picked up in any decent university - care for learning in itself; scepticism about accepted knowledge; the personal qualities of tolerance and friendship; the political values of fairness and social justice. Above all, they should question the notion that their three years of university were not 'real', that university life was somehow 'artificial'. But what is taken as 'real' life

- A mental hospital? Perhaps the Houses of Parliament during the expenses story? A training school for suicide bombers? Or maybe reality television, watching a group of your fellow human beings degrade themselves and each other in front of audiences of 12 million?

I warned them - as I warn you - to beware of the people whom Saul Bellow calls *reality instructors*: You know those people who are always grabbing you to tell you 'What Things Are Really Like': the cops, doctors, judges and journalists who instruct you on how things work 'out there'. The criminological version of 'out there' is sitting in the back of a police van. Allow me then to continue with a narrative of change and continuity which lead up to the work I'm doing now. I promise not to instruct you about what is really real; my subject is rather what is really *important*.

## MORAL PANICS

*Folk Devils and Moral Panics* was surely a child of its time and place.[1] At the end of the Seventies I went to live in Israel for what turned out seventeen years. As this period moved along, so the book and its cultural milieu seemed more and more remote. Even the dumbest and most otiose sociology does not require a theory to 'explain' the differences between Britain in the Sixties and Israel in the Eighties. I am merely trying to think aloud (and in print) about the complex links between biography and external social reality.

In the mid-Nineties, I returned to London and to teaching criminology, deviance and social control courses at the LSE. I tried to reconstruct for my students the texts and contexts of labelling theory, the NDC, new deviancy theory and the new criminology. From my vantage point now, the criticism of our supposed liberal tolerance looks more interesting. The first wave of radical theorists had indeed argued that *too much stuff* was being (to use some

---

[1]    Cohen, *Folk Devils and Moral Panics* 1972.

ugly but useful terms) criminalized, deviantised or problematised): defining deviance up, as this was later called. The point is not whether we approve; nor whether we can sympathize, nor whose side we are on. Nor is everything simply a matter of political stance: non-interventionism can be justified by conservatives (not the responsibility of governments, leave it to the market); liberals (civil rights are threatened, private life is not the business of the State); and radicals (distrust of the repressive State apparatus, the crime problem requires not legal tinkering but radical change of whole society).

The eclectic elements in the original discourse - symbolic interactionism, socialism, restorative justice - hardly added up to a coherent social policy. Social policy is by definition interventionist - which means *doing something* about the problem, for example: moral enterprise to stop the problem from being normalised, further enterprise to draw attention to its seriousness, new laws, prohibitions or sanctions; improving the criminal justice and other social control systems. But these responses only make sense if you have taken the problem seriously. This recognition soon prompted the radical model to develop its own internal self-correction. Therefore the phase of 'left realism' and 'taking crime seriously'.[2]

The pristine rhetoric was 'against' the moral panic: there's no need to panic, calm down, it's not that serious, it's not the end of the world, there are more serious problems. The liberal and radical exposures of moral panic was informed by discovery or recovery of victims - especially under the driving force of feminism. The (still expanding) literature on victims, harm, danger and risk began to examine the empirical base for what has been on the agenda of ethics and moral philosophy for centuries.

---

[2]   Cohen, *States of Denial* 2000.

# DENIAL

The phenomena that concerned me in *States of Denial* were undisputedly serious - torture, genocide, ethnic violence, terror, political massacres, atrocities of all types, 'social suffering' resulting from poverty, racism as well as natural disasters. And just as I had written more about moral panics than folk devils, I was now dealing with reactions to these phenomena (my subtitle is *Knowledge About Atrocities And Suffering*) rather than the phenomena themselves. I don't want to repeat what the book says about how my life in Israel influenced my whole subject, nor about the concept of denial. My viewpoint here is much narrower: the hidden continuities and overlaps between these two books.

The most obvious link, is that the entire human rights enterprise is a product of social construction. The legalistic ownership of the problem is conveyed in the relatively recent term 'human rights violations'. This translates the traditional moralistic language of sin and evil into the legal dialect. In the public realm, however, this translation hardly ever works: participation in genocide, for example, is not convincingly described as a 'human rights violation'. The more pictorial languages of atrocity and social suffering are obviously more appropriate.

In any event, the work of humanitarian organizations and the media is clearly a form of moral enterprise; there are moral crusades and campaigns. But are there moral panics? And is there anything helpful in conceptualizing them as the 'opposite' of denial? I was prompted to ask these questions by current versions of the standard critique that the concept of moral panic is inherently normative, political and value-loaded. The Melanie Phillips version is best known: the left-liberal elitists (who, of course, dominate the media) have simply applied the label of moral panic in a selective and biased way to the wholly justified reactions of ordinary people to real problems.

Hysterical as the 'right realist' position may be, there a peculiar sense in which Phillips is correct. When these left liberals study or support social movements - say, in favour of animal rights or the heavier criminalization of domestic violence - they will hardly describe them moral panics. The category of moral panic is, however, 'objective' in the sense that the criteria for defining some social reactions as moral panics and others not, can be set out and applied by any observer. Thus there can theoretically be 'negative moral panics' (the traditional ones that criminologists so readily detect, expose and criticize) but also 'positive moral panics': the ones that we approve.

The problem, so one argument goes, lies in the particularly negative connotations of the word 'panic': hysteria, exaggeration, crowd behaviour, delusion and - above all - irrationality. Let's see what happens if we use alternative words: yes, it does make considerably more sense to talk of an 'approved crusade' than an 'approved panic'. But this loses the particular connotations of 'panic' that you want to retain!

All these tricky matters become trickier if we compare moral panic with denial. I have argued that denial in the personal realm is morally nuanced and ambiguous; there are defensible and positive functions. In the public realm, however, denial always has to be denounced as the enemy. This, of course, begs the question about the difference between private and public. And in the realms of social life that interest me most - at the interface between the personal and the political - it is near-impossible to use some words in a neutral way: passivity, inertia, silence, normalization, collusion, cover-up, turning a blind eye, the bystander effect, compassion fatigue. The opposite of all this is acknowledgement of the truth and acting accordingly. But to dwell nowadays on matters like 'the truth' is to invite theoretical questions way beyond my reach. Let me rather examine the concept at work.

## CLIMATE CHANGE

The emergence of climate change as a major public problem, no doubt needs setting in the wider discourse about ecology, environmentalist social movements and green politics. I use this only as a more specific case study of denial and moral

panic. I don't know the literature well enough to do more
than list some points of entry:

1.  Climate change seems to fit the social constructionist
    model. There were all the familiar stages in the natural
    history of social problem construction; there are iden-
    tifiable moral entrepreneurs - whether individuals
    (politicians, activists, scientists) and organizations; there
    are claims-makers, contesting not only rival models of
    knowledge, policy and risk-management, but also the
    most basic claims about the problem's existence.

2.  The rhetoric about climate change draws on the classic
    moral panic repertoire: disaster, apocalyptic predictions,
    warning of what might happen if nothing is done, placing
    the problem in wider terms (the future of the planet!).
    According to Tom Burke, climate is: 'the most serious threat
    to humanity since the invention of nuclear weapons.'[3]

3.  Truth claims are made as facts beyond questioning. The
    facts are so obvious, that 'the task of climate change
    agencies is not to persuade by rational argument, but
    in effect to develop and nurture a new 'common sense'.
    *The* 'facts' need to be treated as so taken-for-granted
    that they need not be spoken.[4]

4.  Within the environmentalist movement itself, there is an
    explicit discourse about climate change denial. There is
    a 'Climate Change Denial Website' and a Google search
    yields 390,000 entries. My book on denial is much cited -
    an ironic flattery because I clearly express my own lack of
    enthusiasm about the environmental cause.[5]

5.  The discourse about climate change is quite unusual
    in concentrating so much on what I called *literal
    denial*. The core of the climate change movement is
    the construction of any sort of doubt, qualification or
    disagreement as denial. And they mean not just the
    passive denial of indifference, but the active work

3   Burke, 'Climate Change: time to get real' 2006.
4   Ereaut, *Warm Words* 2006.
5   Cohen, *States of Denial* 2000.

of 'denialists'. Sceptics are demonized: treated like retarded or crazy persons, people who just don't get it. Taking his cue From Al Gore, here is David Miliband: those who deny climate dangers are 'the flat earthers of the twenty-first century'[6] A group of Australian activists and journalists have suggested that climate change denial should become a crime like Holocaust Denial; deniers should be brought before a Nuremberg-style court.[7] We must make them responsible for the thousands of deaths which will happen if global warming alarm not heeded.

6.  Most important of all: the environmental cause is winning hearts and minds. A new part in the moral edifice of society is close to being created. The process of social problem construction is just about complete. Moral entrepreneurs though, will have to remain active - for example, combating climate change denial. But the discourse of the major institutions of society has been changed; for example: the curricula of schools, the public face of big business, the greening of party politics, the very existence of separate government departments of ministries; and of course, the morality plays of the mass media. (A recent *Observer* Sunday Supplement was described as a guide for ethical living. The entire magazine was devoted to environmental causes, instructions on how to live good life. In an ethical life, you learn to put your computer on standby, to give up your electric toothbrush and keep a record of your carbon footprints.)

All this invites two types of question. The empirical question is whether the environmental appeal is competing with humanitarian causes for public support or has its own constituency. The normative question - forgive this Walt Disney simplification - is which of these you would choose to worry about and which you would rather deny.

---

6    Cited in BBC 'Miliband fears on climate Change' 27 September 2006.
7    The Daily Briefing 21/11/05 online at http://webdiary.com.au/cms/?q=node/986.

# MOVING ON

Here, after a journey into the past, is where we have reached:

> The critique behind the concept of moral panics is that too much attention (human resources, moral indignation, social construction) is given to the particular problem at issue. The critique behind the concept of denial is too little attention of the same type is given to a particular problem.

Taking off from denial theory, I am continuing to work on the 'particular problem' of public response to representations (by humanitarian organizations and the mass media) of the suffering of distant others. I am reading more about selective attention, moral judgement and the ethics of responsibility to others. The point is to locate these individual matters in specific social and political contexts.

## Bibliography

BBC 'Miliband fears on climate Change' 27 September 2006 online at http://news.bbc.co.uk/1/hi/uk_politics/5384206.stm

Burke, T. 'Climate Change: time to get real'. Open Democracy 2006 online at: http://www.opendemocracy.net/globalization-climate_change_debate/climate_change_3939.jsp

Cohen, S. (1972) *Folk Devils and Moral Panics* London: Routledge

Cohen, S. (2000) *States of Denial: Knowing about suffering and atrocities* Cambridge: Polity Press

Ereaut, G. and Segnit, N. (2006) *Warm Words: How are we telling the climate story and can we tell it better?* London: Institute for Public Policy Research.

The Daily Briefing 21/11/05 online at http://webdiary.com.au/cms/?q=node/986

# A DISOBEDIENT VISIONARY WITH AN ENQUIRING MIND

## AN ESSAY ON THE CONTRIBUTION OF STANLEY COHEN

### David Scott

*This paper is taken from a special edition of the European Group for the Study of Deviance and Social Control's newsletter to be published in September 2013 commemorating the life and work of Stanley Cohen*

Stan Cohen died on the 7th January 2013. He was a sociologist and moralist whose work epitomised the 'sociological imagination'.[1] Ultimately his writings were characterised by political commitments to social and transformative justice. His work was relevant, interventionist and filled with theoretical insights. Five of his most important works over the last four decades are *Folk Devils and Moral Panics* (1972),

---

[1] Mills, *Sociological Imagination* 1959.

*Psychological Survival* (with Laurie Taylor, 1973), *Visions of Social Control* (1985), *Anti-Criminology* (1988) and *States of Denial* (2000). In reading these books we are, in effect, reading the history and contemporary scope of criminology in the United Kingdom and elsewhere, for many of the axiomatic assumptions, research questions, concepts and problematisations in the discipline of criminology today originate from these texts or in the papers which they bring together.

Stan Cohen was a *founder* rather than a *follower*. The sociology of deviance and criminology has walked in his 'footsteps in the sand'. To talk about criminology today without reference to Stan Cohen is like talking about ethics without reference to Kant. He had those rarest of skills – which have been rightly compared to those of the great socialist thinkers Noam Chomsky and George Orwell – to write to a number of different audiences at the same time and yet deliver a multi-layered analysis carrying the greatest of insights that could be appreciated by all.

In some way it is hard to describe his contribution to criminology because quite frankly it is *so* enormous - his work is of such significance that, perhaps more than any other thinker in the last four decades, it has come to shape and define the discipline of criminology itself. This is quite a remarkable achievement, not least because he was an *anti-criminologist* – that is it was his explicit aim to challenge the 'positivist' or scientific study of crime which dominated the subject in the United Kingdom when he started his career. And yet it would be wrong to say that his contribution or influence is restricted merely to 'critical criminologies' – teachers and researchers from various criminological perspectives and indeed academics, practitioners and activists outside of criminology entirely, have found his work valuable and important. Alongside his friends and colleagues at the *New Deviancy Conferences* [NDC] in the late 1960, Stan Cohen challenged the dominant administrative criminology which closely followed government agendas and rooted its analysis largely in quantitative data, and firmly embedded in the academy a more sophisticated, theoretical and sociologically informed approach to the study of 'crime', deviance and social control. What is taught on undergraduate and postgraduate 'criminology' degrees today would be very different had not Stan Cohen, alongside Jock Young and others, so influentially introduced the sociology of deviancy to the United Kingdom.

Though criminology and its key themes have evolved in the last four decades, the writings of Stan Cohen have remained as relevant and inspirational as ever. His work not only profoundly influenced his peers but also has had an impact on every generation and cohort of criminologists that have emerged since the 1960s. As academic criminology developed in the 1970s his writings on moral panic and the sociology of deviance shaped not only the criminology curriculum in universities but also the key questions posed and addressed in the criminological literature. In *Folk Devils and Moral Panics* Stan Cohen developed the concept of moral panic to explore how certain people, because of certain characteristics, behaviours or social backgrounds, were first defined as a threat to society and then presented as such to the rest of society by the mass media. Drawing upon the insights of Emile Durkheim and Howard Becker, and using the case study of 'Mod's and Rockers', he revealed how moral entrepreneurs subsequently diagnosed and offered crime control solutions that could contain this new apparent threat. An exercise in setting moral boundaries and articulating social anxieties about youth and affluence, for Stan Cohen 'the devil has to be given a particular shape to know which virtue is being asserted'.[2] The focus on moral panics set forth two key ideas that were to run through his many writings in the coming years – first, *why in some places at some times, are certain actions either underplayed or overplayed by the media?* and second, *what is the role of the media in shaping reactions by the social audience?* Both of these questions were to be revisited at length in his book *States of Denial.*

---

[2]   Cohen, *Folk Devils and Moral Panics* 1972:57.

In his broader application of the sociology of deviance, Stan Cohen raised consciousness regarding the problems of radical differentiation and the classification of deviants. Rather than classify or differentiate, which could result in the construction of false hierarchies, he was firmly committed to acknowledging our 'common humanity', albeit with its vast and wonderful diversity. Once again, classification and differentiation would be issues that would be reflected in his research agenda for the next four decades, most notably in *Visions of Social Control*. He wanted to know what were the processes involved in the definitions of deviance and what, perhaps even more significantly, were their consequences. His concern, like that of his American sociology of deviancy counterparts Howard Becker and Edwin Lemert, and the enigmatic French social theorist Michel Foucault, was how social control could play a part in *creating deviancy*. This insight instilled within him a strong intellectual scepticism of both formal and informal mechanisms of social control and its net-widening capacities. His interest in the workings of social control, and especially those organised responses to deviance that are conceived and defined as 'social controls' by those who deploy them, was only to increase as the dark clouds of Thatcherism and neo-liberalism cast their deadly shade across the land.

As the criminology curriculum developed in the 1980s to encapsulate both criminology and criminal justice, his Orwellian inspired book *Visions of Social Control*, what many today consider his *magnum opus*, once again shaped the discipline. Drawing upon a wide range of theorists – Michel Foucault, Colin Ward, Emile Durkheim, David Rothman and Marxist political economists, Stan Cohen delivered his majestic overview of formal and informal control apparatuses in the later stages of the twentieth century. Cohen perceptively warned us that those with the best of intentions could end up promoting policies that had the worst of consequences – and this was a message not just for politicians and practitioners, but also a stark lesson that needs to headed by criminologists of all persuasions, especially critical theorists and abolitionists. Yet despite such scepticism a clear message of hope is retained in his vision – radical activists could also explore the contradictions, unintended consequences and inconsistencies of State practices and policies. Whatever the difficulties and complexities of real life, we must continue to try and 'do-good' when and where we possibly can. This once again was a theme that characterised his perspective.

*Visions of Social Control* is a thoughtful book raising crucial questions regarding contemporary developments in criminal processes and informal interventions devised to address problematic behaviour. Wide-ranging in scope, there is little doubt that one of the primary intentions of the book was to question the moral legitimacy of the current workings of the penal machine. Stan Cohen identified how developments in the 1980s saw a deepening in the intensity of the control mechanisms of the Capitalist State - his warnings about privatisation and the role of volunteers as State agents proving to be particularly prophetic. In moving debates in criminal justice away from a dry and legalistic analysis, *Visions of Social Control* inspired a generation. Drawing upon and synthesising complex and abstract theory, the book delivered an understandable and straightforward analysis and yet at the same was so deeply insightful that it set the agenda for the study of social control for the next twenty and more years. Paradoxically, for the man who so importantly and successfully critiqued classification in criminal process, one of his most important contributions was his ability to classify complex arguments and to draw out their hidden connections. As a critical thinker he was also to use such skills to make clear problems and contradictions of the penal apparatus of the Capitalist State. *Visions of Social Control* identified the early impact of risk assessments and the possible dangers of community interventions, issues that were to dominate the penological literature throughout the 1990s. He foretold of the shift in bureaucratic interests of universities away from scholarship and revealed the growing strength of an 'evaluation' culture that had supplanted the search for the 'cause' of 'crime' and was strangling humane and socially just responses to individual and social problems.

Throughout his career Stan Cohen engaged with one of the most profound tensions within criminology – the relationship between idealism and realism / utopia and immediate humanitarian reforms. One of the most powerful metaphors that Stan Cohen drew upon to explore this tension is the 'tale of the fisherman' by Saul Alinsky in *Visions of Social Control:*

> A man is walking by the riverside when he notices a body floating down stream. A fisherman leaps into the river, pulls the body ashore, gives mouth to mouth resuscitation, saving the man's life. A few minutes later the same thing happens, then again, and again. Eventually yet another body floats by. This time the fisherman completely ignores the drowning man and starts running up stream along the bank. The observer asks the fisherman what on earth is he doing? Why is he not trying to rescue this drowning body? 'This time', replies the fisherman, 'I'm going up stream to see who is pushing these poor folk into the water' ... but Alinsky had a twist to his story – while the fisherman was so busy running along the bank to find the ultimate source of the problem, who was going to help those poor wretches who continued to float down the river.[3]

In *Visions of Social Control* he highlights the centrality of idealist utopias and romantic / sentimentalist anarchist literature in providing the vision we need to create radical socialist transformations of society. Such anarchism, idealism, new deviancy theory and anti-criminology led him to an interest in 'penal abolitionism' – an ethical perspective which challenges the moral legitimacy of punishment. Most penal abolitionists are not 'absolutists' that argue that we should never punish

---

[3]   Cohen, *Visions of Social Control*, 1985: 236-7.

anyone under any possible circumstance, but rather that we should, as Nils Christie puts it, punish with great sadness, regret and a sense of mourning. Rather than feel good about punishment we should punish as little as possible and with a bad conscience because punishment has no moral legitimacy. Stan Cohen wrote extensively about abolitionism in his book *Against Criminology*, edited a special edition of *Contemporary Crises* in 1986 on abolitionism, attended the *International Conference of Penal Abolition* (ICOPA) in the mid 1980s and was a leading member of the abolitionist pressure group *Radical Alternatives to Prison* in the 1970s, where he published the important pamphlets *Prison Secrets* in 1977 (with Laurie Taylor) and *Crime and Punishment* in 1979.

But Stan Cohen was always the 'cautious abolitionist' and though he found the penal abolitionist argument very persuasive he worried about their problems regarding blame allocation and moral responsibility.[4]

Always wise and politically astute, he committed to only a guarded and careful appraisal of the position. At the same he never forgot his social work roots and reminded us of the desperate need for humanitarian interventions in the here and now. I think this tension between trying to change the world so that it is more socially just but at the same time helping those most in need right now runs through nearly all of his work, and indeed perhaps defines it. For Stan Cohen penal abolitionists must be prepared to honestly answer the question *what can we do right now* to mitigate the humanitarian crises confronting contemporary penal practices without abandoning the broader obligation to promote radically alternative responses to troublesome human conduct.[5] Stan Cohen clearly favoured the language of human rights.[6] For him human rights could bridge the realism / idealism divide. Human rights, when codified as legal rights, could provide immediate aid and ease human suffering. They could then

---

4     Cohen, *Visions of Social Control*, 1985.
5     Cohen 'Intellectual scepticism and political commitment' 1998.
6     Cohen 'Social control and the politics of reconstruction' 1995.

act as 'shield' in times of regressive civilisation. But they could also act as a 'sword' – human rights could be bearers of latent utopian ideals and carry with them the ideals of social justice.

Stan Cohen was also concerned about how 'alternatives to punishment' could become even more insidious than the prison. This critique, now one his most famous, has been popularised in his phrase 'net widening', a term he first used in *Folk Devils and Moral Panics.* In *Visions of Social Control* he used the metaphor of 'fishing nets' to explain how more and more people, who have generally committed petty offences, were being sucked into the criminal 'justice' system. As ever, the work of Stan Cohen captivated a number of different audiences. The book connected with radicals working within the State machine, social workers and radical activists, and so once again his influence stretched well beyond the walls of the academy.

As criminology evolved to take a more detailed and analytical approach to 'crimes' of power and State crime his final single authored book, *States of Denial: knowing about suffering and atrocities*, once more led the way. Stan Cohen never lost sight of the importance of drawing our attention to 'unwelcome knowledges' such as human rights abuses and atrocities. In *States of Denial* he asked us some of the most profound questions of the day: *why is there so much suffering yet such little effort to alleviate it? how do people respond to knowledge about the suffering of other humans?* and, *why do some people help?* By asking his reader these questions Stan Cohen highlighted both the general and the particular. In general, the book leads the reader to recognise that 'denial' is something that characterises human life, and in certain personal circumstances may even have a positive impact. In particular, the book is so profound and is written in such an open and honest manner that inevitably the reader will recognise the use of 'techniques of denial' in their own daily lives. His main focus was upon political denial and the failure to act when we have knowledge, whether in terms of personal experiences or via other media. The book was therefore not only a brilliant intellectual overview but also a direct intervention attempting to breach denials. His final book, then, is one of great courage, providing honest reflections of the problems and possibilities of our times, and more than anything else a great endorsement of humanity despite its limitations – for I think he grasped better than most its frailty, beauty and diversity. There was a difference between passivity and moral indifference. We may, as he put it, care intensely and yet still fail to act. It is this insight into the human condition which I think made him such a unique and important contributor to criminology and the social sciences more broadly. It will be this insight which ensures that his work will be of continued benefit to the coming generation of scholars in criminology and related fields.

Indeed, every new generation of academics and students in criminology over the last few decades have engaged with the work of Stan Cohen and the issues he brought to prominence. Not only has he set the criminological curriculum, raised the most pertinent questions, made the most complex of issues understandable through his scholarship, but he also provided the theoretical vocabulary by which the discipline of criminology today engages with its subject matter. Criminology uses his language to explore the problems of today and, I think, also of tomorrow. Where would criminology be without the common language of 'social control talk', 'net widening', 'denial and acknowledgement' and so on and so forth.

Despite his enormous influence I think there is still much that criminology (and related disciplines where his work is of considerable influence) can learn from Stan Cohen. He was never a dedicated follower of academic fashion. We must remember that criminology is inter-disciplinary drawing upon a number of different subjects. Stan Cohen was both a sociologist and a moralist and both should be central to the future of criminology, critical or otherwise. His focus on the 'moral' was not just restricted to 'moral panics'. His moralism, which he referred to as 'moral pragmatism', is outlined in his book *Visions of Social Control*. In this text he wrote about the importance of clarifying our cherished moral values – in other words what do we think are most important, what is it in life that we must protect – what are our key priorities. Among these cherished values for him were social justice and human rights. It is absolutely crucial that criminology continues to focus upon justice, both in its formulation and breach, rather than become obsessed once again with the government set agenda reflecting the interests of the powerful, evaluation studies or securing State funding.[7] But his moralism also goes to the very heart of what it is *to be a criminologist* as a professional vocation today. Stan Cohen recognised that your academic life and who you are as a human being are indistinguishable. In other words the criminologist's biography is important – what you write and talk about should be reflected in *who you are.* Given his writings then, it should come as no surprise that the man Stan Cohen was widely recognised as being gentle, kind and understanding.

He also led the way on his scholarship – he would have read literally everything written on the topic that was available and then carefully present this to the reader. How often in his books do we see the phrase 'I have read thirty books on this topic and they all pretty much say this ...' No stone was left un-turned and as a result his research was exemplary. The message for criminologists is that we ensure that our research and theoretical models are accessible and relevant – the value to cherish is that we should keep our writing style simple – as he put it 'it is always better to adopt the simplest approach'. Further, and at least as equally important, if not more so, we should continue to be critical and raise those questions that need to be answered by those in power. Stan Cohen was a disobedient visionary with an enquiring mind. He told truth to power, and more. He also told truth to the powerless. He did more than most in supporting a view from below. Perhaps here also inspired by Michel Foucault, he encouraged Walter Probyn, a prisoner he had befriended whilst doing the

---

[7]    Cohen, *Visions of Social Control,* 1985.

Durham E Wing Research for *Psychological Survival*, to write his autobiography *Angel Face*. He wrote the introduction and a commentary/ postscript for the book.[8]

For Stan Cohen criminologists should explore human suffering, in its very many manifestations, which have been denied or where there is only limited political action aiming to address such personal troubles. Academics should intervene. They should make their voices heard. In *States of Denial* Stan Cohen makes the case very strongly, and correctly, that academic indifference or silence is not acceptable.

> Intellectuals who keep silent about what they know, who ignore the crimes that matter by moral standards, are even more morally culpable when their society is free and open. They can speak freely, but choose not to.[9]

We live and work in different social and economic times to when Stan Cohen started his academic career. Many universities today, at least in the UK, are run like businesses looking to deliver employability skills rather than focus on education as an end in itself. Outside of the academy the same government orientated agendas that Stan Cohen objected to in the 1960s continue to offer the promise of prestigious careers to ambitious academics, whilst within the academy research careers are increasingly made or broken depending upon the individual's willingness to adhere to the new 'rules of the game' and meet the demands of income generation above all other considerations. Stan Cohen's work has helped us understand the profound changes in that have taken place since this the late 1960s, but the values he cherished then should also be the values cherished by criminologists today. Holding such an approach in academia today can, in the end, mean 'not playing the game': at a time when the economic rational trumps those

---

[8]   See Cohen, 'Introduction' 1977a; 'Commentary (by Stan Cohen): Notes on the reformation of a criminal', 1977b.

[9]   Cohen, *States of Denial* 2000: 286.

moral and political commitments, criminologists should bear in mind that it is not the research grant which is important, but the scholarship and quality of the research undertaken. Scholarship for Stan Cohen was a *cherished value* and the credibility of criminology as a discipline in the future will ultimately depend on how closely it continues to adhere to this value.

## Bibliography

Cohen, S. *Folk Devils and Moral Panics* (London: Routledge) 1972

Cohen, S. 'Introduction' in Probyn, W. *Angel Face* (London: George Allen and Unwin) 1977

Cohen, S. 'Commentary (by Stan Cohen): Notes on the reformation of a criminal' in Probyn, W. *Angel Face* (London: George Allen and Unwin) 1977

Cohen, S. *Crime and Punishment* (London: Radical Alternatives to Prison) 1979

Cohen, S. 'Introduction' in Dronfield, L. *Outside Chance* (London: Newham Alternatives Project) 1980

Cohen, S. 'Footprints in the sand' in Fitzgerald, M. et al *Crime and Society: Readings in history and theory* (Milton Keynes: Open University Press) 1981

Cohen, S. *Visions of Social Control: Crime, Punishment and Classification* (Cambridge: Polity Press) 1985

Cohen, S. (ed) 'Abolitionism' in *Contemporary Crises,* Vol. 10, No. 1, pp. 63-165 1986

Cohen *Against Criminology* (Cambridge: Polity Press) 1988

Cohen, S. 'Intellectual scepticism and political commitment: the case of radical criminology' pp 98-129 in Walton, P. & Young, J. (eds) *The New Criminology Revisited* (London: MacMillan) 1998

Cohen, S. 'Social control and the politics of reconstruction' in Nelken, D. (ed.) *The Future of Crime Control* (London: Sage) 1995

Cohen, S. *States of Denial: Knowing about suffering and atrocities* (Cambridge: Polity Press) 2000

Cohen, S. & Taylor, L. *Psychological Survival* (Harmondsworth: Penguin) 1981

Cohen, S. & Taylor, L. *Prison Secrets* (London: National Council for Civil Liberties and Radical Alternatives to Prison) 1977

Mills, C.W. *The Sociological Imagination* (Oxford: Oxford University Press) 1959

Probyn, W. *Angel Face* (London: George Allen and Unwin) 1977

# 2013 MANIFESTO

## WORKING GROUP ON PRISON, DETENTION AND PUNISHMENT

*In 2012-13 the European Group re-established a number of working groups. This chapter is the Manifesto agreed and published by the European Working Group on Prison, Detention and Punishment. It was originally published in the April 2013 European Group Newsletter.*

1. This European working group provides a network and database for teachers, researchers, students and activists across Europe (and beyond) who have an interest studying prisons, detention and punishment. The working group will provide an opportunity to share our knowledge of sites of confinement and the operation of the penal rationale and help establish new links with activists and academics worldwide who critically engage with the current forms, extent and nature of detention and punishment. The working group will thus provide an opportunity to connect local campaigns with a wider global network through which we can collectively provide solidarity and support. The working group also aims to foster a greater understanding of contemporary penality; offer possibilities for collaborative research; and work towards

emancipatory change. We recognise that, since the inception of the confinement project in the eighteenth century, the boundaries between different sites of detention have become increasingly blurred: prisons house foreign nationals and recalcitrant mental health patients; high security hospitals hold the 'criminally insane'; immigration centres are run like prisons. The working group is committed to the abolition of penal confinement and other sites of involuntary detention. We also aim to challenge the logic and assumptions of the penal rationale and propose the development of non-repressive means of handling social problems and conflicts.

2. In many countries around the world there has been a proliferation in sites of confinement. More than ten million people are confined in prisons and many millions more are housed in other forms of detention. However, the rise of global hyper-incarceration and the analytical frameworks that underscore its assumptions have been challenged by a growing number of academics in their teaching and research, and by social workers, anti-prison activists, social justice-inspired social movements, members of the radical penal lobby, progressive members of the public, socialist politicians and students. An increasing number of organisations all around the globe are now directly challenging hyper-incarceration. The European working group aims to contribute to the development of abolitionist and anti-prison activism and to highlight the limitations of the current application of confinement. We acknowledge that the mobilisation of grass roots activists is absolutely necessary for any sustained radical transformation of current penal and social realities.

3. The working group aims to encourage members to formulate intellectual interventions and direct activism that can systematically expose the brutal realities of detention, penal confinement and community

punishments and facilitate a reduction in the stig-matising effects and collateral consequences of the application of the penal rationale. We recognise that it is essential that the experiences and voices of detainees are given a platform to air their views and that the brutal and inhumane realities of sites of confine-ment are brought to the attention of the wider public and those in positions of power. The working group supports the rights of activists and citizens, including those sections of the voluntary sector that are pursuing social justice and penal reductionism, to pursue their goals without domination by governmental or profit-making interests.

4.  The working group prioritises the critical scrutiny of the justifications of the punitive rationale; punish-ment in the community, semi-penal institutions and probation hotels; and the wider moral and political contexts of the deliberate infliction of pain. The justi-fication of detention of people in the *interests of others* should be critically scrutinised and located within its given social, economic, political and moral context. This does not mean we believe that nothing should be done, or that all forms of detention or deprivation of liberty are necessarily unjustified (especially those forms of detention provided for the *best interests of the detainee*), but rather that imprisonment and many forms of detention are an illegitimate response to wrongdoing, social harms and social problems. Sites of confinement fail to uphold human rights, meet the demands of social justice or provide transparent or accountable forms of State governance. The increasing reliance upon involuntary detention, prisons and other forms of detainment in recent times also draws attention to its very real threat to democracy. All forms of detention have faced consistently high death rates and intentional self injury; institutionalisation and disculturalisation; bullying and sexual violence; staff

moral indifference; institutionalised racism; masculinist hierarchies of power; and broader vulnerabilities to systemic abuses through torture and inhuman and degrading treatment. What the different institutions also seem to share is an historical broad inability to satisfy the *duty of care* owed to those who they detain. We acknowledge also that detainees are predominantly poor, in bad physical and mental health, unemployed, and badly educated. It is the less fortunate, vulnerable and needy who are disproportionately detained and this draws direct connections with the need for a more socially just world.

5. The organisation of the European working group on prisons, detention and punishment is undertaken by a steering group that will consist of at least the following: a working group coordinator; the coordinator of the European Group for the Study of Deviance and Social Control; the secretary of the European Group for the Study of Deviance and Social Control. Members of the working group may also be invited to join a steering group. The working group will meet every year at the annual conference of the European Group for the Study of Deviance and Social Control and members are encouraged to organise other events, meetings and conferences throughout the calendar year to help generate ideas, networks and direct interventions. Such events may be full meetings for the whole working group or specially convened meetings of local activists in one given region / nation. A separate mailing list will be maintained and other European Group media sources, such as Facebook, YouTube, Twitter and Crimspace, will be used to disseminate information about the working group and its activities. The working group coordinator will be elected at the European Group annual conference and full details of the membership of the working group will be detailed on our website (www.europeangroup.org)

6. Members of the working group are committed to the reversal of the proliferation of sites of confinement and the utilisation of strategies drawing upon direct action and abolitionist praxis to facilitate radical penal and social transformations. Though strategies of engagement will vary from place to place depending upon local circumstances, we believe that to achieve our aims we must propose a number of direct interventions that are feasible here and now and that can exploit contradictions in the operation of penal power. We call for the following general interventions as a means to facilitate a long-term and radical reduction in the populations of those detained in sites of confinement.

   i.   An international moratorium on building new sites of confinement (prisons / asylums / immigration centres) and on the allocation of existing buildings and spaces as locations of involuntary detention

   ii.  An end to the privatisation of sites of confinement and the insidious expansion of the carceral State via the voluntary and private sector

   iii. A detailed and critical interrogation of existing State detention, followed by a systematic call for governments to close the most inhumane, degrading and torturous sites of confinement without opening new houses of detention

   iv.  A virtual end to pre-trial detention and the abolishment of the antiquated notion of bail except for those who present a serious threat to society

   v.   The safeguarding and expansion of the legal rights of detainees. Post incarceration ex-detainees must be recognised as full citizens and given full and uninhibited access to employment, housing, other social and financial services and full access to political and civil society

   vi.  The decriminalisation of victimless and harmless acts, such as alcoholism, deviant sexualities between consenting adults, substance misuse and drug taking. The criminalisation of sex workers (who are often from working class backgrounds) is harmful and victimising and we propose alternative responses that protect and prioritise the safety of the men and women who engage in this work.

vii. The decriminalisation of infringements of migration laws

viii. To raise the age of criminal responsibility in all countries in the world to the age of at least 16

ix. To divert people with mental health problems, learning disabilities, severe physical disabilities, the profoundly deaf and people with suicidal ideation from the criminal process whilst at the same time ensuring any alternative interventions are both 'in place' of a penal sanction and are not merely forms of 'trans-incarceration' to other sites of confinement

x. To immediately remove those people most vulnerable to the inherent harms and pains of confinement from places of detention

xi. To formulate and advocate radical alternatives to the criminal process and social injustices for individual and social harms that are feasible and could be implemented immediately or within a short period of time

xii. To propose that all governments prioritise meeting human need, recognising common humanity and facilitating social justice as the most effective means of preventing / dealing with human troubles, conflicts and problematic conduct

# SECTION B

CRITIQUE

the power and legitimacy of the State. *Critique* means more than being just 'critical'. For the authors showcased in this section, critical theory must be grounded within socio-economic and political contexts, linked with the work of grass roots social movements (or interpreting their interventions) and intended to facilitate emancipatory change.

In chapter thirteen Sebastian Scheerer questions the rationale behind the introduction of new laws to meet the challenges of terrorism and political violence. Drawing upon historical cases, Scheerer focuses on the response of the State to socialist inspired political violence. He suggests that given the extensive sheaf of already existing laws it cannot be plausibly argued that *new laws are necessary* to combat political violence, thus opening the debate for alternative explanations of law formation. Scheerer identifies that in an "ideological *state of siege"* anti-terrorism laws are presented in the 'national interest' to solidify existing moral boundaries and re-legitimate the State. This *state of siege* is likely to increase social polarisation, deepen intolerance of deviance and create new 'enemies within'. Yet paradoxically it may also act as a conduit to radicalise marginalised populations and reignite dormant utopian ideals. Scheerer's central argument is that the *state of siege* must be contextualised within an understanding not only of the perceived threat to the State but also the relative weakness and fragility of political legitimacy in western liberal democracies. Acknowledging that all political violence can potentially undermine the States monopoly of violence, Marxists and Anarchists are considered as presenting a particular danger. This is not because of the harm or instability wrought through their political violence– the State has legislative power enough to contain socialist activism - but rather because socialists offer to *fulfil the principles and values* of democracy, justice, freedom and equality. The State is thus presented with a dilemma when dealing with socialist inspired political violence - anti-terrorist legislation may strengthen the internal powers of administrators and expand the remit of the penal apparatus of the Capitalist State but is unlikely to be effective in its stated aim of controlling political violence. Further, to abandon entirely its commitment to democracy would only increase the potency of socialist critique and further exacerbate the legitimation crises. Liberal democracies are therefore shackled by their need to offer at least lip service to the principles of democracy, thus leaving legal loopholes that can be exploited by pro-democracy campaigners. Indeed, the more repressive the interventions of the State, the greater the attractiveness of socialisms and their critique of actually existing democracy.

Emma Bell explores the impact of neo-liberalism on the role, scope and application of the criminal law and welfare provision in Britain in chapter fourteen. Bell shows us that though there are continuities with an earlier interventionist social democratic 'welfare state' regarding the application of the criminal law – notably that it continues to target the 'crimes' of the poor whilst 'crimes' of the powerful are largely ignored – policies in neoliberal Britain have undoubtedly become more invasive and punitive. For Bell, we have not only witnessed a major expansion in the penal apparatus of the Capitalist State – new surveillance technologies, extensive regulatory powers and the rise of out-of-court penalties – but there has also been an extension of punishment through welfare. In short, in recent times a new 'security-industrial complex' has emerged. Representing a contemporary re-articulation of the Gramscian analysis of the Capitalist State, Bell argues that the increasing emphasis on authoritarian populist 'crime policies' must be located within the socio-economic and political contexts of the current historical conjuncture. Central is the relationship between neo-liberalism and State legitimacy. Neoliberalism, with its emphasis on the 'free market', has exacerbated social divisions and rendered the State impotent to intervene. This raises questions regarding the legitimate role of government for under the logic of neoliberalism: the State can no longer intervene in the economy or promote progressive welfare interventions for those at the bottom of the social structure. Further, neo-liberalism has also demanded massive public spending cuts and welfare retrenchment which are likely to undermine public support and exacerbate social divisions. This crisis of legitimacy has been accommodated on a number of levels. First, as indicated above, to appeal to the electorate increasing emphasis has focused on the control of criminals and immigrants. Second, there has been a shift towards a more 'managerial' approach; the reconstruction of welfare recipients as 'consumers' and a transformation of the State from provider to facilitator of social services. Consequently there has existed a 'correspondence of interests' between the neoliberal governments and the private sector which has led to the privileging of market solutions and increased emphasis on the privatisation of crime control. Yet accommodations to the neoliberal condition remain shot through with contradictions, erode civil liberties and fail to adequately address the most pressing social harms of our day. Rather than being effectively policed, the crisis is likely only to deepen.

In the chapter fifteen Dany Lacombe explores the co-option of 'critique' by coercive forces and agents of the State. Lacombe is concerned with how the State uses moral arguments (as well as scientific research discussed further in following chapters) to construct social problems. Lacombe's central focus is an analysis of the Canadian State's decision in the mid 1980s to take pornography seriously. Lacombe explores the role civil society, especially feminist orientated interest groups, performed in the criminalisation of pornography and how support from below was orchestrated to increase State repression. In particular Lacombe emphasises how the debate was won and what lessons can be learned to resist similar interventions in the future. In so doing she highlights how pornography in Canada in the mid 1980s became contested terrain for ideological struggle. For Lacombe feminist anti-pornography activists performed a central role connecting women's lived experiences to the demands for criminalisation by a conservative patriarchal State. To illustrate her arguments Lacombe focuses upon the *Fraser Committee Report* (1985). She explores how in this official report feminist arguments were

re-shaped so that they became consistent with the 'legal structures of the present state'. Feminist arguments inconsistent
with the interests and agenda of the State – such as socialist
feminism and anti-censorship feminists - were de-legitimated.
Lacombe identifies how moral concerns informed official
discourse and how the meanings of certain key aspects of the
pornography debate, such as 'erotica', were redefined to reflect
heteronormativity. Whilst the official discourse promoted
the criminalisation of pornography as a means of facilitating
great gender 'equality' what remained marginal were: considerations of the structural and political constraints on women's
lives; the role of media in the construction of idealised femininity; and deeply engrained sexist attitudes towards women
in wider culture. The anti-pornography position, feminists
included, therefore ignored gendered power differentials and
promoted criminal law interventions in the name of equality.
Although she provides a critical account of the failure of feminism in this particular instance, for Lacombe understanding
the role feminists performed in the criminalisation of pornography is crucial on at least two levels: it provides insights into
(1) the boundaries and limitations of State power and (2) the
important role interest groups perform in State policy formation. Both of these insights could inform and motive future
resistance and emphasise the potential of feminist analysis.

Ase Berge's explores the failure of male dominated social
sciences to adequately understand men who perpetrate sexual
abuse or acknowledge the gendered meanings and embodi-
ment of victims of sexual violence in chapter sixteen. For
Berge, malestream criminological knowledge of perpetrators is characterised by superficial masculinist explanations
grounded in individual pathologies resulting in simplistic
policy solutions. Berge argues that feminist analysis could
offer a more sophisticated theoretical toolkit and help inform
alternative and more progressive policy agendas. She starts her
analysis with an exploration of Sandra Harding's 'three levels

of the gender concept': symbolism, structure and identity.[1] Significantly 'science' itself is conceived as an ideology rooted in patriarchal-androcentric gender-symbolism assumptions. Indeed the production of 'scientific knowledge' performs an integral role in maintaining and developing conceptions of 'femininity' and 'masculinity' in ideology and culture. Most notably Berge points to how the assumption that men's sexuality is an 'uncontrollable impulse' has heavily influenced 'scientific' research on sexual violence. This has 'made it possible that violence and power-relations in sexuality are kept largely invisible' or the harm and injury inflicted reinterpreted or downplayed. Berge reminds us that most [sexual] violence is perpetrated against partners or former partners. [Sexual] violence, in the main, is familial / relational and situational: the perpetrator is often intimately known by the victim, in a relationship with them or a family member; the perpetrator may only be violent to those he is sexually attracted. The 'paradoxical situation [is] that an offender may well be a 'normal', 'ordinary' man'. Masculinist scientific knowledge fails to take this into account, nor can it account for wider moral and political contexts. Feminist analysis can present a sophisticated understanding of both the sexual and violent dimensions of 'sexual violence'; account for the normalcy of perpetrators; the distinct differentials in power between perpetrator and victim; problematise masculine sexuality and the difficulties it presents regarding identity and emotional adaptation and the conflicts it generates; and locate the treatment of victims of sexual violence by professionals within the wider structures of gender and power. For Berge, 'as researchers and in the interests of stopping and preventing all kinds of reactionary cries for strong prison sentences, it is a serious task to take responsibility for this state of affairs.'

Claus-Peter Behr, Dietlinde Gipsen, Sabine Klien-Sconnefeld, Klaus Naffin and Heiner Zillmer follow up the previous critiques of the State and 'criminological knowledge' in chapter

---

[1]   Harding, *The Science Question in Feminism*.

seventeen with an important analysis of the use of 'scientific knowledge' to legitimate State planning activities. The authors locate the 'misuse of science' by the State within its wider social and political contexts. Rather than focussing on the co-option and manipulation of individual researchers, Behr et al explore how the 'Interventionist State' carefully constructs its research projects and how the knowledge gleaned from them is then applied to maintain and extend State control. They illustrate their concerns through examining two inter-related case studies in Germany in the late 1970's – (1) the State initiated 'origins of terrorism' research project and (2) how the State utilised different sources of 'scientific knowledge' to inform the creation of new high security units for terrorists, latterly referred to as 'therapeutic individualisation'. In so doing the authors powerfully evidence the problems that may arise by bringing together separate research project findings on one particular aspect of policy. Their key concerns regard both *what* the researcher is being asked to do and *how* the knowledge derived from their study is then used by the patron. Anticipating some important theoretical work on State bureaucracies in the late 1980s, Behr et al explore how State research agendas can be separated into a number of small projects but then collated holistically to be used by the State. Moving beyond a consideration of individualised research ethics or political orientation, Behr et al identify how those undertaking research for the State are merely tiny cogs in the State machine working towards a State orientated project. Whilst individual researchers may have some control over the research process itself, their independence is fatally undermined as they operate within the definitions of the State and have no control over how their findings may be used. Accepting State definitions of a given set of social circumstances rules in and rules out certain realities, thus shaping legitimate knowledge. Researchers are free to perform tasks, but not the tasks of their own choosing. Behr et al therefore remind us of the importance of reflecting upon the 'big picture'. The authors conclude by highlighting key values and principles for individual researchers – research findings should never be used against those on which the research has been undertaken; we must explore the research question independently, aim to uncover the truth and have solidarity with the researched; research must not be explored in isolation but located in its appropriate contexts; emancipatory knowledge and praxis should be the ultimate aim of the research rather than servicing the State machine.

Chapter eighteen takes the unifying theme of 'critique' further by exploring and problematising the very framing of social problems through the language of 'crime' and the meaning and scope of the discipline of criminology itself. Previous chapters have highlighted how 'criminological knowledge' has been co-opted to serve the interests of the State. With this problem in consideration, Paddy Hillyard presents us with the argument that we need to move *beyond criminology*. Whilst we continue to work within 'criminology' we will always be bound by the definitions of 'crime' and criminality dictated by the State. As a discipline criminology perpetuates myths about the nature and extent of 'criminal conduct'; excludes many of the most harmful events; and provides legitimacy to existing power relations and the penal apparatus of the Capitalist State. Hillyard argues that the only effective strategy to challenge the discursive power of 'crime' is to establish a new separate discipline grounded in the study of harm that would provide a new language or counter-discourse to that of criminology. Hillyard refers to this approach as zemiology, the name of which arose from discussions at the 1998 European Group Annual Conference, which would locate inequality, poverty, disadvantage, racism and sexism at the centre of its approach. Unlike 'crime', Hillyard maintain that 'harms can be counted and have a material and ontological reality'. Hillyard's main interests in this chapter are to chart the new disciplines progress in the last fifteen years and to explore the reception of zemiology by criminologists. In terms of the latter, Hillyard presents us with a 'tongue-in-cheek topology' of five different reactions by criminologists to zemiology: Colonialists, Imperialists, Nationalists, Reluctant Nationalists, and Misguided

Nationalists. He identifies how the reception of zemiology has been largely sympathetic but that the over-riding attempt has been to co-opt or incorporate harm into the discipline of criminology itself. Through his analysis of the five different types of reception Hillyard presents a robust counter-defence of zemiology against its criminological critics and reasserts the importance of this approach for conceptualising contemporary social problems.

## Bibliography

Harding, S. *The Science Question in Feminism.* (Boston), 1986.

# LAW MAKING IN A STATE OF SIEGE

## SOME REGULARITIES IN THE LEGISLATIVE RESPONSE TO POLITICAL VIOLENCE

### Sebastian Scheerer

*This paper was originally delivered at the Bremen conference in 1978 and published in the 'Working Papers in European Criminology: Volume 1 Terrorism and the Violence of the State.'*

## UNNECESSARY LAWS AND THE LEGISLATIVE SEQUENCE

With some regularity legislative bodies are assigned the task of meeting the challenge of terrorism. At first glance the arguments in favour of legislation seem convincing, for do not extraordinary situations require extraordinary executive counter-measures? Indeed, who else but the legislature can ensure that 'officials who must act against disorder, terrorism, and political violence have the legal means at their disposal to take all measures that may be necessary to meet such contingencies as may arise'?[1] But a closer look at the crimes committed by terrorist's show that they have already been outlawed for some time. With blackmail, manslaughter and murder being established crimes in the statutes, terrorist violence seems to indicate a deficit in the implementation of existing laws rather than demanding the creation of a new criminal statute. From a pragmatic point of view, new anti-terrorist laws, so often passed after sensational acts of political violence, seem unnecessary.

Nevertheless, sensational political violence can be shown to have a 'triggering' effect on legislative activity. The pattern of political events resulting in this specific kind of legislation has remained essentially unchanged over the last 100 years of European history. In its first phase the legislative sequence involved a single or series of provocative political crimes resulting in a rapid spread of news via the mass media. The social segment hitherto excluded from access to power, institutions, and channels of communications thereby conquers at least the latter, forcefully entering into a dialogue with political decision-makers and the public.[2] The second phase is shaped by social and governmental reaction involving both a highly and acutely irritated public and a quick and harsh legislative reaction. Jean Maitron's history of the French anarchist movement points out the fact that when the *Socialist International* began to show signs of revitalisation after the defeat of the Commune in Paris, the law Dufaure was voted without hesitation in March 1872. Two days after the firebomb attack on the Chamber of Deputies by Auguste Vaillant in 1893, two anti-terrorist bills were introduced and accepted; and when president Carnot was assassinated half a year later the formu-

---

[1]   National Advisory Committee on Criminal Justice Standards and Goals Task Force, *Report on Disorders and Terrorism*, 1976:77. Identical forms of argument like 'extraordinary situations call for extraordinary laws' can be found anywhere and especially in places where there is an interest to conceal the true, political motives behind legislative initiatives.

[2]   We must not forget that neither anarchists nor terrorists enjoy full freedom of speech and there is only limited representation of their interests in the mass media. Due to their extreme political positions their only means of 'getting on television' is by exploiting the built-in sensationalism of the media.

lation, introduction and passage of a third anti-terrorist law took also only a few days.[3] In Germany, the legislative bodies were hardly left more time for deliberation when Bismark introduced the 'Socialist Law' after the attempted assassinations of the Emperor in 1878 by E. H. Max Hodel on May 11, and by Dr Carl E. Nobiling on June 2. The first draft bill was laid before the Reichstag on May 20. To secure optimal chances of parliamentary success for the second bill, Bismarck dissolved the Reichstag and held elections before introducing the Socialist Bill on September 9 1878.[4]

# GENERIC CONDITIONS
# THE STATE OF SIEGE

The situations triggering the legislative sequence show a high degree of conformity, demonstrating that the functional mechanisms of institutionalised rule tend to resemble each other even in their appearance and that they can be traced back to a single set of generic conditions. Successful introduction of anti-terrorist legislation is preceded by a systemic condition which may be described as an ideological state of siege. In a physical state of siege, the outside threat to the social system's existence increases both deviancy and inner-group solidarity. Typically, the everyday duty of the system's members not to actively endanger the cooperativeness of the system is being reversed in the state of siege to actively engage in the systems maintenance. The prevailing ideology is that of a common cause and a common interest to which all members must subscribe - those who do not actively proclaim their identification with the system's belief and value structures, let alone voices dissent or even organises opposition are severely rejected by the system. In other words there is an increase in the level of rejection of deviants. The variety of legitimate behaviour is restricted and

---

[3]   Maitron, *le mouvement anarchiste en France: des origines a' 1914*, 1975: 56-86, 252.
[4]   For a good political analysis of both assassination attempts see Carlson *Anarchism in Germany: The Early Movement*, (1972: 115-172).

the negative sanctions applied to deviancy are increased; the potential costs involved in dissenting communication and organisation are escalated for even simple non-support of the prevailing ideology; the moral boundaries of the system become contracted, thus securing broad popular compliance as well as the definition and production of a socially visible antagonistic out-group of 'enemies'. There is thus the elimination of neutrality.[5]

The polarised plot of a zero-sum game, where the cost of one group exactly equals the benefit of the other, becomes the theoretical formula of any state of siege and can be found in any pre-legislative situation. Although the State tends to physically react to terrorist attacks by enlarging and improving the control apparatus, terrorists do not physically besiege the social system, but rather symbolically challenge the legitimacy of its institutionalised rulers. It is therefore the State's perception of a direct confrontation with radically violent groups that decide the proclamation of emergency. If the government's image of societal order is not close enough to the zero-sum game plot, the chances for successful anti-terrorist laws are dim.

After the Hodel assassination attempt, the bullets of which had gone far astray, the situation was characterised by the absence of a credible image of a threat to the cooperativeness of the system itself. 'On the evening of the assassination attempt the Emperor, after a formal dinner accompanied by his children, the Crown Prince and the Grand Duchess of Baden attended the opera, the National Theatre and a concert at the Zoological Garden. Wherever he went, the public gave him a jubilant reception. People rose to their feet and broke out singing "Deutschland Uber Alles" - It is clear that this scenario was hardly what was needed for the

---

[5]    Whereas in the state of peace a system can afford to let many of even most of its members live in an undecided situation, the state of siege pulls members so tightly together that the possibility to remain neutral or otherwise outside the confrontation is eliminates. Members are individually put into a situation where they must openly decide for or against the given social order and/or political rule ("Entscheidungszwan"). See Simmel *Conflict*, 1955:87.

passage of an anti-terrorist law.'[6] The successful attempt to pass an anti-Socialist law was preceded by a scenario that had dramatically changed inside a few weeks. Within two weeks after the Reichstag had rebuked the first bill, a well-planned second attempt at the life of the Emperor was carried out, heating the situation up to boiling point and turning Berlin 'into a city that was garrisoned as though it were in a state of siege.'[7] The government, visualising itself as being immediately and directly threatened by the socialists succeeded in spreading this generalised belief among the public and thus put pressure on the Liberal Party to support the Socialist bill. According to Maitron, the same was true of the French situation immediately preceding the Lois des Scelerates of 1893, when the government, shaken up by the attack on the Chamber of Deputies, believed that it was targeted by the anarchists.[8]

## ORIGIN OF THE STATE OF SIEGE

Aware of the consensus-building mechanisms set in motion by an external threat, governments may contribute their share to the construction of a siege-scenario in order to strengthen their position. Whereas party and interest rivalries lie out in the open in the absence of external threat, the state of siege makes party differences disappear from the face of political life. At the same time, political arguments are made illegitimate as 'disturbing the public order' or the solidarity of all well-meaning members of society. This situation allows the most influential parties and interest groups to pursue their goals with much less consideration of rival parties and/or groups than would be necessary in peacetime.

Deprived of political argumentation, minor coalition partners or interest groups are in no position to question the wisdom of the decisions taken in the name of the common

---

[6]    Carlson *Anarchism in Germany: The Early Movement*, 1972:124.
[7]    Ibid. 142.
[8]    Maitron *le mouvement anarchiste en France: des origines a' 1914*, 1975:232.

good without risking of being labelled enemies, deviants or at best well-meaning security risks who simply failed to take the common goods and values into consideration. It is well documented how the Bismarck government took advantage of the assassination attempts only to pursue its own political goal of the ruin of the Liberal Party and the Socialist Party.[9] The power interests of governments even, it may well be assumed that it is generally to the help of governments threatened by some form of de-legitimation that political violence is styled to a zero-sum game or state of siege.

But even if governments tend for reasons of their own political survival to feed, reinforce and channel the image of a state of siege in cases of political violence, this explanation does not go far enough in terms of a causal analysis. There arises the question of the specific conditions which make governments susceptible to politically violent threat. A possible answer lies in the radical de-legitimisation connected with a challenge of the State's monopoly of physical violence. If legitimacy of institutionalised rule is no more than the absence of organised radical opposition within a social system, the violent attacks on symbolic office holders of a political system above all symbolise the withdrawal of legitimacy by those who carry out the attack and by those who help them and/or sympathise with them. But how can withdrawal of legitimacy by small radical groups have such an enormous effect on the State?

The question would remain unanswerable if efforts aiming at an explanation were limited to the immediate dangerousness

---

[9]   Carlson, *Anarchism in Germany: The Early Movement,* 1972: 126, 155 Carlson shows rather accurately how the Sozialistengesetz was an anti-terrorist law not only aimed at anarchists and revolutionary socialists, but also and - indirectly, but on the political level foremost - at the strong Liberal Party, which was more annoying to Bismarck's plans than all revolutionaries together. With strong public feelings behind them, the proponents of "law and order' can under all circumstances use terrorism to gain political profit. If they are strong enough to pass a bill, they can stigmatise all presumed spiritual fathers' of terrorism (and thereby all political adversaries) and suppress unwelcome opposition, cf Demagogengesetze of 1819/20 in Germany, and Sozialistengesetz of 1878. If they are not in power, they can provoke the Liberals or Socialists in power to pass a - slightly more lenient - anti-terrorist law and at the same time discredit the 'leniency' of the political competitors by introducing a bill that contains twice as many repressive measures.

of the small group to the power holders.[10] Indeed, an explanatory attempt should incorporate the whole picture of power generating and maintaining mechanisms in democratic societies. It would have to consider that the ice layer of legitimacy that lies atop a few undercurrents of sheer power is very thin, even in Western style democratic societies. Even when using power-maintaining mechanisms like zero sum plots in which the potential costs for dissenting opinions, organisations and actions are radically increased by coercive measures, the State is never sure of its order. Further, it cannot be sure of this so long as there exist transcending political models that can successfully claim to be the better realisations of democratic principles. The student revolt of 1968 was an insurgent attempt from within the societies in the name of a better accomplishment of commonly shared values like democratic self-government, participation, and so on and so forth. Student uprisings; large industrial 'wildcat' strikes; radical ecology movements; the fashion of farm communities: all these point to the thinness of legitimacy of institutionalised rule.

Symbolic violent action is not an isolated phenomenon, but refers to all these phenomena, drastically reminding the State of the permanent possibility of de-legitimation. By forcing the State to respond to the provocation of this power system by unconcealed use of violence, the challengers thrust the system backwards to the earliest stages of the development of the State and the Law and by subjugation and building a clientele in the midst of rival autonomous groupings.[11] To gain an impression of the magnitude of the latent state of siege in which the State finds itself, it is not unimportant to consider

---

[10]   Whatever the Liberals and/or Socialists in power decide to do, they are caught on the horns of a dilemma if they don't pass legislation, they will easily become victims of a political campaign and lose their electorate, if they pass a relatively 'moderate' anti-terrorist law, the conservatives can easily denounce their 'weakness' with the introduction of a tougher bill, passing a tough bill they would give themselves up.

[11]   Cheerful delegation of competencies plays the smallest part in the emergence of power and the State. It is important to know that 'consensus' and 'legitimacy' are best described not as a deep-rooted love for the State, but the simple grudgingly performed act of legal compliance, if one wants to explain the enormously destabilising effects of small groups of offensive challengers of the given institutionalized rule. It is the thinness of legitimation that makes political systems react so exceedingly apprehensive.

the 'literary movements' that spread de-legitimising general conceptions long before their actualisation by acts or waves of manifest action. Virtually all great anarchist theorists dedicate much space and diligence to the problem of the Law as the principle coercive instrument of the State.[12] Anomic spontanistic theories of anarchism constitute a permanent radical challenge to the Law and the State,[13] and even those who leave a place for both in their utopian models must radically deny any repressive function of the law in future societies.[14] The anarchist literary movement is a dormant force as long as it finds no objectivation in reality. In periods of manifest action though, it suddenly gains relevance as the focal point of reference for all challenges of the system. Its position is further helped by the eradication of 'floating' members of the social system whose position towards the system is hardly defined. The polarisation of the political structure in the wake of social control responses to political violence leaves but the most radical focus of opposition as a gathering and reference point for those rejected by the system as radical deviants.

## ANTI-TERRORIST LEGISLATION IN A STATE OF SIEGE

Anti-terrorist legislation can be seen as the eminent instrument of coercive social control in the context of the functional mechanisms of institutionalised rule. Constantly and latently under a state of siege by transcending ideologies often for a long period of time only incorporated in literary movements, the State reacts to outbursts of political violence with the acute need to contract the moral boundaries and to produce greater in-group solidarity by intensified rejection of 'neutrals' and

---

[12]   See Proudhon, *Oeuvres compl tes* 1870:138, 215.

[13]   For an example of anomic-spontanistic anarchist theories on the law see Godwin, *An Inquiry Concerning Political Justice and its Influence on General Virtue and Happiness* 1793: 81.

[14]   Proudhon, Bakunin and BR Tucker were all tolerant of state and law even in their future visions, but were still radical enough to be perceived as terrible villains by the rulers. See Tucker, *Instead of a book by a man too busy to write one: A fragmentary exposition of philosophical anarchism* 1893: 312.

'dissenters'. The laws are not directed against the minimal threat of terrorist actions, but are instrumental in raising the potential loss involved in refusal of active support by the governed. They are aimed not at the political criminal, but at the on-looking public.

The principal aim of anti-terrorist legislation is a decisive change of the expected payoffs in social conflict. Administrative and penal laws promise such discouraging negative sanctions for dissenting opinions/organisations that whatever benefit the social actors might expect from unruly behaviour, this benefit simply fades in the face of the expected sanctions. To achieve this chance of expected payoffs:

    i.   *laws are designed to improve efficiency of the control agencies inner laws*

Many a police reform owes its birth to the repercussions of a state of siege. Many of these "inner" laws of security do not directly affect the citizens. Others, like shifts in the power balance between prosecution and defence before court do affect at least the accused and the status of the defence lawyers.[15] Laws concerning the status of public officials and their special obligation towards the general belief and value structures of the system affect the implementation staff at all levels of public employment.

    ii.   *laws are designed to extend the social space controlled by penal law outreaching laws*

---

[15]   As a rule, both the formal legal rights of the defence and the accused and the implementation of the existing statutes are being modified so as to disadvantage the defence. Typical legal innovations in this field of criminal procedure are trial of the accused in absentia, control of contacts between the accused and his lawyer, exclusion of defence lawyers transfer of judicial privileges to the state attorney. The whole repertory has come to new honours in the German history as well as that of other countries. Typical modifications in the implementation of existing statutes are denials of defence requests ordinarily granted by the court. These techniques have an uninterrupted tradition in all countries with a terrorist history. For France see Maitron, *le mouvement anarchiste en France: des origines a' 1914*, 1975:232. For the Hodel case in Germany in 1878, see Carlson, *Anarchism in Germany: The Early Movement*, 1972, 125.

Extension and amplification of the control apparatus are a necessary background for the extension of the controlled social space. Between coercion and consensus as a means of social control there exists a substitutive relationship. The further coercive measures grow, the smaller the social space left to the sole forces of consensus and - vice versa - the lesser consensus to be found in society the more the system will have to rely upon coercive control. The extension of formal control can be shown in the outreaching function.

The aim of the last outgrowths of the law is not the violation of rights, but these laws attempt to prevent the communication of ideas on power, justice, authority and violence, thereby maximising the risk for dissenters.[16] Typically, anti-terrorist legislation addresses the social space of communication, stretching a net of coercive control over a realm normally reserved for the self-steering mechanisms of public opinion and informal control. Both the *Frens lois des scelerates* and the German *Sozialistengesetz* were aiming at the sphere of communication rather than of manifest acts. The first *lois des scelerates* was directed against the liberty of the press whereas its predecessor of 1872 had only prohibited the instigation to violence, the new law of 1893 prohibited the mere verbal apology of acts qualified as crimes. A second anti-terrorist law was directed against criminal conspiracies, making it a punishable offence to agree on a crime, even if no manifest preparations are made. A third law still enlarged the definition of 'conspiracy'.[17] Patterns in the legislative response to political violence followed the same path in Germany in 1894 and in 1976.[18]

---

[16] Whenever laws try to secure consensus by raising the risk of articulation and organisation of dissensus, whenever laws tend to positively prescribe a behaviour or even sentiments, the discrepancy between the normal expectations of the functions of law and its sudden aspirations to play a role in the socialisations of individuals inspires cartoonists to denounce this extension of coercive social control. The cartoon illustrates the criminalisation of verbal behaviour towards crimes and violence and the State. Article 140 of the German Penal Code prohibits the public approval of crimes.

[17] Maitron *le mouvement anarchiste en France: des origines a' 1914,* 1975: 262.

[18] In 1894, a legislative project wanted to fight the influence of the spiritual ancestors of revolution. In 1975 and 1976 a legislative project wanted to fight the same bad influences that were made accountable for terrorism by an article prohibiting any approval of violent acts. Full realisation of the 1894 as well as the 1975/6 proposals was prevented by intellectuals', writers' and journalists' protests who saw their work as well as the work of classical poets and other well-respected people endangered.

# EFFECTIVENESS

Anti-terrorist legislation can successfully repress political violence against the government if: the statutes at the disposal of the enforcement apparatus are comprehensive and leave no loopholes that can be used to organise dissent; if these tight laws are being implemented with evenly rigid vigour over a long period time; and if they do so in the face of a small segment of the population that has no resources for a longer underground activity. Given the present political situation in most Western European countries, chances for such uncompromising anti-terrorist laws are dim. Given the alienating nature of legal coercion, anti-terrorist laws must be perfectly effective to reach their intended goals of repression. Any intensification of State coercion, that does leave loop-holes for the communication and organisation of dissent, produce the de-legitimisation of its own power and also provides the channels for agitation and organisation of radical opposition. The foreseeable effect of non-perfect anti-terrorist legislation is, then:

- greater rejection of deviants ('scapegoats' or 'enemies of the state');
- elimination of political third parties (i.e. of moderate and/or undefined intra- or extra-parliamentary opposition);
- emergence/growth of radical violent groups;
- greater in-group solidarity ('solidarity of all democrats');
- de-legitimisation by increased State coercion (grudging over the government, the parties, retreatist, escapist and rebellious reactions).

Mid-range effects of imperfect anti-terrorist legislation will include the development of a strong extra-parliamentary opposition and, an increased need for the State to compensate for the loss of legitimacy by increased coercion in place of informal consensus building mechanisms. As increased coercion is likely to build up counter-pressure, government influence on the construction of consensus (i.e. manipulative techniques) becomes more likely after the in-effectiveness of sheer coercion becomes evident. Such political violence and legislative response are likely to lead to government attempts at more control both by coercion and by manipulation.

Laws pertaining to the social space of communications are most likely to meet with resistance within the social system itself and therefore, to be typical examples of imperfect anti-terrorist laws, the *Sozialistengeaetz* of 1878 prohibited the publication of socialist books, pamphlets and periodicals. Meetings of party members had to be approved of by the police; agitators of the social democratic party were being expelled from their towns.[19] But still, the law was full of loop-holes and therefore so counterproductive that membership of the party soared enormously during the twelve years of its prohibition. Laws that address the freedom of the press, the arts and the sciences are at the core of such counterproductive laws: their chances of success in parliament vary considerably. Once accepted by the legislative bodies their effects are:

- the eradication of individual symbolic opponents by direct implementation of the law;
- the compliance/conformity of most hitherto unde-cided members of the system to the institutionalised rule;
- radicalisation of the remaining protest;
- de-legitimisation of institutionalised rule.

## CONCLUSION

Sensational political violence by terrorists regularly provokes typical forms of legislative response that aim at centralisation of social control and the suppression of radical opposition. The main target of penal anti-terrorist legislation is the social space of communication as the most rudimentary of all visible

---

[19]   Mere agitation was so feared that from Berlin alone, at least 294 persons with about 500 family members were expelled. In many towns, the expelled party members again assembled, founding clubs like the "United Expelled from Berlin in Hamburg and Environment" and the like.

forms of political opposition. Meetings, publications and discussions about violence and authority, other than in an affirmative manner, are made punishable offenses since these acts are seen as threats to the given (institutionalised) rule. The nature of the threat is described in this paper as a latent ideological state of siege, threatening the power-holders with de-legitimisation and symbolic rupture of a vague and only factual consensus, which is upheld by coercive prevention of public articulation and organisation of dissent.

Anti-terrorist legislation is part of a power-maintaining mechanism that involves the contraction of social control in order to regain system stability. Contraction of social control implies centralisation and enlargement of the formal control agencies, a shift of moral boundaries towards the elimination of third parties, thus productive of a two-party zero-sum game with the necessity for each system member to decide for or against the given form of institutionalised rule. With penal sanctions outreaching far into the realm of (normally) informal means of social control, the expected payoffs for individual political decisions are so altered that conformity will be likely to be restored. But as contraction of social control also presupposes an increase in the level of rejection of deviants, those segments of society which are being rejected will tend to emerge as radical out-groups or terrorists, thus perpetuating the need for, or the legitima-tion of, continued State coerciveness. In legal-democratic societies anti-terrorist laws are likely to remain imperfect in so far as statutes contain loop-holes for the organisation and communication of dissent and their implementa-tion is likely to be erratic, rather than static. Continuous intensified erratic repression is likely to produce greater conformity of group members through production of radical out groups as a threat to institutionalised rule and, also a loss of legitimation with the general population as a result of intensified coerciveness and a lowered level of integration by consensus-building mechanisms.

## Bibliography

Carlson, A.R. *Anarchism in Germany: The Early Movement,* (N.J.: The Scarecrow Press), 1972.

Godwin, W. *An Inquiry Concerning Political Justice and its Influence on General Virtue and Happiness* (London: Peregrine), 1793.

Maitron, J. *le mouvement anarchiste en France: des origines a' 1914* (Paris: Maspero), 1975.

National Advisory Committee on Criminal Justice Standards and Goals Task Force, *Report on Disorders and Terrorism,* (Washington, DC: Printing Office), 1976.

Proudhon, P.J. *Oeuvres completes* (Paris: Librairie Internationale), 1870.

Simmel. G. *Conflict* (Glencoe: Free Press) 1955.

Tucker, B.R. *Instead of a book by a man too busy to write one: A fragmentary exposition of philosophical anarchism* (New York: B.R. Tucker), 1893.

# NEOLIBERAL CRIME POLICY
## WHO PROFITS?

### Emma Bell

---

*This paper was originally delivered at the 2010 European Group conference in Lesvos, Greece, and 'a longer version of this paper was published in the subsequent edited collection of conference proceedings entitled 'The Politics of Criminology' (papers from the 38th European Group Conference).*

In order to answer the question posed in the title of this paper, it is first necessary to define exactly what is meant by neoliberal crime policy. The focus here is on the British context, although variants of neoliberal crime policies can of course be detected across most Western nations today. In many ways, neoliberal crime policy is not dissimilar to crime policies of the past: it targets the 'usual suspects', namely the poorest and most disadvantaged members of society, whilst largely turning a blind eye to the crimes of the powerful; it continues to rely on imprisonment to punish convicted offenders and to deter future offenders; and it aims to send out a moral message about the State's limits of tolerance. However, in contrast with penal policies of the past, particularly those associated with social democracy, neoliberal crime policy is supported by a greatly-extended penal apparatus in the form of new surveillance technologies, extensive new regulatory powers and the rise of out-of-court penalties. This intensification of the punitive capacity of the State is justified by the need to prevent crime, before it occurs. Whilst the optimism of the previous era centred on the State's capacity to rehabilitate and reintegrate offenders, contemporary penal optimism centres on the State's capacity to control risky behaviour.

Consequently, a wide range of punitive, exclusionary and disproportionate penal measures have been adopted in recent years, notably under the New Labour government.[1] Yet, neoliberal crime policy need not necessarily lead to punitiveness. Indeed, the logic of homo economicus according to which rational individuals commit crime only when the benefits of crime are greater than the costs incurred, crime policy should focus on increasing the relative costs of criminality by rendering punishment more certain and severe.[2] Such logic clashes with disproportional sentencing. As Joseph Stigler, a key neoliberal economist explained, where such sentences are used 'the marginal deterrence of heavy punishments could be very small or even negative'.[3] This would suggest that disproportionately severe punishment such as we are witnessing today is not intrinsic to neoliberalism itself, as experts such as Loïc Wacquant have suggested.[4] It is instead argued here that penal severity results from the peculiar political conjuncture that neoliberalism produced in the United Kingdom.

That peculiar conjuncture was one where the two major political parties in the UK were suffering severe crises of legitimacy. In 1993, the year to which the so-called 'punitive turn' is usually dated, the Conservatives were struggling to deal

---

[1]   See Bell, *Criminal Justice and Neoliberalism,* 2011.

[2]   Becker, 'Crime and Punishment: An Economic Approach', 1968; Zedner, 'Opportunity Makes the Thief-Taker: The Influence of Economic Analysis on Crime Control', 2009.

[3]   Stigler, 'The Optimum Enforcement of Laws', 1970: 527.

[4]   Wacquant, *Punishing the Poor: The Neoliberal Government of Social Insecurity,* 2009.

with the socially destructive legacy of Thatcherism, whilst the Labour Party was attempting to come to terms with neoliberal hegemony and to shed what it had come to consider as its left-wing baggage. The Conservatives' crusade on crime was part of a wider campaign to rebuild the moral foundations of society, creating what Harvey has described as 'social glue'[5] capable of uniting the nation around a common project – that of neoliberalism. For New Labour, adopting a tough stance on crime was a way for it to divest itself of its unjustly-earned image as being 'soft on crime' whilst providing it with an issue that could appeal to voters across class lines, thus also enabling the party to shed its lifelong association with the working classes and move into the political mainstream. Indeed, once the party had reconciled itself to the new neoliberal order, it found itself relatively powerless to assume the key function of the Social-democratic State as it had been understood since the beginning of the 20th Century – guaranteeing the social security of its citizens. Although, in government, it did attempt to manage the socially deleterious effects of neoliberalism, thus inaugurating a new, less destructive 'roll out' neoliberalism in opposition to the 'roll back' neoliberalism of the Thatcher era,[6] its commitment to neoliberal orthodoxy, which focused on individual rather than State responsibility for social problems, rendered any attempt to tackle social injustice entirely futile. Crime policy can thus be understood as a way of managing the neoliberal transformation of the State from provider of social security to facilitator of market solutions.[7]

Indeed, as David Garland has argued, toughness in the face of the crime problem is a means for the State to demonstrate its capacity to protect citizens from the risk posed by crime whilst it remains relatively powerless to protect them from the various risks posed by what he describes as 'late

---

[5]    Harvey, *A Brief History of Neoliberalism*, 2nd edn, 2007.
[6]    Jamie Peck and Adam Tickell, 'Neoliberalizing Space', 2002.
[7]    Leys, *Market-Driven Politics: Neoliberal Democracy and the Public Interest*, 2nd edn, 2003.

modernity'.[8] Rather than speaking of late modernity, I think it is more appropriate to speak of neoliberalism, which is surely the overarching political orthodoxy of contemporary times. It is specifically neoliberalism which has both exacerbated social problems and rendered the State impotent in face of them. It has done this by forcing a profound restructuring of the labour market and also by fostering a culture of hedonism in the economic sphere whilst simultaneously encouraging a culture of authoritarianism in the social sphere. Ironically, as irresponsibility has come to characterise the world of finance, increasing focus has been placed on the need to encourage individual responsibility for social problems. Consequently, all of New Labour's attempts to tackle the social problems which it identified as key causes of crime were focused primarily on the need to encourage, or even force, individuals and families to take responsibility for turning their lives around. In the penal sphere, welfarist measures were underpinned by coercion, leading to the extension of punishment through welfare.

It is in this sense that the State 'profits' from neoliberal crime policies. The profits are not pecuniary – indeed, spending on law and order has been increasing wildly in recent years – but should rather be understood in terms of the legitimacy they can confer on those States which apply them. It is true that in practice New Labour failed either to foster a culture of responsibility or to successfully legitimise its own power. It has instead fostered a culture of irresponsibility towards others by fostering a form of exclusive, egotistical individualism. Moreover, no matter how tough New Labour governments got on crime, it was still perceived to be 'soft' in this respect. Nonetheless, in the context of the neoliberal transformation of the State, crime, like immigration, represented one of the few 'popular' issues which it could regularly invoke in an attempt to appeal to the public at large. It may thus be understood as an attempt at legitimation at a time when governments can no

---

8   Garland, *The Culture of Control: Crime and Social Order in Contemporary Society*, 2001.

longer seek legitimacy by presenting themselves as providers of social and economic security.

Yet, the State is not the only one to profit from neoliberal crime policies. The private actors who form part of the 'security-industrial complex' also benefit considerably. They have influenced the punitive direction of these policies and then reaped the benefits, using crime control to protect their own commercial imperatives. Increasingly, as government has come to see its key role as facilitator of market solutions, it has, according to Joe Sim (2010) come to share what Hall and Scraton (1981) once described as a 'correspondence of interests' with the private sector.[9] Governments in post-war Britain tended to share commonality of interests with civil service and academic élites, both of whom tended to see themselves as the 'platonic guardians' of the public interest, entrusted to govern the country as they saw fit.[10]

Today, neoliberal governments have come instead to share an interest with the private sector, promoting market solutions wherever possible. For New Labour in particular, forging close links with the private sector was a way of proving its competence in economic affairs to the electorate. In terms of criminal justice, both parties benefited when criminal justice services were opened up to contestability. The government was able to appear to be offering good value for money whilst the private sector has been able to make substantial profits from the management of a range of criminal justice and security services. The private sector has also benefitted more indirectly from such policies since a focus on the kind of crime and antisocial behaviour, which harms business, has diverted attention from the crimes it may itself perpetrate. Indeed, whilst there has been an increased regulation of the crimes of the poor, there has been a significant deregulation of crimes perpetrated by

---

[9]  Sim, 'Review Symposium: Punishing the Poor' 2010; Hall and Scraton, 'Law, Class and Control' 1981.

[10]  Loader, 'Fall of the 'Platonic Guardians': Liberalism, Criminology and Political Responses to Crime in England and Wales', 2006.

the powerful.[11] According to Tombs and Whyte, there is a serious 'crisis of enforcement' as State agencies routinely fail to effectively regulate breaches of health and safety regulations in the workplace.[12] Joe Sim[13] refers to this as the 'non-governance' of social harms. Indeed, the law is more usually employed to protect businesses, especially as business has become a key partner not just in the delivery of punishment but also in the development of policy. For example, under the 1998 *Crime and Disorder Act*, members of locally-based Crime and Disorder Reduction Partnerships (CDRPs) are obliged to develop anti-crime policies together with representatives from local businesses. In some areas of Britain, known as Business Improvement Districts (BIDS), private companies have even been given total control over developing strategies to fight against antisocial behaviour in order to encourage commerce. It is now often private companies which can determine what is to be considered as 'public space'.

Under the influence of corporate interests, the British government has been applying a form of what Rene van Swaaningen[14] has described as a form of 'revanchist urbanism' whereby the poor, rather than being incorporated within public spaces, are held responsible for crime and the decay of the inner cities and are thus deemed to have forfeited their right to inhabit 'public' space.[15] Meanwhile, control of these spaces is handed over to private business. Business is thus granted further opportunities for profit maximisation whilst government can vaunt the benefits of urban regeneration projects.

Despite the managerialist rhetoric about the need to satisfy the 'consumers' of criminal justice services, it is this group of people who profit the least from neoliberal crime policies.

---

[11]   Coleman *et al.*, 'Capital, Crime Control and Statecraft in the Entrepreneurial City', 2005.

[12]   Tombs and Whyte, *A Crisis of Enforcement: The decriminalisation of death and injury at work*, 2008.

[13]   Sim, *Punishment and Prisons: Power and the Carceral State*, 2009: 88.

[14]   Van Swaaningen, 'Public Safety and the Management of Fear', 2005.

[15]   Ibid.

It is useful here to ask who exactly the government is referring to when it speaks of the 'consumers' of these services.
For New Labour, the consumers were clearly considered to be
the victims of crime and the public at large in whose interests
the criminal justice system needed to be 'rebalanced'. The
interests of the other 'consumers' of criminal justice services
– namely offenders themselves – were, however, routinely
ignored. Laws intended to protect the interests of the former
tended to undermine the interests of the latter, such as the
abolition of the 'double jeopardy' rule.[16] Yet, in practice, none
of these groups have benefitted to any significant extent from
neoliberal crime policies. Although the voice of victims of
crime is now more likely to be heard by the courts via, for
example, Victim Personal Statements which allow courts to
hear about the impact of certain crimes on their victims, legal
conflicts very much remain the property of the State.[17] This
fact is demonstrated by the hijacking of restorative justice
programmes by the State.

The general public also fails to 'profit' from neoliberal
crime policies in any significant way. As taxpayers, the public
suffers considerable pecuniary loss through increased expenditure on the criminal justice system. It is not even possible to
argue that this is good value for money since it is notoriously
hard to prove any link between such expenditure and falls in
crime rates. Furthermore, government failure to tackle social
injustice and the structural causes of reoffending has meant
that the poorest and most vulnerable members of society –
those who suffer most from crime and antisocial behaviour
– are even more likely than ever to become victims of crime.
Despite New Labour's professed commitment to 'left realism',

---

[16]   This legal rule, according to which an offender cannot be tried twice for the same crime, was
effectively abolished by the *Criminal Justice Act 2003* which permits the Court of Appeal to
annul an acquittal and order a new trial when there is 'new and compelling evidence against
the acquitted person in relation to the qualifying offence' provided that a new trial would be 'in
the interests of justice'.

[17]   This is contrary to Nils Christie's advice delivered almost 35 years ago in 1977 in Christie,
'Conflicts as Property' 1977.

the poorest tenth of the population[18] are considerably more likely to be murdered than the rest of the population, whilst those living in the poorest areas of England and Wales are more likely to feel that they are affected by anti-social behaviour.[19] It might also be argued that they are also more likely to suffer from unofficially-defined forms of antisocial behaviour perpetrated by companies which employ them in dangerous, low-paid jobs without respecting health and safety regulations. Society as a whole has also suffered from the general erosion of civil liberties which, it has been claimed, is the price to pay for greater public protection.

Finally, whilst some offenders have experienced a slight improvement in the material conditions of their detention (such as the end of slopping out), many more others have found themselves subject to worsening conditions in over-crowded jails or to an erosion of the centuries-old protections designed to protect them from miscarriages of justice – we mentioned the abolition of the double jeopardy rule above, but we can also list the admission of hearsay evidence into criminal trials, the limitation of the right to choose trial by jury, the decline in the quality of legal protection offered to defendants on account of the severe limitation of legal aid; not to mention the blurring of the boundaries between the civil and the criminal law via the creation of hybrid measures. We might also note the disgraceful treatment of those suspected of having committed, prepared to commit, or merely promoted acts of terrorism.

It might be asked whether a change in direction in penal policy is at all likely under the current coalition government in the UK. I would suggest, rather pessimistically, that the chances of this occurring are slim. Despite the coalition's declared commitment to civil liberties and the new Justice Minister's much-publicised indirect criticism of the 'prison works' philosophy which has dominated sentencing policy since

---

[18]    Dorling, 'Prime Suspect: Murder in Britain', 2006.
[19]    Thorpe and Hall, "Public Perceptions", 2009: 101.

at least 1993,[20] it would appear that neoliberal crime policies will remain in place. The coalition's commitment to neoliberalism is firmly anchored. It would be a mistake to regard plans to increase State regulation of the financial sector as a retreat from neoliberalism. As Dardot and Laval[21] point out, neoliberalism cannot be reduced to the notion of laissez-faire. Furthermore, just like the State interventions in the economy in 2008 and 2009, which involved the part-nationalisation of the banks, future interventionist measures are likely to be regarded as emergency measures only, designed to ensure the survival of the neoliberal order rather than to herald the beginning of a fundamental transformation of capitalism.[22]

Yet, as I suggested earlier, punitiveness in penal policy is not intrinsic to neoliberalism. Nonetheless, given the renewed crisis of legitimacy of the neoliberal order, it is likely that the coalition, as the New Labour governments before it, will turn to issues such as crime and immigration in a desperate attempt to appeal to the electorate across class lines and consequently try to secure its legitimacy, particularly in the context of massive public spending cuts which will inevitably exacerbate social and economic insecurities and undermine its already fragile popularity. Indeed, in the recent general election, these issues continued to be a hot topic for debate amongst all three major contenders for office, situated in second and third places behind the economy in the public's list of 'Most Important Issues' facing the country.

A closer analysis of the detail of crime policy reveals that a more libertarian approach in this respect is skin-deep only. It is only the civil liberties of the law-abiding that appear to be of concern to the current government. Rather than repealing legislation, which has led to the blurring of the boundaries between the civil and the criminal law and the rise of out-of-court justice, the coalition government plans to extend the arsenal already

---

[20] Ministry of Justice, *Breaking the Cycle: Effective Punishment, Rehabilitation and Sentencing of Offenders,* 2010.

[21] Dardot and Laval, *La nouvelle raison du monde: Essai sur la société néolibérale,* 2009.

[22] Callinicos, *Bonfire of Illusions: The Twin Crises of the Liberal World,* 2010: 128-9.

available to the police, reducing 'timewasting bureaucracy' and amending the health and safety laws that 'stand in the way of common sense policing'.[23] This would suggest that the civil liberties of offenders are somewhat less sacrosanct. Indeed, the Conservatives promised to repeal the *Human Rights Act 1998,* which they claim has rendered the fight against crime more difficult by protecting the human rights of criminals.

Furthermore, plans to halt the current wild expansion of the prison population are likely to be difficult to pursue in practice: both parties to the coalition support the toughening up of community sentences which is likely to mean that such penalties will continue to act as additions rather than alternatives to imprisonment. A commitment to 'honesty in sentencing' may mean that prison sentences will continue to lengthen. It is finally important to note that business will remain an important partner in the formulation of crime policy and the delivery of criminal justice services. Indeed, its role with regard to the latter is to be extended in the context of current budget cuts. Government is thus likely to continue to share a considerable 'correspondence of interest' with the private sector in prosecuting the crimes of the powerless whilst ignoring those of the powerful. Both parties will continue to profit from neoliberal penality.

## Bibliography

Bell, E. *Criminal Justice and Neoliberalism* (Basingstoke and New York: Palgrave Macmillan), 2011.

Becker, G. 'Crime and Punishment: An Economic Approach' *Journal of Political Economy,* 76(2), 1968: 169-217.

Callinicos, A. *Bonfire of Illusions: The Twin Crises of the Liberal World* (Cambridge and Malden: Polity Press), 2010.

Christie, N. 'Conflicts as Property', *British Journal of Criminology,* 17(1), 1977: 1-15.

Coleman, R., Tombs, S. and Whyte, D. 'Capital, Crime Control and Statecraft in the Entrepreneurial City', *Urban Studies,* 42(13), 2005: 2511-2530.

---

[23]   HM Government, http://programmeforgovernment.hmg.gov.uk, 2010.

Dardot, P. and Laval, C. *La nouvelle raison du monde: Essai sur la société néolibérale* (Paris: Éditions de la Découverte), 2009.

Dorling, D. 'Prime Suspect: Murder in Britain', *Prison Service Journal*, 166, 2006: 3-10.

Garland, D. *The Culture of Control: Crime and Social Order in Contemporary Society* (Oxford and New York: Oxford University Press), 2001.

Hall, S. and Scraton, P. 'Law, Class and Control' in Fitzgerald, M., McLennan G. and Pawson, J. (eds.) *Crime and Society* (London and New York: Routledge), 1981.

Harvey, D. *A Brief History of Neoliberalism*, 2nd edn (Oxford and New York: Oxford University Press), 2007.

HM Government http://programmeforgovernment.hmg.gov.uk/ [accessed 26 May, 2010].

Loader, I. 'Fall of the 'Platonic Guardians': Liberalism, Criminology and Political Responses to Crime in England and Wales', *British Journal of Criminology*, 46(4), 2006: 561-586.

Leys, C. *Market-Driven Politics: Neoliberal Democracy and the Public Interest*, 2nd edn (London and New York: Verso), 2003.

Ministry of Justice, *Breaking the Cycle: Effective Punishment, Rehabilitation and Sentencing of Offenders*, Cm7972 (London: HMSO), 2010.

Peck, J. and Tickell, A. 'Neoliberalizing Space', *Antipode*, 34(3), 2002: 380-404.

Sim, J. 'Review Symposium: *Punishing the Poor – The Neoliberal Government of Insecurity* by Loïc Wacquant', *British Journal of Criminology*, 50 (1), 2010: 589-608.

Sim, J. *Punishment and Prisons: Power and the Carceral State* (London and Thousand Oaks: Sage), 2009.

Stigler, G. 'The Optimum Enforcement of Laws', *Journal of Political Economy*, 78(3), 1970: 526-536.

Thorpe, K. And Hall, P. "Public Perceptions" 2009. Quoted in Walker, A. *et al.* (eds.) *Crime in England and Wales 2008/09 Volume 1: Findings from the British Crime Survey and police recorded crime* (London: Home Office).

Tombs, S. and Whyte, D. *A Crisis of Enforcement: The decriminalisation of death and injury at work*, (London: Centre for Crime and Justice Studies), 2008.

van Swaaningen, R. 'Public Safety and the Management of Fear', *Theoretical Criminology*, 9(3), 2005: 289-305.

Wacquant, L. *Punishing the Poor: The Neoliberal Government of Social Insecurity* (Durham and London: Duke University Press), 2009.

Zedner, L. 'Opportunity Makes the Thief-Taker: The Influence of Economic Analysis on Crime Control'. Quoted in Newburn, T. and Rock, P. (eds) *The Politics of Crime Control: Essays in Honour of David Downes*, 2nd edn (Oxford and New York: Oxford University Press), 2009.

# THE DEMAND FOR THE CRIMI- NALISATION OF PORNOGRAPHY

## A STATE-MADE IDEOLOGICAL CONSTRUCTION OR A DEMAND ARTICULATED IN CIVIL SOCIETY?

**Dany Lacombe**

*This paper was delivered at the Vienna conference in 1987 and was based on what was then a recently completed M.A. thesis by the author and published in the Working Papers in European Criminology: Volume 9, Justice and Ideology: Strategies for the 1990s pp 83-91.*

Pornography is not a problem which has suddenly emerged in the 1980s. It has a long history in terms of the debate it created, the disputes it involved and the philosophies it implied. In 1983, however, the Canadian Government designated pornography as a 'social problem', and created a committee, the Fraser Committee[1], to enquire about the problems posed by pornography as well as the views of Canadians on what the government should do about it. The designation of pornography as a 'social problem', which needs to be dealt with by the government should not be treated as non-problematic. Why is it that the public outcry in the 1960s against pornography was not treated as seriously as it is in the 1980s? Why is the government so active today in fighting what it has now come to define as the source of violence against women? This revival of interest in pornography by the Canadian State leads to other important questions regarding the reaction of interest groups in society. For example, are interest groups in society responding to the threats posed by pornography or to the widespread belief that pornography is infiltrating their lives and becoming more and more violent, as is suggested by the Canadian State?

## THE CONSTRUCTION OF SOCIAL PROBLEMS

These questions pertaining to the role of the State in the construction of 'social problems' need to be addressed if we are to understand the making of criminal justice policy. This chapter attempts to do so by presenting some of the findings of my research on the larger social and political forces involved in the recent debate over pornography in Toronto, Canada.[2] Specifically, I propose to examine the theoretical significance attributed to the role of the social control culture in the creation and/or manipulation of 'social problems' for the establishment of a repressive order. This will be followed by an attempt to explain the process by which a politics of sexual repression is created. Efforts to resist this politics of sexual repression will also be offered.

The Marxist debate on the role of the State in capitalist

---

[1]    Fraser Committee. *Special Committee on Pornography and Prostitution Report*, 1985.
[2]    This research is based on my published Master's thesis *Ideology and Public Policy: the case against pornography.*

societies and the growing intellectual interest in the influential work of Antonio Gramsci[3] were translated in the field of criminology into a desire to understand the ideological significance of 'criminal justice issues' for the State and to locate them within the historic conjuncture. One of the most important criminological works of the 1970s addressing the relationship between ideology, crime and the State is *Policing the Crisis*.[4] Hall et al. brilliantly demonstrated that the State can no longer be treated as a neutral entity simply responding to the pressure of social forces in society. Instead, they attempted to illustrate the active role of the State in securing its hegemony during periods of economic crisis. Through the ideological manipulation of a criminal justice issue, the State, it is argued, generated mass support from below for the establishment of a strict social order. Presenting the social realities of pornography and its link to crime as a pure ideological construction by the State and its apparatuses, in order to displace and contain conjunctural crisis, is an approach which can be criticised for its functionalism, and for its implication that little resistance is possible.[5] In order to avoid such a fallacy I decided in my research to concentrate at the micro level and investigate in detail the interest groups involved in the pornography debate.

I have examined in an empirical and analytical way the views of the most vocal groups in Toronto involved in the debate over pornography. One of the arguments I was able to make on the basis of my study was that the site of cultural hegemony is not, as suggested by Hall et al., solely located in the State. I do not want to suggest that the arguments put forward

---

[3] For the Marxist debate on the State see Ralph Miliband, *The State in Capitalist Society,* 1969, Ralph Miliband, 'The Problem of the Capitalist State', 1972. Nicos Poulantaz, *Political Power and Social Classes,* 1973. For an overview of Gramsci's influence on the Marxist debate see Antonio Gramsci, *Selection from the Prison Notebooks*, 1971 and Ernesto Laclau and Chantal Mouffe, *Hegemony and Socialist strategy: Towards a Radical Democratic Politics,* 1985.

[4] Hall, Clark, Jefferson, Critcher & Roberts, Policing the Crisis , 1978.

[5] For an excellent Marxist critique of the theoretical and methodological problems of the thesis presented in *Policing the Crisis,* see Colin Sumner, 'Race Crime and Hegemony', 1981: 277-291.

in *Policing the Crisis* concerning the active role of the State in creating 'social problems' which can lead to support for law and order campaigns for the establishment of a strict social order is wrong. On the contrary, my case study illustrates how active the Canadian social control culture is in articulating an ideological conception of pornography serving to repress any form of sexuality outside the confines of monogamous hetero-sexual marriage. My empirical evidence, however, refutes Hall et al.'s argument that the State is creating a 'social problem' to which interest groups are simply 'responding'. Instead, my case study illustrates the presence of various social forces in civil society that are not part of the 'State apparatus' but are also very active in the construction of pornography as a 'social problem'. By attempting to define pornography, to locate its causes and to suggest solutions to eradicate it, these social forces are ultimately trying to convince politicians, policy makers and the general public about the adequacy of their analyses so that a consensus can be established in support of their views. Feminists have, for example, convincingly demon-strated the existence of misogynist and heterosexist culture by analysing how most cultural productions, such as those found in the media, language and the most extreme forms of sexist sexual presentations, sustain and maintain norms of male dominance and female submissiveness. In sum, by examining the interest groups involved in the debate over pornography my study demonstrates that rather than being the result of a recent State-made ideological construction, pornography is a contested terrain.

The argument that the State is capable of ideologically transforming a social issue into a moral panic to which people are simply reacting is problematic for another reason. It implies that ideologies are manipulative, that they are designed by the ruling elite to fool and deceive people. This model of manipulation from behind the scenes is also indica-tive of a poor understanding of the subject and consciousness. It suggests that people are empty entities blindly 'responding' to any ideas. Things or ideas make sense to people only when these resonate with their lived experience. Consequently one cannot assume that a dominant ideology is shared by all people or that there is a one-to-one correspondence between such ideology and people's attitudes. This can only be demonstrated through empirical evidence. Fieldwork and interviews with people involved in the porn debate led to the rejection of the notion that Canadian's are fooled by the social control culture into supporting a repressive demand for the criminalisation of pornography. The support from below for a strict social order is not the product of manipulation by a ruling class. It is a much more complex process which involves the participation of various social forces in civil society. The following example will briefly illustrate how feminist groups are orchestrating the support from below for a repressive order.

## FEMINIST INTEREST GROUPS

The 'social problem' referred to as pornography by feminist groups is substantially different from the conservative analysis of it. For feminists the issue is misogynist presentations, whereas for conservatives it is non-patriarchal sexuality. While there is divergence at the level of conceptualisation, there seems however to be agreement at the level of practice. In effect, when it comes to solutions, both groups are advocating the criminalisation of pornography.[6] It is by developing an analysis of pornography, which inevitably leads to the argument for censorship, that the feminist anti-pornography movement allows its analysis to be co-opted by conservative forces. The feminist anti-pornography movement articulated a conception of pornography that does not take into consider-

---

[6]   Not all feminists agree on the best strategies to combat misogynist/heterosexist sexual presentations. Feminists adhering to the theories of radical feminism and liberal feminism on the oppression of women tend to argue for censorship. My research demonstrates that the anti-censorship position advocated by socialist feminist groups is the most sophisticated approach to pornography. See Lacombe, *Ideology and Public Policy: The Case Against Pornography*, 1988:78-83.

ation the social relations in which it is organised. Pornography is studied as a 'thing out there', having the possibility of directly affecting men's actions and attitudes. The resulting effect of this de-contextualisation is the subsequent treatment of pornography as the problem instead of the social relations organising and producing pornography and its meaning. Consequently, pornography becomes the product of an aggressive male nature desirous to oppress women. Such conceptualisation of pornography is based on an essentialist view of sexuality which, in turn, is premised on the need to control and/or repress sexuality for the protection of women. There are similarities between this view and the one shared by conservatives. While it is true that the feminist demand for repression of misogynist sexual presentations is significantly different from the conservative demand for repression of sexuality, both demands are however predicated on empowering the social control culture whose practices, as is demonstrated in my study, are essentially for the preservation of traditional values characteristic of a strictly patriarchal order. Such practices are, therefore, anti-feminist, anti-gay and anti-lesbian sexualities.

The participation of anti-pornography feminists in the elaboration of a discourse premised on the need to repress a certain form of sexuality sheds light on the argument concerning the sole responsibility of the State and its apparatuses in the creation and manipulation of an issue to which people are reacting. Instead of 'responding' to a crisis, the feminist anti-pornography movement is one force among others orchestrating the support from below for a repressive order. It follows that had this movement produced an analysis of pornography not premised on the repression of sexuality it would have made it very difficult for the State to co-opt, transform and manipulate its analysis. The discussion below details the mechanisms by which a politics of sexual repression was articulated in Canada. It does so by comparing some findings of my research[7] with those provided by the Fraser Committee, since we both analysed the same groups involved in the debate. This examination, it is hoped, will illustrate the role of the feminist anti-pornography movement in this process.

## A CRITICAL EVALUATION OF THE FRASER COMMITTEE (1985)

The sexuality of sexual repression is articulated in the 1985 Fraser Committee report in the following three ways:
1.  through the marginalisation of groups that offer a significant challenge to the criminalisation of pornography;
2.  through the establishment of a variety of vague consensus amongst Canadians; and finally
3.  through the empowerment of a social control culture.

The Fraser Committee establishes three categories of opinion into which most of the interest groups in the pornography debate fall namely, the conservative, liberal and feminist approaches to pornography. What they refer to as the conservative and liberal approaches to pornography correspond to my usage of the terms. The feminist approach is defined differently and warrants further examination.

Though it attempted to encompass all the variations in the feminist views of pornography in the end the Fraser Committee focuses primarily on the analysis of radical feminists that have been translated - in the political arena by the feminist anti-pornography movement - into legal demands to address specifically the 'new pornography'.[8] The Committee simply omits the views of feminists whom they cannot accommodate. For example, they disqualify the views of anti-censorship feminists who are said to 'have a Marxist orientation'[9] and/

---

[7]    Lacombe, *Ideology and Public Policy: The Case Against Pornography* ,1988.
[8]    The 'new' pornography is distinguished from the 'old' by its explicit violent and sexist content.
[9]    Fraser Committee, *Special Committee on Pornography and Prostitution Report* ,1985:19.

or who share 'what could be termed a socialist viewpoint'[10] because it is said that their critique of sexism is not related to the politico-legal context characterising liberal democracies. Instead of objectively summarising their views, the Committee delegitimizes the anti-censorship feminists by reducing their analysis of pornography and sexism to the revolutionary abolition of capital. My examination of the anti-censorship feminists' position on pornography and sexism demonstrates that their analysis is much more sophisticated than the Committee pretends. The marginalisation and distortion of Marxist/socialist feminist analysis needs not be interpreted however in a conspiratorial fashion. It is rather a structural effect of the privileging of another feminism, whose discourse had more resonance with the liberal world view of the Committee, and could therefore be better accommodated to the legal structure of the present State.[11] This suggests, once again, that if the feminist anti-pornography movement had analysed pornography differently, the Fraser Committee might not have been able to accommodate it and to purge it of its progressive aspects.

Another mechanism by which the politics of repression is articulated in the Report is through the establishment of a variety of consensus among Canadians. In its effort to produce a workable definition of pornography which would please the majority of Canadians, the Committee asserts, for example, that most Canadians 'appreciate' sexuality *i.e.* that they agree with the principle that humans enjoy and benefit from sexual relations characterised by mutuality and respect.[12] From this assertion the Committee concludes that it found little support for the repression of sexuality as a mean of eliminating pornography. While my case study would not negate the 'appreciation' conservative groups have

---

[10]  Ibid 22.

[11]  It is however not far-fetched to suggest that the Committee's reliance on the crudest reductionist version of anti-censorship feminists is indicative of the extent of the threat the analysis of patriarchal and capitalist social relations represent for the Committee.

[12]  Fraser Committee, *Special Committee on Pornography and Prostitution Report*, 1985:23-26.

for sexuality, it would qualify it. Conservative groups seem to understand so completely the power of depictions of sexuality that want regulation which will bolster the values that they see as fundamental in society - that is, traditional values characterising patriarchal social order. The following statement of a founding member of Canadians for Decency, a Presbyterian Church organisation, illustrates this point well:

> I see the terrible danger in our society coming from television. And I see the undermining of family values for sure in comedies and in many areas which are not obscene or indecent but are very dangerous. And the policeman is often portrayed as a fool and the minister is for sure a fool, and most sexual relationships are not married and often they are not one on one, they are among several groups. So all these things we (Canadians for Decency) see as a danger, but, I cannot address the issue when I make a speech on pornography, but I say be aware. This is the undermining of family values.[13]

Consequently, the conservative 'appreciation' of sexuality is based on repression. Feminists 'appreciation' of sexuality, on the other hand, is expressed through their demand for erotica instead of pornography. While not all feminists agree on the forms erotica will take, they are all advocating at a theoretical level sexual explicitness. The Fraser Committee, by defining sexuality only in terms of its appreciation rather than expression or presentation, establishes a consensus which upon further examination appear to stand on shaky ground. Moreover, to affirm that all Canadians 'appreciate' sexuality says very little on how such a value can regulate pornography or justify its criminalisation. This is the case because this value says nothing about the way sexuality can or cannot be presented. The divergence of opinion amongst and between

---

[13]    Cited in Lacombe, *Ideology and Public Policy: The Case Against Pornography,* 1988:66.

conservatives, feminists and liberals, as I demonstrate in my research, indicate the total absence of consensus on what constitutes acceptable sexual expression. The Committee avoids discussing the complex issue of sexual expression by stating the existence of another dubious consensus. It is argued that feminist and conservative groups are for the production of erotica, which they both define in a compatible way. The Committee states that:

> The position of most feminist groups, and some church organizations, was that erotica, which they describe as sexually explicit material which contains no violence or coercion and in which the participants were there by choice, was acceptable.[14]

My research clearly demonstrates that the sexually explicit material feminists call erotica is substantially and politically very different from what conservatives consider to be erotica. Sexual images challenging patriarchal sexuality, such as expressions of consensual sex between lesbians, are unacceptable for conservative groups. Not only is lesbian sex unacceptable for conservatives, but so is explicit sex between heterosexuals as is illustrated in the following statements:

> Does erotica have to have a penis going into a vagina? No I don't think it has to have that myself.[15]

> Well, you see this (erotica) on restricted movies all the time, even in adult films. You see a relationship and then you see them in bed. No, it embarrasses me very much. I don't want to see them in bed. I don't want you in my bedroom, and I don't want to be in yours and to find this on a big screen. No, I would not necessarily find this immoral but I

---

14   Fraser Committee, *Special Committee on Pornography and Prostitution Report,* 1985:63.
15   A member of Project P, the special anti-porn squad in Canada, cited in Lacombe, *Ideology and Public Policy: The Case Against Pornography,* 1988:61.

would find it embarrassing and trivializing to have
a whole bunch of people sitting with their mouths
open watching, to see how he does it.[16]

On the basis of such conservative understandings it is
difficult to affirm that a consensus on erotica exists between
them and feminist groups. The Fraser Committee's attempt
to establish a variety of consensus is one which glosses over
major differences and disagreements amongst and between
groups. They ultimately serve to camouflage and silence the
complexity surrounding the issue of sexual explicitness giving
the false impression that the criminalisation of pornography
will not be based on the repression of sexuality. It will become
obvious in the following that this is not the case.

In its preface to the Report the Committee affirms the
complexity of pornography and prostitution and stresses on
various occasions the limitation of legal strategies, particularly the usage of the criminal law, in eradicating what it
considers the 'social problems' responsible for the oppression
of women. It is therefore with caution that it makes a case for
the criminalisation of pornography. The Committee is very
critical of the research on the alleged effects of pornography
on behaviour, especially the connection which is often made
between pornography and the carrying out of violent crimes.
In effect, it would have been suicidal for the Committee to use
this rationale for the criminalisation of pornography since
the research on the effects of pornography has been highly
criticised for its inadequacy and inconclusiveness.[17]

Since scientific evidence cannot justify the criminalisation
of pornography in the eyes of the Committee, it establishes a
new rationale – this time based on morality instead of science
– for the criminalisation of pornography. It argues that the
criminal law ought to be used against any sexual presentation

---

[16]   A founder member of Canadians for Decency cited Ibid:68.
[17]   For a thorough discussion of the highly inadequate equation between pornography .and the
       acting out of violent behaviour, see Thelma McCormack, 'Machismo in Media Research, a
       Critical Review of Research on Violence and Pornography', 1978.

which undermines the fundamental values Canadians adhere to. One of these values is the right to equality as asserted in the *Canadian Charter of Rights and Freedoms*. The Committee argues that, if women have not yet achieved equality, it is due to the perceptions of women as inferior beings. According to this logic, the eradication of pornography will ensure women greater equality. At a time when women's secondary status in the political, economic and social spheres is questioned by various social forces in society, a position for the improvement of women's status is ideologically and politically very significant. However, the assertion that the lack of equality for women is simply a matter of sexist attitudes precludes the Committee from addressing the important structural inequalities sustaining women's oppression. This indicates that the commitment to women's equality undertaken by the Committee is somewhat superficial, if not dubious. This becomes more apparent when the Committee argues that the sexist attitudes responsible for women's lack of equality stem from pornographic material, rather than media portrayals of women and, therefore, that control should only apply to pornographic materials. This logic suggests that the Committee is trying to clamp down on sexual rather than misogynist presentations. This inconsistency also casts doubts on the seriousness of the Committee's justification for using the criminal law against sexual depictions. If sexist depictions are said to have a harmful effect on equality, a fundamental value which ought to be upheld and protected by the criminal law, then it logically follows that they should all be banned. The Committee's refusal to use the criminal law to rid the media of 'false depictions of women'[18] contradicts such logic. In addition it suggests that the Committee is interested more in criminalising pornography as such rather than upholding the fundamental value of equality.

The last mechanism used by the Fraser Committee in its articulation of a politics of sexual repression consists of the

---

[18]   Fraser Committee, *Special Committee on Pornography and Prostitution Report*, 1985:263.

recommendations it makes for the empowerment of the social control culture. Such recommendations are based on the Committee's findings regarding the availability, content and resulting effects of pornography in Canada. The following will briefly present them in order for the reader to assess the inconsistency existing between the Committee's findings and its subsequent recommendations. The Committee's findings indicate that the availability of pornographic material has increased over the years. It attributes such increase to the fact that more stores carry such material today than they did before.[19] While this finding validates the claim of both conservative and feminist groups concerning the increased availability of pornography, it strongly negates its violent content and harmful effects. The Committee explicitly states that:

> The research which has been conducted on magazines and videos does not confirm the overwhelmingly awful picture presented by some groups and individuals in their briefs to the Committee. The view that large amounts of violent pornography or child pornography are being consumed IS not substantiated by research (and) the idea that a great deal of the pornography has taken on the worst possible characteristics of the genre is unconfirmed at this time.[20]

To this it adds that:

> While both types of videos (adult and triple X videos) do contain scenes of sexual aggression, violence and domination are not predominant themes. Rather, mechanical sexual relations, i.e. an absence of affection, love or passion and

---

[19]   Ibid: 88.
[20]   Ibid: 93.

concentration on the pure mechanics of sex between two adults of the opposite sex were by far the most common portrayals.[21]

Such findings are antithetical to the recommendation the Committee makes to the Canadian Government to give higher priority than it actually does to the control of the importation of 'material, which is so extreme or harmful in its depiction that is qualitatively different from the general context'.[22] Why after challenging the claims that extreme violent pornography IS infiltrating Canadians lives and affecting their behaviour does the Fraser Committee suddenly focus on this form of pornography? Why has it not focused on the material that is mostly available in Canada? This sudden shift in emphasis suggests that the Committee is an active participant in the discourse on the regulation of sexuality.

Other recommendations substantiate this claim. For example, while the Committee previously noted the limited extent of the importation of extremely violent sexual material, it strongly recommends extended power, as well as increasing funding to customs officers in order to better prevent the accessibility of such material. No effort is made to examine the actual list of prohibited goods or definitions used to prohibit material entry to Canada. The numerous court cases against Canadian Customs suggest that the criteria used to prohibit material entry to Canada are discriminating against lesbian and gay sexual presentations. My case study demonstrated that Law enforcement officers do not distinguish between the titillating materials used by homosexuals such as *The Joy of Guy Sex* and images of bestiality or child sexual abuse. The heterosexism characterising the practices of law enforcement officers casts serious doubts on the possibility of establishing guidelines that will not discriminate against attempts to produce forms of sexual presentation that go against the

---

21    Ibid: 95.
22    Ibid: 264.

grain. Such practices also contribute to the maintenance of gay and lesbian sexualities in a subordinate position. Ultimately these practices regulate our sexual desires. The Fraser Committee, by requesting more power to custom officers without seriously analysing the agency's heterosexist and anti-feminist practices suggests that the Committee is indeed participating in the making of what Foucault termed a repressive apparatus designed for the surveillance and discipline of 'sexual deviants'.

## CONCLUSION

As concluding remarks I would like to state once again the argument presented in this paper. The demand for law and order, as is exemplified by my study on pornography in Toronto, Canada, is not the sole product of a manipulation by the State and its apparatuses. It was demonstrated that the demand for law and order was also generated by various social forces in civil society, one of which is the anti-pornography feminists. In other words, rather than being a State–made ideological construction, the demand for the criminalisation of pornography corresponds instead to the articulation of the views of various social forces in society. This of course is not an argument for the neutrality of the State. It is demonstrated in this paper that the Fraser Committee, which was appointed by the government, was indeed quite active - through the marginalisation of progressive viewpoints, the establishment of vague consensus and the manipulation of information – in producing a definition of pornography which essentially necessitates legal control.[23]

The making of criminal justice policy is therefore a complex process which requires that we pay more attention to the relationship between the State and civil society. A conspiratorial and functionalist view of the State and of ideology, as

---

[23] My research also illustrates in detail the active role of two state apparatuses, the Ontario Censorship Board and Project P, the special anti-porn squad in Canada.

it is somewhat implicit in *Policing the Crisis,* glosses over such complexity and leads to the unfortunate conclusion that little resistance is possible.

## Bibliography

Fraser Committee. *Special Committee on Pornography and Prostitution Report,* 1 & 2, 1985.

Gramsci, A. *Selections from the Prison Notebooks* London: Lawrence and Wishart, 1971.'

Hall, S., Clark, J., Jefferson, T., Critcher, C. & Roberts, B., *Policing the Crisis, Mugging the State and Law and Order.* (London: Macmillan), 1978.

Laclau, E. and Mouffe, C. *Hegemony and Socialist Strategy: Towards a Radical Democratic Politics,* London, Verso, 1985

Lacombe, D. *Ideology and Public Policy: The Case Against Pornography.* (Toronto: Garamond Press, Network Basic Series), 1988.

McCormack, T. 'Machismo in Media Research, a Critical Review of Research on Violence and Pornography', *Social Problems,* 25, 1978 pp 544-558

Miliband, R. *The State in Capitalist Society,* New York, Basic Books, 1969,

Miliband, R. 'The Problem of the Capitalist State' in Robin Blackburn, *Ideology and Social Science,* 1972.

Poulantzas, N. *Political Power and Social Classes,* London, New Left Books 1973.

Sumner, C. 'Race Crime and Hegemony, a Review Essay', *Contemporary Crises,* 5 1981 pp. 277-291

# SEXUAL VIOLENCE

## THE GENDER QUESTION AS A CHALLENGE TO PROGRESSIVE CRIMINOLOGY AND SOCIAL THEORY

**Ase Berge**

*This paper was delivered at the 1988 conference in Norway and published in 'Working Papers in European Criminology: Volume 10 Gender, Sexuality and Social Control' pp 151-165*

'Somehow anger and frustration, as well as growing understanding of what is wrong, must be transformed into words.'

## INTRODUCTION

It is not easy to stand up against the overwhelming tradition of male dominance and definitions of women's sexuality. This tradition is not only part of culture, but also has a stronghold in science. In confronting the problematics of sexual violence, the challenge to existing knowledge, concepts and theories is of more than academic interest to most feminist writers. Discussions on definitions and premises of theory have political and practical implications: they are part of the gender questions in society.[1]

To address gender-symbolism in the socially constructed concepts and categories of sexuality, requires us to confront androcentric science and, in particular, notions of objectivity. As feminists we must ask if and how concepts and theories take account of gender. In addition, a concept of gender implies that gender-relations constitute some power inequality between men and women: gender-relations make up a special type of social hierarchy. In the problematics of sexuality and sexual violence, the introduction of a gender concept at different analytical levels is necessary to de-construct and reconsider existing bodies of scientific and professional knowledge. Consequently in this chapter I explore the 'three-level gender concept' as defined by Sandra Harding, an American feminist science critic.[2]

Following a brief outline and definition of the 'three-level gender level concept', I address four problematics, which ought to be given more attention, that in different ways amplify the gender concept at two of these three levels. The role of scientific knowledge in our culture is also commented upon in the context of sexuality and gender relations. The foci of the four problematics I have chosen to illustrate Harding's gender concept are:

1. Imaginary sexuality - the blending of fictional images and reality;
2. Gender symbolism in scientific knowledge and research on sexuality (sexology) and sexual violence;
3. What constitutes violence in sexuality and how the notion of violence/power in this phenomenon itself is deeply gendered;[3]
4. The gendered structure of the knowledge we have - who we know of and who we do not. Here lies what some feminists call the 'gaps and hidden agendas' in this field.

---

[1]    Liz Kelly discusses these problems in 'What's in a Name? Defining Child Sexual Abuse', 1988.
[2]    Harding, *The Science Question in Feminism*. 1986.
[3]    MacKinnon, *Feminism Unmodified,* 1987.

Finally, I sum up the situation today as the Three Paradoxes, as regards the status of knowledge in research and its relation to the public.

# THE THREE-LEVEL GENDER CONCEPT

Throughout this chapter I draw upon Sandra Harding's understanding of the 'three level gender concept' and, like her, I am also inspired by anthropological/cross-cultural analysis of gender symbols. Harding's three levels that analytically differentiate gender are:

1.  The gender *symbolism* (or totemism) of each culture (or epoch in history) - myths and symbols - that construct meaning and structure in metaphors, religion, art, literature and language. In short, this level of analysis explores how symbols, meaning and interpretations are ascribed to gender and what signifies masculinity and femininity; as in "the holy family" notions of Motherhood. Most symbols and gender metaphors operate on a pre-rational level and survive as such also in the modern rational life world of daily perception;[4]

2.  Gender *structure* – or gender division of labour; including how gender roles are developed and organised in society, family and division lines between private/public – is the basis for attributing masculine/ feminine characteristics in the social-cognitive order (e.g. women bear emotional responsibilities, men are instrumental, and distinction between productive/ reproductive roles). Most social science research on women refers to this level of studying gender, whether described as sex roles or gender differences;

3.  Individual gender *identity* - masculine/feminine personalities in each culture – where the level of analysis is on how identity is developed in each gender. Until quite

---

[4]    French feminist theorists such as Helen Cixous, Luce Irigaray and Julie Kristeva all have a basic theoretical interest in how language transmits masculine symbols and metaphors, and therefore is inseparable from our way of thinking in that language.

recently concepts of sex differences in identity-cognitive structures referred to a more generalised (ungendered) concept of socialisation, except in the work of Piaget. This has now changed. Carol Gilligan found girls/women's identity, structure and moral thinking to be different from boys/men. Frigga Haug's work on female socialisation - the process of becoming 'feminine' - on the image of body and formation of self to others provides examples of gender reflected ways of how femininity is being individually constructed in our society.

As regards theorising and concepts in the field of sexuality and sexual violence, the interconnections between gender *symbolism* and individual gender *identity* in each culture, are of special interest. My contention is that they are possibly stronger than have hitherto been suggested.

How should we understand the role of science in shaping contemporary culture? To feminist and women researchers, it is important to analyse science's role in the social structure as part of maintaining and developing ideology and culture. In the analysis of Harding and other critics of modern science, we come to see the degree to which the production of scientific knowledge today is an integral part of culture. As modern men/women, we think of ourselves as rational beings who appreciate only knowledge labelled as 'scientific' knowledge.

In a historical perspective, this is a trend of reduction in the variety of knowledge forms and thus, also a reductionism of the modes of human existence. Only what can be known by rational thinking and measured by objective standards counts as knowledge. Our way of thinking, of perceiving and making order of life-events are greatly influenced by the scientific rationale, but we might have trouble in seeing this. This is even more so when it comes to our common-sense notions about sexuality, sexual violence or sexual 'deviance'.[5]

---

[5]   The German sociologist Frigga Haug in *Female Sexualization,* 1987 argues about our 'notions of sexual fulfilment or non-fulfilment as root causes to happiness. We treat such interpretations as common knowledge that has the effect of a natural law. In reality, however, they derive from psychoanalytic constructions, applied and lived out in everyday life.'

# SEXUALITY: BLENDING OF
# FICTIONAL IMAGES AND REALITY.

As human beings - men or women - we have a body. But we also have an image of that body, unlike animals, and our image will somehow reflect a gender-image of our body. We can think of how we might value beauty in our body, or look on our faults, as well as what we experience as pleasurable, desirable or painful. Imagination, therefore, is part of our bodily existence, our emotions and our perceptions. Sexuality is a powerful incarnation of this blending of bodily existence, emotions and imagination. We will experience great trouble trying to think ourselves 'out of" living in a post-Freudian/post-Kinsey era of portraying and speculating about sex. Somehow - and this is essential to sexuality, its humanness - our images of sex make up an integral part of what we experience as our sexuality.[6]

Pornography is one type of materialisation of masculine culture's imagination of sexuality, of images of the body and human relations in sexuality. Another would be the images of sexuality associated with marriage. As Andrea Dworkin found, after working in pornography's world of pictures for three years:

> The photographs I had to study changed my whole relationship to the physical world in which I live. Pornography has infected me. Once I was a child and dreamed of freedom. Now I am an adult and I see what my dreams have come to pornography.[7]

In the analytical schema of Harding's gender concept, pornography is an important part of contemporary gender-symbolism in sexuality - as in earlier history. But the propaganda intent of contemporary pornography has become much more effective and large-scale through modern technology. In this

---

[6]   The same doubleness is intricately part of the problem of defining sexuality, as discussed by Haug (Ibid) who states that to define what sexuality is, 'I find myself about to invent it'.'
[7]   Dworkin, *Pornography*, 1982.

world of images, particularly those of the TV-video-world, we will be unsure of the blending of symbols and meanings attached to common signs of 'femininity/masculinity' - in movies, advertisements, literature, language or pornography and our actual sensations and acts.

I remind you of the 'image message' of Marilyn Monroe. As a woman, a body and a movie star she has formed a concept of what is most 'sexy' to millions for decades. The strength of the movie-made image of Marilyn Monroe is more powerful than the knowledge of what her real life was like, her troubles in sexual life and her struggle for an identity of her own. Aspects of her struggle for identity reveal some of the general mechanisms behind women's development of a sexual identity of their own within the overall picture of 'femininity' in culture. Catherine MacKinnon observes from Norman Mailer (sexist male writers might be very truthful when speaking their mind) "She is the mirror of the pleasure of those who stare at her".[8] And MacKinnon comments, "Suppose this is true and she knew it and killed herself. A Feminism that does nothing about that, does nothing for her, does nothing."[9] Marilyn Monroe, her image message, as mirror of men's adoration (and of many women as well), of their projection of sexual desire, shows us the impossibility of the 'real woman'.

Another example of our daily-lived world can be drawn from a movie commercial for chocolate in Norway. A male car-driver sees a pretty young girl in a yellow mini-dress walking on the pavement, the camera focusing on her 'sexy' bottom and legs. The car-driver becomes so upset and aroused by her very appearance that he 'loses control' of himself and the car, which crashes through the windows of the nearest chocolate shop. The taken-for-granted message in the few pictures is very clear to us as regards gender-symbolism in sexuality. Men's sexuality is uncontrollable, an impulse or 'drive' which is directly stimulated by the view of sexy women.

---

[8]   MacKinnon, *Feminism Unmodified*, 1987:16.
[9]   Ibid.

And the girl in a mysterious way is completely de-personified (like the man) and portrayed as a sign of sexual stimulus to men, a picture of femininity. The effect of gender-symbolism, of portraying the 'stimulus' definition of sexuality is much stronger than the attraction of a specific chocolate. That is why gender-symbolism, directed to our emotions and unreflected commonsense, is so often used in commercials.

If one aspect of sexuality is it's imaginary or fictional nature, then the questions of which pictures, what kind of fiction and images our culture exhibits and maintains and how, are more pivotal to the problem of social change and the transformation of gender-symbolism in fictitious images. This also pertains to images of sexuality in scientific theories and the practice of actual research. As men have had the power and the opportunity to create images, symbols and meanings in relation to the concepts and words surrounding sexuality - as in the case of the female body - we are left with an imaginary culture of gender-symbolism which is deeply patriarchal – androcentric. Trying to think about these difficult aspects of sexuality, I feel I understand what the French feminist theorists mean when they say, in the words of Lacan 'Feminite n'pas existe, pas q'une vision'.

## GENDER-SYMBOLISM IN SCIENTIFIC KNOWLEDGE AND RESEARCH ON SEXUALITY AND SEXUAL VIOLENCE.

Harding says:

> Surely it is 'bad science' to assume that men's problems are everyone's (and society's) problems, thereby leaving unexplained many things that women find problematic and to assume that men's explanations of what they find problematic are undistorted by their gender needs and desires.[10]

---

[10]   Harding, *The Science Question in Feminism*, 1986.

Men's needs and desires, as the more powerful in
defining sexuality, have deeply influenced research
and what counts as scientific explanations in the
problematics of sexual violence.

The history of psychology/sexology, from Freud's *Zur Aeti-*
*ologie der Hystria,*[11] to Kinsey's *On the Sexual Behaviour in the*
*Human Male*[12] and from *The Human Female*[13] to contemporary
sexology, is a history of how androcentric scientific inquiry
starts from androcentric premises about what gender is.
While this tradition of research on sexuality (and occasionally on sex/violence) does recognise sex-roles and gender, it
employs a male concept of objectivity and is unaware of the
complex nature of gender differences. The gender-symbolism
underpinning the very concept and theories of the nature
of sexuality – as in gender differences in sexuality - is never
discussed as an analytical and theoretical problem. The male
scientist's concept of objectivity in research is caught by his
own tale of metaphors and symbols in language and culture.
  Although both Freud and Kinsey pay a lot of attention to
gender (or sex) differences in sexual personalities and behaviour in both men and women, the underlying concepts of
sexuality, which they use, are based on men's experiences and
ways of seeing/thinking. The voices of women are either not
heard at all or constituted 'a special problem' - as in Freud's
work. In addition, this history of scientific work is the hidden
story of how it came about that science itself, as ideology and
culture, made it possible that violence and power-relations
in sexuality were kept largely invisible. Sigmund Freud, as a
young (male) scientist, 'saw', empirically speaking, the sexual
violations of children in his patients.[14] But the scientific
community was not able to 'see' this in the context of its definitions of what constituted 'scientific' knowledge at that time,

---

11   Freud, *Zur Aetiologie der Hystria*, 1896.
12   Kinsey, *On the Sexual Behavior in the Human Male*, 1948.
13   Kinsey, *The Human Female*, 1953.
14   Miller, *The Drama of Being a Child*, 1981.

or later. Likewise, Kinsey found, even in his special objective measurement of human behaviour (or sexuality 'as you like it'), that more than 20 per cent of female respondents had experienced 'adult-child sexual contact' before puberty.[15]

In all cases the abuser was a man. Kinsey's survey on men did not ask about adult-child sexual contact, therefore the boy-victims were kept completely invisible. Moreover, in Kinsey's schema, one wonders if such contacts would be viewed as part of homosexuality and as such a type of variation in sexual behaviour. Yet out of all the intense discussions and scandals following the publication of his reports in moralist-puritan America, not one public debate focused on findings relating to adult-child sexual contacts.

To Kinsey's 'objectivity', concepts of abuse, incest or sexual violence were moral concepts and as such 'irrational', and to be kept out of scientific research and interpretation. In keeping with this, many of Kinsey's followers 'explained away' rape and sexual assaults as mere reflections of society's moral restrictions on 'free' sexuality.[16] Kinsey's moral view of women's role in sexuality - her femininity - is of special interest. To make free sexuality possible, Kinsey argued, women, who seem to adhere to norms of morality more than men, should 'let go' of their cultural/moral inhibitions and make themselves properly accessible to men who are 'stimulated' and in need of 'sexual outlet'. It seems his 'stimulus' definition of sexuality cannot be realised unless women are made to feel responsible for men's satisfaction. So, there are moral/social norms to adhere to for women in realising their femininity - female sexuality is not one of 'biological drives'.

In Kinsey's idea of un-reflected gender-symbolism and American culture's 'femininity/masculinity', the problem of sexual violence would best be solved when no moral restrictions hamper 'free' sexuality. This is the judgement and

---

15    For further discussion see Russell, *The secret trauma: Incest in the lives of girls and women*, 1986; Herman, *Father-daughter incest*, 1981; MacLeod & Saraga, *Child Sexual Abuse: Towards a Feminist Professional Practice*, 1988.
16    See Dworkin, *Pornography* 1982.

theoretical model of the 'libertarian era'[17] and also seems to be present in much progressive criminology and its 'sister-discipline', victimology. However, the experiences of the 1960s and 1970s, as summed up by the women's movement and the greater visibility and amount of sexual violence in Western culture, provides little empirical support for Kinsey's view.

Much victimology bears the marks of Kinsey's and the libertarians' 'stimulus' model of sexuality. In so doing, they have built up and reinforced the same gender structure in how to theorise and explain sexual violence.[18] Even a critical, reflective sociologist such as Finkelhor[19] in his review of research on children as victims, analyses how such studies can help teach children to better avoid and disclose adult sexual abuse. He further asks what children can learn from who was approached and how they succeeded in escaping the abuser. Another strategy is to learn from molesters themselves how and why they chose their victims.

Again, what we have here is a research strategy based on traditional victimology's frantic search for the 'victim-type' woman for rape or battering. Should we really look for the 'victim-type' child knowing that there is no specific type of family or social class that victim-prone? We know all too well how this tradition maintained and aggravated the 'stimulus' model of male sexuality. Likewise, researchers (and therapists) are looking to prevention programmes for children, and for parents, to rescue them from being abused. This way, responsibility is placed on the possible victim - the child - whereas no claims are heard that place definite responsibility on male sexuality and men's relationship to children, their own or others. Such strategies are signs of desperation and it should come as little surprise that treatment programmes for abusers so far have been of little success. Yet whatever the overall consequences for society and in our way of understanding sexual abuse, the assumptions of this tradition remain influential.

---

[17]    MacLeod & Saraga, *Child Sexual Abuse: Towards a Feminist Professional Practice* ,1988.

[18]    Examples are M Amir in the USA. Kurt Weis (GFR) gives a critical overview of the same tradition in German victimology in *Die Vergewaltigung der Opher*, 1982.

[19]    Finkelhor, *A Sourcebook on child sexual abuse*, 1986.

Aspects of prevention programmes also show the marks of gender-symbolism. Finkelhor points to the fact that of those educators and parents who are open to information and training on child sexual abuse, the overwhelming majority are women and mothers. The author remarks on this as an important policy question and notes the silence on the subject in literature. Even so, accepting the fact that women take the responsibility for childcare, he comments that 'certain undeniable benefits might accrue from making it a priority to recruit men, one in particular being to discourage men from becoming abusers'. So, he just drops the problematic of masculinity right where it is, instead of looking for strategies which might make men more responsible for their sexuality and for children's integrity.

Another problematic of great interest to the gender concept is how gender differences in socialisation are patterned - how individual femininity/masculinity is structured. In recent years more research interest has been directed to gender-specific socialisation and identity. The work of Gilligan[20] is an important contribution to the understanding of how women perceive, and try to solve, moral dilemmas. Her concepts and theories show interesting aspects of gender-identity and ways of interpreting inter-/intrapersonal relations - as in the abortion study. In-depth research on boys/men's identity problems and conflicts in relationships could likewise give better clues to understanding masculinity.

Frigga Haug[21] and her research group studied 'feminine' socialisation, focusing on the 'sexualisation' of the female body and the formation of self. Haug's special methods of 'memory work' and 'transcription' are examples of a multi-dimensional concept of sexuality-body and images, as well as a reflected concept of gender-symbolism. Haug is trying to untangle some of the interconnections between levels 1-3 in Harding's analytical gender concept.

---

[20]   Gilligan, *In a Different Voice*, 1982.
[21]   Haug, *Female Sexualization*, 1987.

Responsibility seems to signify a core concept in feminine identity, whether regarding the moral-cognitive set-up of Gilligan[22] or the relationship of the body-emotional-sexuality complex of Haug. Even though Gilligan points to dependency in interpersonal and love relations as the 'test of maturity' in adult men, there is still little knowledge on how men try to cope with such conflicts and how these are solved. What we do know is that most violence (except wars) is perpetrated by men within personal relationships, often inflicted on women they have, or have had, a relationship with. Both Gilligan and Haug's results indicate that gender-specific morality and gender identity ought to be paid more attention to when researching sexuality and sexual violence.

## WHAT IS VIOLENCE IN SEXUALITY?

Possibly, professionals providing help and therapy for victims of sexual violence are correct in saying that the ideology in scientific research should be forgotten. The question of why violence in families and in sexual relations of all kinds has been rendered invisible should also be forgotten. But feminist researchers, working with the aim of understanding and de-constructing the mechanisms and characteristics of patriarchy, cannot afford to forget. We must read and interpret the texts of Kinsey, Ellis, and those of modem family systems' theory, depicting the emotional role of the Mother as if modern women all still lived within the classical gender symbolism of patriarchy or the 'holy family', even though professionals think themselves 'freed' from such symbols. When feminist theorists attack the unreflected gender-symbolism, they also challenge the gendered structure of knowledge which is produced in this field. Acknowledging that the very perception and experiences of our body, including violence in sexual relations, are gendered, feminist and other critical researchers are raising new questions and seeking new avenues to establish knowledge.

---

[22]   Gilligan, *In a Different Voice*, 1982.

What constitutes 'violence' or force in sexual relations, or in adult-child relationships? And following this question is it possible to theorise or even to measure or observe empirically what sexual violence is unless we as researchers have a moral starting point? A Norwegian psychologist, Soergaard, working with child victims of sexual abuse, asks 'Is it possible for instance to "see" violence the same way as you "observe" acts or behaviour otherwise? To be able to "see" violence, acts must be observed through a filter which is also somehow morally coloured.'[23] Kinsey and a lot of empirically-oriented researchers, including therapists, have no professional view of such a 'filter' because they claim to be 'objective' - or in the case of the therapist, 'neutral'.

Soergaard argues that child sexual abuse in his profession, as in psychiatry, 'is mainly seen as a phenomenon of pathology, not as a moral one'. To assess particular acts and to characterise the adult-child relationship, you (as a professional), or in culture, have to refer to some criteria of what constitute children's rights. Unless the child is seen as a person and a person in the making, then the definition of what can be done to children is left to the parents, or other grown-ups, to decide upon as a matter of individual choice. That is the real tragedy of our individualistic, private/public split culture; children are viewed as their parents' personal property and responsibility. There must exist - culturally, as a collective responsibility - some sort of limit to what can be done to children beyond which actions constitute violations of the child's integrity, bodily and mentally. That is, this limit or set of standards constitute some notion of morality on the behalf of society, of institutions and for individuals of what it is to be a parent.

The same line of argument could be taken regarding the human rights of women within marriage and their right to personal and sexual integrity. As we know, in many European countries such as England and Western Germany, and in some

---

[23]  Knut Soergaard, Norwegian psychologist, working in Norway, in an article for the periodical of Norwegian Psychological Association, Nov 1987.

states in the USA rape in marriage is not a legally defined offence.[24] A typical example of not 'seeing' the characteristics of violations to children in sexual abuse is a Swedish court psychiatrist, Ahlstroem,[25] who gives his expert view on the effects of sexual acts done to children and minors. From his research data Ahlstroem cannot find evidence of high levels of violence and direct force and therefore draws the conclusion that there is only minor harm to the child, providing society's reactions do not disturb the child more than the act itself. In his definition of personal/physical integrity for a child, he sees no sexual integrity in its own right for children (as distinct from a bodily/physical integrity) because children have not yet developed a personal sexuality. To some extent he might be excused since, even in 1976, little research literature was known in Scandinavia of the disturbances and traumas in emotional, psychological and/or sexual development in children who had been sexually abused by adults. Still, we might wonder how it comes about that an 'expert' psychiatrist might be able to think in such terms. Unless one uses a distant mode of abstraction (as a type of formal logic), sexuality and its emotions - its personal meaning - are materialised in that same body. But Ahlstroem seems to think that the sexuality of children cannot be violated - or that actions could affect the development of their future adult sexuality; bodily experiences do have a meaning for children and as they grow up will be part of their image of that body.

An even more serious reminder of cultural gender-symbolism and the ultimate lack of rights for children and their integrity is the still common routine in criminal courtroom procedure. In a review of incest verdicts dealt with by the High Court in Norway,[26] the researchers found that compliance on behalf of the child (*i.e.* the idea that she willingly took part in the acts) is frequently at issue - used of course as an argument

---

[24]   Please note that this situation has changed since the original date of publication. Rape in marriage has been recognised in England since a landmark ruling by Lord Lane in 1991.

[25]   Ahlstroem in SOU, 'Policy report for the Law Ministry in Sweden', 1976.

[26]   Agerup, A. & Mauseth, *A Report to Norwegian Council for Social Sciences,* 1986.

by the defence. Consequently, the sentences vary according to whether the abuse involved physical violence or the 'consent' of the victim. However, the idea of a child 'freely' accepting sexual acts by adults is not part of the definition of sexual violation of children or incest. Therefore the issue of evaluating the graveness of the crime should be simply a question of whether force/abuse occurred or not with no in-between measures. Of course, the 'double-talk' of the court and the penal law practice is just reflecting this same cultural or common-sense model of male sexuality in which also the child body is being sexualised. Cultural norms - or the lack of them - seem to be stronger than the wording of the law.

The gender relations in culture, as a power relation, deeply interfere with the morality systems in that culture, as in the above example from the courtrooms. These issues have long been a hidden agenda and of little interest to social scientists and professionals. In the professions and health service it is defined as an individual problem, or one of pathological families. This means, so the politicians seem to think, that we can leave it to psychology, to professionals, thus losing the collective-cultural dimensions. But feminist researchers might also have trouble analyzing and reflecting on gender specific aspects of sexuality and violence in sexuality.

A second question arises from the insight of how morality in these matters is a gendered morality.[27] This presents us with problems of both definition and interpretation. For some time now the women's movement, in the light of growing research on men who rape, has argued that rape is an act of violence, not a sexual act. This definition, they argue, attacks the patriarchal/male monopoly hitherto, in law as well as in 'common-sense'. Women feel that in this way we have managed to get across to men more effectively what the real meaning of rape is to us women. Also, this definition identifies more important aspects of the motives of men who rape.[28] However,

---

[27]    Haug, F. 'Morals have also got two Genders', *New Left Review,* 1984.

[28]    Groth, A.N with Birnbaum, J. *Men who rape: the psychology of the offender,* 1979.

the problem here is one of gender-specific meaning and experiences of sexuality, of what constitutes violence in sexual acts and relations. A definition of rape as 'only violence', bereft of any sexual connotation, is at best a simplification or an under-communication of the gender-based complex of sexuality, power relations and violence in society. From Groth and other sources (like pornography) we know that the fantasy and exercise of power, violence and dominance is perceived as sexually arousing - what for men who rape, or might rape, 'turns them on' sexually. MacKinnon states:

> So long as we say that these things (rape, sexual harassment, battering etc.) are abuses of violence, not sex, we fail to criticize what has been made of sex, what has been done to us through sex, because we leave the line between rape and intercourse, sexual harassment and sex roles, pornography and eroticism, right where it is.[29]

Confusing the gendered definitions of sexual meaning, the women's movement has, accidently, abstracted the actual violence of forced intercourse as 'not sexual' - only violence. That might work for the analytic mind, but not for the body and sexual feelings of the raped woman. MacKinnon surely does not have a one-dimensional definition of sex as only a 'biological drive'. Rather her cultural criticism of 'what has been made of sex' comes nearer to Foucault's understanding of sexuality as a cultural discourse and how its meaning and practice is formed and developed as an historical practice - the social ordering of the power that the individual is socialised into. It is therefore important to be careful when using gender-neutral concepts in this field. We must not fall prey to making the world easier or less complex and less evil to look at than is the case.

---

[29]    MacKinnon, *Feminism Unmodified*, 1987.

# THE GENDER-STRUCTURE OF KNOWLEDGE: ON THE GAPS AND HIDDEN AGENDAS IN THE FIELD OF SEXUAL VIOLENCE.

The last decade has made the extent and seriousness of conflicts of sexual violence more visible and part of the discourse in the professions and in society more generally. And latterly - because children are always 'the last ones' in adult conflicts when interests are twisted - the prevalence and reality of sexual assaults on children have come on to the agenda. In the subsequent social turbulence and public shock, feminist researchers find themselves bewildered and unsure of how to interpret and make use of existing knowledge, professional views and research strategies. It is difficult to establish definitions and theoretical concepts and to decide which strategy to follow that can combine the need for better knowledge and a feminist policy.

The English feminist researchers MacLeod and Saraga observe the many dilemmas and give us some comfort:

> We need to have confidence in our ability to read and interpret. Rather than believe in 'experts' who imply they know it all, we must look for the gaps and hidden agendas. If knowledge and power go hand in hand, it is the responsibility of feminists both to acquire knowledge and to transform it.[30]

They go on to sum up the situation as regards research about child sexual abuse and find "there has been a deafening silence on why it happens".[31] Most research of the kind looks for characteristics of the children's families – class/income, abuse of alcohol, marital relations, emotional atmosphere, etc. But as Finkelhor concludes, the results so

---

[30] Cited in Cameron and Frazer, The Lust to Kill, 1987.
[31] MacLeod, M. & Saraga, E. *Child Sexual Abuse: Towards a Feminist Professional Practice*, 1988.

far are a bunch of non-significant correlations, giving few clues to the questions of why or what causes the 'sexualisation' of children.

So, the first question is what kind of knowledge do we have? Do we have knowledge that can help us enter a more serious discourse on what steps to take, to make a strategy that does not put the responsibility (in practice) on women/children or their mothers alone? We have learned a great deal more about victims - of different kinds of sexual violence and from prostitution - that they are all kinds of women, and all kinds of children (the great majority, girls.) More importantly, we have learned a lot more about victimisation - what the effects and dynamics are when violence and sexual/physical abuse occurs. The type and amount of knowledge of course has been facilitated by the women's movement and victims' own claim for help and more adequate treatment and intervention programmes.

However, we still do not know much more about the men - the abusers - what 'type of man' he is in terms of masculine identity/psychological make-up or about those individuals who commit sexual violence and who abuse wives.[32] Groth has contributed greatly with his studies on men who rape, but they were a prison/treatment population, as are almost all studies of child abuse perpetrators. Part of the problem is the huge number of unreported violent acts, whether battering, child sexual abuse or rape. No reporting means that the variation of masculine characteristics among men not having criminal behaviour in other respects remains unknown. No serious research strategy has so far been discussed to investigate the problem of masculine sexuality in today's society; to look for the differences and problems in masculine identity and emotional adaptation; to investigate the signs of conflicts that might lead to violence; or understand how men cope with and solve these conflicts. The pattern of knowledge we have shows

---

[32]   Kristin Skjarten, Norwegian sociologist, Institute of criminology University of Oslo, is the first to interview men who admit they have been or are battering their wives/partners.

us there is a specific structure of gender and power as regards sexuality and its place in public discourse. It is closely linked to the way society and professions meet with and work with victims and the double effect of help and administration of rights. You have to convince and declare that you are a victim and how and why etc. In cases of sexual abuse of children, it is the heavy responsibility of the professional supporting the child to evaluate the parents and state of affairs within the family to convince the system that the child is a victim. The offender/abuser is left out in darkness for the professionals; he/she is left to the legal authorities. Similarly, the refuges for battered women provide opportunities for knowing more about survivors of abuse and for research of all social groups, ethnicity and types of family. Not so for the men who mistreat them as so few incidents are reported.

A radical interpretation of this state of affairs is to say that power and ideological hegemony always try to hide themselves - it is the power of the hidden agenda. The anonymous (unchangeable?) power is the unknown of male sexuality and identity problems, as in 'what has become of male sexuality'. An unspoken consequence too is a silent acceptance that the traditional, androcentric model of male sexuality in terms of 'stimulus' behaviour and the traditional gender symbolism it carries, continues to have its effect in culture. We have a responsibility to change an attitude of resignation, that male sexual violence 'just happens', like an accident to someone. This attitude of course lets it stay within the ontology of male sexuality as just 'drives' - uncontrollable unless the mother, the wife, the child, women at large, or law, take the responsibility to help him control it. The strategy for potential child victims - hitherto being how they should better learn how not to become victims - tells us of our culture's defeat in protecting children. So it comes to absurdity.

The claim for better knowledge should be the claim to learn more about characteristics of masculine identity and sexuality. Today it is urgent that research and administrative policy (and criminal law practice) make it easier to study men who commit sexual violence/abuse, and also groups of men who are not reported or 'caught up' by professionals and treatment programmes.

To sum up I have chosen to point to the situation of the Three Paradoxes; the 'unknowns' of male sexuality - the why and what kind of man? - have resulted in a serious and bewildered relation between scientific and 'expert' knowledge and the public. The result is misunderstanding and confusion among ordinary men and women as parents. In this picture the women's movement has also to take some responsibility. What messages have scientific research and feminists given to the public?

> *Paradox 1* - the men who rape/might rape, being not a 'deviant', the classical type (lack of impulse control, not having satisfying sex in an acceptable way). Most of them might be otherwise well adapted (even if they might be under the influence of serious stress.) But, alas, which man is not, at times?

> *Paradox 2* -the violent husband/lover ('how do you find out about him before you marry him?') not being violent or dangerous to others but only towards the woman he is emotionally/sexually attached to.

> *Paradox 3* - the child abuser/incest perpetrator, not the majority, the 'deviant', the paedophile proper, poorly educated, alcoholic, perverse, but also men/ fathers of all classes, socially well-adapted, reliable in work. Incest-fathers even, on average, more intelligent than other men.

To us, as researchers and in the interests of stopping and preventing all kinds of reactionary cries for strong prison sentences, it is a serious task to take responsibility for this state of affairs. Logically, we know this paradoxical situation in that an offender may well be a 'normal, ordinary' man but this is not the same as saying all men are potential rapists, child molesters or mistreating their wives. We know, on the contrary, that it means we know too little. We do not know the 'the unknown factors'.

## Bibliography

Agerup, A. & Mauseth, A. *Report to Norwegian Council for Social Sciences.* (Oslo), 1986.

Ahlstroem, A. 'Policy report for the Law Ministry in Sweden', *SOU,* 1976.

Cameron, D. and Frazer, E. *The Lust to Kill,* (New York: New York University Press) 1987.

Dworkin, A. *Pornography* (The Women's Press Ltd) 1982.

Finkelhor, *A Sourcebook on child sexual abuse* (London: Sage Publications) 1986.

Freud, S. *Zur Aetiologie der Hystria.* (Berlin) 1896.

Gilligan, C. *In a Different Voice,* (Harvard University Press), 1982.

Groth, A.N. & Birnbaum, J. *Men who rape: the psychology of the offender.* (Michigan: Plenum Press), 1979.

Harding, S. *The Science Question in Feminism.* (Boston), 1986.

Haug, F. 'Morals have also got two Genders', *New Left Review.* (London), 1984.

Haug, F. *Female Sexualization,* (London: Verso), 1987.

Herman , J.L. *Father-daughter incest.* (Cambridge, MA: Harvard University Press) 1981.

Kelly, L. 'What's in a Name? Defining Child Sexual Abuse', *Feminist Review,* 28, (Spring 1988)

Kinsey, A.C. *On the Sexual Behavior in the Human Male.* (Ishi Press) 1948.

Kinsey, A.C *The Human Female.* (Ishi Press) 1953.

MacKinnon, C. *Feminism Unmodified,* (Harvard University Press), 1987

MacLeod, M. & Saraga, E. *Child Sexual Abuse: Towards a Feminist Professional Practice* (P.N.L. P.) 1988

Miller, A. *The Drama of Being a Child* (London: Virago) 1981.

Russell, D. *The secret trauma: Incest in the lives of girls and women.* (New York: Basic Books),1986.

# STATE CONTROL

## THE USE OF SCIENTIFIC DISCOVERIES.

### Claus-Peter Behr, Dietlinde Gipsen, Sabine Klien-Sconnefeld, Klaus Naffin & Heiner Zillmer

*This paper was originally presented at the 1978 conference in Bremen and a version published in 'Working Papers in European Criminology: Volume 2 – Terrorism and Violence of the State' pp 95-120. Some sections of this chapter have been rewritten during the editing of this version.*

What I have in mind is the police as a diagnostic instrument of society. I am in a position, like a doctor, to feel the pulse of society and to keep up dynamically our judicial system with the help of rational understanding … these sources are available to us. We describe the present situation; we describe what is coming, what dangers might arise, what has developed and how the actual conditions are.[1]

---

[1]    Herold, Chief of Criminal Investigation (BKA), 1980: 36-37.

The requirement for 'knowledge of planning' is intensifying in 'Interventionist States'. Consequently the demand to identify 'failures' in direction and planning are greater than ever, highlighting the need for legitimation. To address this mounting necessity for use-orientated knowledge that can satisfy changing State interests, we have witnessed an extension of research sectors owned and controlled directly by the State. At the same time we should not underestimate the alarmingly eclectic habit of mishandling scientific knowledge. As a result, independent research is less capable of competing with State research. The unscrupulous handling of scientific knowledge fails to protect *any* social or sociological research project from being misused politically. With consideration of this misuse of science by the State, we discuss the following:

1. research on terrorism, initiated and developed by order of the 'Bundesminister des Inneren' (BMI - Minister of the Interior);
2. the 'scientific' development of high-security units special treatment of prisoners, belonging to the 'terrorist' scene;
3. theses on organisation of research processes.

## RESEARCH ON TERRORISM ORDERED BY THE MINISTER OF THE INTERIOR (BMI)

Critical scientists were involved in a large research project on the problem of 'terrorism' that was funded by the Minister of the Interior (BMI). This project came to light after the publication of a letter by Peter Paul Zahl.[2] In this letter Zahl, as a person involved in so-called 'trials of terrorism', explained why he refused to partake. He argued that "there is no 'decent' person who is able to inform the participants of such

---

[2]    Zahl, Peter Paul. Terrorismus etc in *Arbeiterkampf,* 170 vom 28,1 1980, S 50f.

a project,"[3] obviously supposing, "that scientists' who engage themselves in such an enterprise, could be no more than corrupted 'accomplices' of their patron and his 'terrorist' institution of persecution."[4] As the scientists involved in the project were generally known to be supporters of critical positions, we cannot entirely agree with the concerns of Zahl. The patron/employer alone cannot present a sufficient indicator of manipulation or bias, for even 'independent science and research' is not completely disinterested. Science has long lost its innocence, if it has ever possessed one. It should also be noted that there are numerous examples of State research producing critical results. The image portrayed by Zahl of corrupt scientists manipulated by the State is naïve and unsuited to a subtle organisation and utilisation of science. Considering the critical potential of the scientists involved, we are not concerned with the problem of an individual's liability to corruption and direct manipulation. Unlike Zahl, we believe that it is possible that the interests and functions, formulated by the participant scientists, may be contrary to those ones of the State. Rather, we are concerned with the interests and functions of the whole project in its political and scientific context.

### BMI – projects on the research into 'terrorism' in their political and scientific context

There are general fears that research projects dealing with 'terrorism' could create new powerful instruments for the social control of 'troublesome' people and the isolation of 'deviant' social movements. The State already has access to data-material and is free to co-ordinate individual results in an increasingly subtle and integrative way. We cannot avoid the impression that the State did not show enough concern in the objective causes of terrorism and that more and more

---

3   Jager, "Ambivalenz von Staatsforschung in der Kriminologie", 1980.
4   Ibid.

uninvolved citizens were exposed to stricter control. In view of this, the main function of the project could be to prove *symbolically*, in retrospect and completely independent of continued rearmament by the State and the extension of State social control, that the State is also involved in critical consideration of the objective causes of terrorism.

In September 1978, the team 'Work in public against terrorism' organised a model-meeting under the theme "Terrorism" in the BMI. The purpose of the meeting was to push on the 'intellectual-political' confrontation and discussion with 'terrorism'. The project is defined by the BMI as follows:

> Notable scientists from different research fields are working in the scientific project-group 'research into the origins of terrorism' – criminologists and psychologists, sociologists and politologists, legal scientists and philosophers. Therefore interdisciplinary co-operation, independent of the special fields, is a characteristic of this research project. Furthermore, the investigation of origins of terrorism is meant to be based on concrete empirical material. Important research-subjects in the framework of the whole project are: (i) the analyses of personal records; (ii) group processes; (iii) conditions of society; (iv) ideological influences, and (v) international connections. They will be investigated in corresponding sub-projects ... The sub-project 'analyses of personal records' will collect and analyze biographic data of people, who have performed or have supported terroristic acts of violence, considering both 'right wing or left wing terrorists'.[5]

According to our research, approximately 250 personality dossiers collected by the BKA will be analysed in this sub-project and prisoners and their contacts will be interviewed.

---

[5]    Junkers, 'Ursachen des Terrorismus' 1978:42.

The project now seems largely restricted to 'left-wing terrorism'.

In a second sub-project, problems of group formation and group processes are to be analysed. It is concerned with the formation, recruitment, and forms of terrorist organisations; with the role of group pressure; the negation of social-reality; and with isolation-processes. Furthermore the social conditions of terrorism are to be investigated, that is, problems of the loss of legitimation and authority, of the lack of social integration and the reciprocal effects of terrorism and State reaction. Finally, ideological differences between terrorist groups are to be worked out by international comparison. 'The fight against terrorism by means of the police, legislation and justice is aimed at already existing terrorism. The intellectual and political confrontation implies that the fight starts much earlier, *namely with the formation of extremist attitudes in order to prevent such attitudes developing further*' [emphasis added].[6]

The members of the project say that they are guaranteed the uncensored publication of preliminary results. Independent of that, all reports delivered to the employer (patron) in the framework of the project work are the employer's property. In such cases the employer is usually free to use the completed work, together with the results, however they wish. The patron retains the right to copy, distribute, exhibit, recite in public, send through the mail or to broadcast in picture or sound the works and the results. Additionally the right to make available to the public or use the work and results in a processed or modified form, without having to seek permission from the original researcher is usually obtained.

The political context in which the whole project 'Origins of Terrorism' is placed is determined by the simple knowledge that a planning, Interventionist State needs knowledge and control of society, groups and individuals to be competent.

---

[6]    Ibid: 43.

The result of this, among other things, is a strategy of preventive social control by means of using discrimination against politically 'different' behaviour.

Within the framework of the 'political and intellectual confrontation with terrorism' a 'double-strategy' is operating in the way that the apparatus/bureaucracies of control itself are built and furnished in the preventive sense. Information systems are constructed which can 'prevent problems before these occur ... before they start to be dangerous'.[7] In a destructive way, the sanction-bureaucracy is adjusted to the 'modern' discoveries which adds to the suspicion that 'terrorism' is not the subject of research but serves as a pretence to 'get hold of' protest movements in general. The State is thus initiating a new research project giving precise instructions that go much further than the formulation of hypotheses. The assignment by the patron State of isolated themes to various researchers in incompatible fields is producing a dangerous mixture:

1. A non-explicit unscientific definition of terrorism as stated by the employer is accepted as such by the scientists. This definition evidently originates from the interests of governmental security organs which, true to their ideological background, are minimising extremism from the right;

2. Discussion is being stifled at birth when it comes to the question under which circumstances and in what shape resistance could be necessary and legitimate;

3. The research questions and the direction of the preventative measures of the State are aiming at the 'thoughts' and 'feelings' of the individuals. Quoting the president of the BKA: 'The police, as a governmental body being confronted with reality more and more immediately than other State organs, is in a uniquely privileged position to obtain insight into a multitude and variety of behavioural patterns which deviate from the norm and which are anti-social. The police can also "feel"

---

[7]   Herold, "Gesellschaftlicher Wandel – Chance der polizei?" 1973:21.

structural defects of society and the legality of mass behaviour ... They therefore should have to change from being a subjugated hidebound body with the mere function of enforcing law and order to being subject to changes in society. This necessitates a radical change from the limitations of their traditional functions. It also would require a radical intellectual rebirth, a turning to a different self understanding, in short, to the police as an institution for re-adjusting society';[8]

4. There is the further danger that regarding social conditions and the reciprocal effect of terrorism and State reactions to be no more than the background for the individual perception of the 'terrorists', but not stimulus and origin in a process of direct interaction. These fears are further justified by the 'well-balanced' selection of scientists. The explosive effect of the mixture results from the fact that the areas of reaction and of social conditions have been filled with critical scientists.

## Legitimation by participation – remaining doubts

The fact that we do not share the optimism, uttered by some of the participants, that the State could learn from this kind of knowledge in order to practice voluntary self-restriction of its selective definition and sanction power, may be due to different analyses of State interests and State actions. There is then a question - because of the structure of the results of the research - of whether the State patron/employer will be able to use the knowledge and, if so, how it will be possible to extract sufficient justifications in order to develop more subtle control-mechanisms avoiding unwanted side-effects. This is the discussion of faith at the moment. Yet illustrations of such critical-intended questions extending knowledge around social movements are to hand. The fact that this

8    Preuss, "Strategien staatsburgerlcher Diskriminierungen", 1978: 48.

knowledge is placed in context of the formation of terrorist groups, does, in fact, alarm us. In this we see a chance for the State apparatus of propaganda to justify scientifically the well-known thesis on the so-called 'sympathizer-scene' and to generalize and apply it to other social movements, a mechanism, surely not intended by the participants. The attraction of such an opportunity increases with the possibility to quote critical scientists as a proof of truth, even against their will. Furthermore, we are afraid of a far more indirect legitimation effect by the participation of critical scientists in Luhmann's sense of 'Legitimation v Action'. The pure participation in a project of this nature implies beyond individual intention that the problem of terrorism is accepted in the way it is defined by the State. In other words, it feeds the assumption that it is as an *extreme extension* of social movements and not the result of a *separation* from social movements.

The realisation of the danger to produce a mixture of individual results at the expense of the critical potential becomes apparent; particularly as research problems and their contexts are defined by the employer precisely in advance, therefore assuming that the 'origins of terrorism' are already known. Besides the legitimation-effects of science in general, the aim of the investigation then seems to be to gain differentiated detail-knowledge about the functioning of individual mechanisms in order to change this knowledge to suit the more directed, preventative way.

## THE SCIENTIFIC DEVELOPMENT OF THE HOCHSICHERHEITSTRAKTE (HIGH-SECURITY UNITS)

High-security units/tracts in the Federal Republic of Germany [FRG] are a highly developed form of the 'therapeutic prison'. By their example we want to show how it is possible to develop instruments of individual and social control from the combination of findings/discoveries of different disciplines of social sciences that present a new quality of destructive power.

Well-meaning scientists have collected findings in their disciplines which in themselves are harmless. However, when combined and handled by competent and powerful people, effects may come to light that were never intended to be displayed by the scientists and may even have been rejected by them with dismay. We outline the main characteristics of the high-security units and different scientific research contributions that influenced their construction and highlight these concerns with the following questions:

1. What is the importance or significance of the experimental high-security units for the development of a new system of social control in general?
2. How should research be undertaken methodologically and how should it be organized so that its results are of use to any extent desired, i.e. even destructively?

## Wohngruppenvollzug – residential groups in prison – the highest developed form of high-security units

The treatment of prisoners from armed groups in the FRG can be divided roughly into three phases which are marked by an increasing intensification, systematization and flexibility. It indicates the way that resistance of any kind will be treated in future.

The authorities have learnt that isolation over years does not sufficiently promote the wanted effect of sensibility and weariness, but that alternating between isolation and contact, hope and then again resignation ... promises perhaps more success. A large number of prisoners have lived through this, alternating both solitary confinement over months, then confinement in small groups, suddenly transported to a provincial prison where solitary confinement continues until the prisoner by chance obtains by fighting 'integration' – which means then that

intensified measures of supervision are extended
to all prisoners.[9]

Late in 1979 parts of West Berlin's prison Moabit were
rebuilt into, firstly, fifty 'highly secured' cells, which were all
occupied. According to the motto 'highest possible security to
the outside, highest possible freedom of movement inside',[10] a
tract was established which, if required, could divide the area
into four individual units, the smallest of which consisted of
three cells. There were common rooms where groups could
meet, however all were watched by cameras and microphones.
Because of the 'danger of suicide' corridors and solitary cells
were controlled with the assistance of monitors.

To the tried principles of therapeutic individualisation and the specifically personality oriented most effective
treatment (isolation, pressure, reward, drugs, therapy etc.),
are now added the planned concentration of different individuals in a tract, totally separated from the outside, and the
systemic application of group dynamic processes. By changing
the combination of individuals and sub-groups, conflicts
and sympathies are directed and further used on purpose.
Intended is the alternative between the utmost destruction of
the psychic identity (even suicide as a last degree of freedom to
behave is suppressed) or to abjure and convert (which means
giving up one's own identity).

Distinct research, aiming at the isolation and manipulation of people's abilities and needs to bring about a change
in personality or some of its factors, is liable to manipulation. One possibility would be to use the treatments against
the person without them realising it; or even to win over
the person for cooperation in their own manipulation. This
kind of research is able to be used for the construction of the
'high-security units' - and for the regulation of 'normal social
processes' in the interest of the status quo. Scientists have

---

9    Autonomie 1c, p. 100f.
10   Berlin's Senator of Justice, Meyer, FDP.

constructed this 'therapeutic prison', the basic principles of which originate in the following disciplines of social sciences: sensory deprivation; research on behaviour theory; research on the concentration camps; research on 'brain-washing'; total institutions; psychotherapy; and group dynamics and isolation of small groups. Let us now briefly consider some of these fields of research that contributed to the construction of high-security units.

> It is an axiom of behavioural science that the better one can control the environment of an organism, the better one can control its behaviour. The only possibility to gain the total control over a person's behaviour then, of course, is the total control of its environment. The experiments with sensory deprivation show that we should be able to do this exactly.[11]

The main question in the investigation into the situation of concentration camps has been, 'in what way do stress-factors in an extreme situation affect different personalities?' This question can quite easily be twisted into the question, 'which stress-factors do I need to influence a certain person the most (up to his destruction)?'

Investigations on the Chinese brainwashing eventually initiated the development of a technique of control that should become the guiding example for the construction of prisons. For this, the knowledge of social and environmental factors is essential for any experiment to modify behaviour by social manipulation and to fill people with new aims. When these investigators met with Erving Goffman,[12] they studied the admission-ritual, the alterations in the patients' behaviour, their subculture and the behaviour of the keepers in American psychiatric clinics. In discus-

---

[11]    McConell, "Criminals can be brainwashed – now", 1970.
[12]    Goffman, *Asylum*, 1972.

sions with Goffman the brain-washing specialists realised that the mechanisms they had studied as brain-washing had long been developed more or less 'naturally', in the form of the reality of these 'total' institutions. Since then, the problem of the total institutions has been analysed and investigated to make it accessible to planned alteration and manipulation.

The human and economical aspect of research on deprivation has been emphasised by scientists in this field. Prison scientists make use of two principles out of this research. Firstly, there is the therapeutic individualisation – the selection of the most effective form of treatment to undermine personality. Secondly, there is the planned mixture of individuals.

> With the help of partition walls it would be possible to isolate whole groups as well as individuals. If somebody was prepared for normal treatment, he would be taken into the normal process. Special privileges – from light, switched on for longer time, to vacations – could perhaps be promised to certain individuals beforehand. With the separation of individual groups as well as with the separation of individual prisoners, tension within the groups could be promoted or reduced at any time.[13]

*What are the implications of the 'experiment'*
*high-security unit for the development*
*of new systems of social control?*

In capitalism the liability of the social and economical system to disturbances grows with its increasing differentiation and its fast changing processes. To keep up the complex social organisation one has to presume that human beings are created and accepted as a multifunctional, highly

---

13   Senator of Justice, Meyer, Berlin.

adaptive stem. The human being is no longer allowed to be simply the receiver of orders. He has to understand, accept and perform changing tasks relatively autonomously, but without becoming autonomous to such a degree that he himself wants to contribute in the formulation of the tasks and aims (e.g. partly autonomous teams in production).

Thus social conditions and dispositions of behaviour have to be provided, which – on the one hand – allow a complex, adaptive self-regulation of the individual, but on the other hand – prevent the autonomous regulation of all individual and social needs.

The control of individual members of society by exterior means like the setting of norms, the acceptance of norms in the early socialization process, supervision and control on the keeping up of norms by organs of control like the police, justice etc., is not sufficient any more. The system of exterior control has to be completed by a highly adaptive control-system of a new quality. The high-security units are – besides their direct task to isolate and destroy resistant people – a significant experiment on the development and testing of new forms of general social control. Possible transfers of experiences from the high-security units on social movements are only recognizable in their outlines. The basic principle of the residential groups in prison nevertheless indicates the new direction of highest possible security to the outside and highest possible freedom of movement inside. Transferred, this principle could mean maximal self-regulation of individual and social behaviour with aims, set and formulated from outside the individual. The power of definition for the setting of social tasks and aims remains with the centres of power of economy, State and politics. Social groups and individuals have to accept the set aims, but they are more or less free in the performance of the tasks.

# THESES ON ORGANISATION OF RESEARCH PROJECTS

How should the scientific process of research be organized and what quality should scientific results have, so that they cannot be used in any way against the interest of the concerned people?

1. The 'golden method' of scientific research which could guarantee that its results are not to be used against the interests of the researched people and against the intention of the researcher, does not exist;

2. The social scientist is obliged to engage himself really in the question and in the persons or groups, which are researched. The personal and social history of the concerned people has to be included, understood and kept;

3. The distinction of subject and object of research, i.e. of researcher and people being researched, should be diminished. Research has to become a solidarity process of all involved people in which commonly defined problems are solved in the sense of commonly formulated aims. Solving problems is not the result of a unique act of application of knowledge, but a toilsome process of analyzing situations, by acting in solidarity and by learning from errors;

4. Research should be formed as a dialogue of autonomous partners. The one partner, the person concerned in certain problems, are the first experts in their living conditions. They have the most complex perception of all aspects, which are involved in the problems to be solved. The other partner of the dialogue, the social scientist, is especially responsible for the following criteria of research;

5. The scientists have to be fully aware of the whole research-project and should not leave the connection of isolated results to alien decisions;

6. Scientists take part in the interests and needs of their partners. But they have to use their own position – not being integrated into the social structure of the research area – to make available the existing

knowledge in order to promote the aim of the research project, as well as the development of knowledge. They are obliged to look for 'true' findings;

7.  'True' findings and discoveries have to prove their quality in praxis by really helping to improve social and individual problems according to commonly formulated criteria. Depending on the problems, it takes different times until the truth of findings and discoveries work out in practice.

## Bibliography[14]

Autonomie No. 10 *Die neuen Gefangnisse,* 1979.

Autonomie Sonderheft, Januar, *Sicherungsverwahrug,* 1980.

Bundesministerium des Inneren, Arbeitsstab 'Offentlichkeitsarbeit gegen Terrorismus' (Hg) *Geistig-politische Auseinandersetzung mit dem Terrorismus,* (Bonn) 1979.

Cobler, Sebastian Herold [Chief of Criminal Investigation (BKA)] "Gegen alle Gespreache mit dem Prasidenten Bundeskriminalamtes", in *Transatlantik* No. 11 pp 29-37, 1980.

Goffman, E. *Asylums,* (Frankfurt: Penguin) 1972.

Herold, Horst "Gesellschaftlicher Wandel – Chance der polizei?" In Schafer H (Hg) *Kriminalstratigie und Kriminalistik, Bd II* (Hamburg) S 21f, 1973.

Jager, Herbert Zur "Ambivalenz von Staatsforschung in der Kriminologie", in *Kriminologisches Journal* no 3 S 228f, 1980.

Junkers, Maire Therese, Bericht uber das Bund/Lander-Forschungsprojekt 'Ursachen des Terrorismus', in *Bundesminister des Inneren Geistig-politische Auseinandersetzung.* a. a. o. S 41f., 1978.

McConnell, J. "Criminals can be brainwashed – now", in *Psychology Today,* S. 14f, April, 1970.

Preuss, Ulrich K. "Strategien staatsburgerlcher Diskriminierungen", in 3 *Internationales Russel-Tribunal Zur Situation der Menschenrechte in der BRD Bd I,* (Berlin) 1978.

Preuss, Ulrich K. "Wissenschaftsfreiheit contra Gedankenpolizei", in *Kritische Justiz* No 1 S 44f, 1978.

Zahl, Peter Paul. "Terrorismus" in *Arbeiterkampf* No. 170 vom 28,1 S 50f, 1980.

---

14    Note from editors: The bibliography for this chapter has been published as closely as possible to that in the original paper, including author first names on occasion, to aid those wishing to follow up references.

# ZEMIOLOGY REVISITED

## FIFTEEN YEARS ON

### Paddy Hillyard

*This chapter was commissioned for this anthology. A longer version of the paper was presented at the European Group annual conference in Chambéry, France, September 2011.*

## INTRODUCTION

In the late 1990s a group of academics[1] at Bristol University working in social policy and teaching some courses in criminology began to be increasingly concerned about the expansion of criminology as a discipline while at the same time more and more social problems and behaviours were being constructed within criminal discourses and their solutions determined through the criminal justice apparatus. Even the delivery of social policy was being increasingly linked to the reduction of crime.

---

[1]    David Gordon, Paddy Hillyard, Christine Pantazis, Simon Pemberton.

Critical Criminology and conferences of the European Group have played a significant role in fostering a much broader approach to the harms people suffer beyond the narrow terrain of traditional criminology. But whereas even critical criminologists were content for criminology to embrace within the discipline an ever expanding group of social harms, the Bristol Group wished to move beyond criminology in order to be able to challenge the discursive power of crime, criminal justice and criminology. They took the position that only through the establishment of a separate discipline could the shackles of criminology be jettisoned and a radical approach to a variety of social harms, many of which were not perceived as criminal, could be developed. The Group struggled with a name for a new discipline. 'A social harm approach' or a 'social harm perspective' did not sound as grand or as appealing as 'Criminology' or indeed 'Sociology'. In any event, 'social harm' was a key concept within criminology and every new form of social harm was likely to be appropriated within that discipline.

In 1998 the European Group held its annual conference on the Greek island of Spetses. A few of the Bristol Group were chatting in the sun with Professor Vassilis Karydis and I asked him what was the Greek word for harm and he said it was zemia, hence zemiology. The study of harm as a new comprehensive discipline distinct from criminology was therefore born. A year later the Bristol Group held a conference under the title *Zemiology: Beyond Criminology* at Dartington in Devon, England. Some years later in 2004 we published *Beyond Criminology: Taking Harm Seriously*,[2] which provided a critique of criminology and examples of a social harm approach to key issues.

Hillyard and Tombs (2004) suggested that there were nine principal criticisms of criminology:

1. *'Crime' has no ontological reality.* There is nothing intrinsic to any particular event or incident which permits it to be defined as a crime;

---

[2]   Hillyard, Pantazis, Tombs and Gordon, *Beyond Criminology: Taking Harm Seriously*, 2004.

2.  *Criminology perpetuates the myth of 'crime'.* In general, the discipline has not been self-reflexive about the State-defined and culturally given definitions of crime while rendering numerous other social harms invisible;

3.  *'Crime' consists of many petty events.* The majority of events which are defined as crimes are very minor and would not score particularly highly on a scale of personal hardship. Much policing, prosecution and court time is taken up processing these behaviours;

4.  *'Crime' excludes much serious harm.* Many events and incidents which cause serious harm are either not part of the criminal law or, if they could be dealt with by it, are either ignored or handled without resort to it. For example, poverty, hyperthermia, malnutrition, occupational injury and death, pollution, corporate corruption, State violence, and medical negligence are seldom embraced by the notion of 'crime';

5.  *Criminology constructs 'Crime'.* In the absence of any intrinsic quality of an event, the criminal law uses complex tests and rules to define a 'crime'. At the heart of these tests is the notion of the responsible individual. Corporations, State and other organisations are generally excluded;

6.  *Criminalisation and punishment inflict pain.* They therefore create further harm;

7.  *'Crime' control is ineffective.* The criminal justice system does not work according to its own aims. It is highly negative. It is about arrest, detention, prosecution, punishment;

8.  *'Crime' gives legitimacy to the expansion of crime control.* The universality of narratives of crime and fear of crime facilitate the further expansion of the system and the construction of even more 'crime';

9.  *'Crime' serves to maintain power relations.* It plays a fundamental role in upholding the existing unequal social structures by a focus on the behaviours of the poor and marginalised groups in society.

The aim of this chapter is twofold: to provide a brief background to the continuing expansion of criminology within British and Irish Universities and the much slower development of zemiology and to focus upon criminology's reaction to the emerging discipline of zemiology.

## THE GROWTH OF CRIMINOLOGY AND ZEMIOLOGY

Criminology has expanded rapidly in recent years in British and Irish Universities. In 1969 there were just two postgraduate courses - one at Cambridge University and a new one at Keele University. There were no undergraduate degrees in criminology. By 2011 there were 94 Universities and Colleges which offered criminology degrees in the UK, totaling between them just under 1,000 separate single, joint and minor degree courses. The University of Sunderland offered no fewer than 138 criminology degrees including 'Criminology and Dance' 'Financial Management and Criminology' and 'Tourism with Criminology'.[3] In 2013 the number of Universities and Colleges hosting criminology dropped to 88 and the range of courses has become more restricted.[4] However, even if each degree course only produces 10 graduates each year, this would suggest that British Universities graduate around 8,000 criminological students every year.

The number of books published in criminology has followed the same upward trend. The British Library website shows the total number of books catalogued for particular subject areas. For criminology, some 2720 books have been catalogued and of these over 1000 have been published after 1997.[5]

The growth in criminology has therefore been phenomenal. In contrast the growth of zemiology has been very modest and has mainly involved postgraduate work. One of the first studies

---

[3]   Whatuni.com, 2011.
[4]   Whatuni.com, 2013.
[5]   See British Library website http://www.bl.uk/ . Accessed September 2011.

to use a zemiological perspective was carried out by Michael Naughton for a PhD in the early 2000s. He analysed miscarriages of justice defined in terms of wrongful conviction and explored the social, psychological, physical and financial harm of the consequences of successful appeals in British courts and has since published his thesis as a book. [6]

Two further PhDs - one at Queen's University Belfast and the other at Bristol University – have now been completed. The former was by Sarah Machnieski, entitled *Social Harm and Older People in Northern Ireland*. Of particular significance, it was found that out of 568 violent deaths of older people only three died from 'crime' harm. This suggests that instead of making older people's houses more secure, harm to older people would be more effectively reduced by helping them with their shoe laces, crossing the road or taking away old medicines.

The other thesis, by Lynne Copson, entitled *Archaeologies of Harm: Criminology, Critical Criminology, Zemiology* makes a significant contribution to teasing out the similarities and differences in the conceptualisation of harm in criminology, critical criminology and zemiology. Her key argument is that there are fundamental differences in the notion of social harm adopted by the three disciplines, reflecting different ideas and assumptions around issues of justice and liberty in the context of the fulfilment of human need. The novelty of the zemiological approach, she argues, "lies not in its centralisation of the concept of harm, but, rather, in its employment of an alternative concept of harm to that of conventional and/or critical criminological approaches". She argues that by invoking a conception of harm based on non-fulfilment of human need, zemiology identifies harm as:

> A composite component of individual subjectivity, constituting individuals' capacities for autonomous action in the first place and thus enabling a broader

---

[6] Naughton, *Rethinking Miscarriages of Justice: Beyond the Tip of the Iceberg*, 2007.

account of the causation of such harm than that offered by the conventional criminological approach.[7]

Simon Pemberton and Chris Pantazis have continued to develop the discipline of social harm. They are editing a book series called *Studies in Social Harm*, published by Policy Press. The first book is entitled *Nation States and the Production of Social Harm* which is being written by Pemberton and the second is by Rob White on *Environmental Harm*. Further books are planned to cover *Harms of Poverty, Corporate Harms, Harms of the Criminal Justice system* and *Harms of the Economic Crisis*. In addition, they are hoping to obtain shortly a contract for a new journal on social harm.

There is a growing interest in social harm in other disciplines. For example, Linklater (2011) has used the notion of social harm to explore international relations.[8] In medicine, Nutt and his colleagues[9] on the UK Advisory Council on the Misuse of Drugs identified sixteen harm criteria – nine related to the harms that a drug produces in the individual and seven to the harms to others both in the UK and overseas. The key challenge for zemiology is to bring together all the existing work into a single disciplinary perspective.

## THE RESPONSE TO ZEMIOLOGY BY CRIMINOLOGY

Zemiology has now received much attention from criminologists. As the discipline of criminology takes it operating framework from the State, a tongue-in-cheek topology based on different types of supporters of various State forms has been adopted to describe the different reactions which zemiology has received. The five types are: Colonialists; Imperialists; Nationalists; Reluctant Nationalists; and Misguided Nationalists.

---

[7]  Lynne Copson, *Archaeologies of Harm: Criminology, Critical Criminology, Zemiology:* 2011 8-9.
[8]  Linklater, *The problem of harm in world politics*, 2011.
[9]  Nutt, et al, 'Drug harms in the UK: a multicriteria decision analysis', 2010.

## Colonialists

Colonialists search to impose control or governing influence over an independent country, territory or people. Boundaries or borders for colonialist criminologists are invisible or ignored. For colonialists any form of harm, whether defined as criminal or not, can be incorporated within the discipline of criminology. As an example, consider the work of Roger Hopkins Burke. In the second edition of his *Introduction to Criminological Theory* he has a section entitled "Critical Criminology and the Challenge of Zemiology". It opens with the statement:

> A significant and fast expanding contemporary variant of critical criminology has been zemiology or the study of social harm: the intention is to significantly extend the *legitimate* (emphasis added) parameters of criminological study away from a limited focus on those injurious acts defined as such by the criminal law ... and to establish that a vast range of harms, for example, sexism, racism and imperialism and economic exploitation, could and should be included as the focal concern of criminological investigation.[10]

As with so many colonialists, there is no attempt to recognise the boundaries or history of zemiology or even the origins of the term. There is no reference to any of the papers presented at the Dartington Conference, where the term was first used in a conference title and no reference to *Beyond Criminology*. By coupling zemiology as a discipline concerning social harm but positioned outside criminology with the social harm approach, which had emerged within criminology, it ignores the argument that there is a need to move beyond the borders of criminology itself. This is perhaps not surprising as he appears not to have read any of our work.

---

[10]    Burke, R.H., *An introduction to criminological theory,* 2005: 1790.

A more sophisticated form of colonialism is seen in the work of Gordon Hughes. To his credit he has read the arguments for a zemiological perspective but he rejects the right of zemiology to exist. In his review of *Beyond Criminology* he raised a number of substantial criticisms.[11] More recently Hughes in a section entitled 'Arguing against Criminology' he notes that "Foucault's typically magisterial and 'radical totalitarian' critique of criminology is taken by zemiologists as proof of criminology's sins, past and present."[12] He goes onto suggest that "this verdict is seen as especially pertinent given mainstream criminology's 'handmaiden of the State' role in the contemporary context of a 'mass criminalizing State' and neo-liberalism's 'socially destructive trends.'"[13]

Hughes rejects this position because he suggests few mainstream criminologists would dissent from the claim that 'State and corporate crimes, as well as the ills bought by an unequal and divided world, are, indeed, key concerns of criminology'.[14] He then goes on to suggest that:

> zemiology both sets up a 'strawman' (of 'orthodox/ mainstream criminology) to critique, which parodies much of the actually existing, plural forms of contemporary criminological work today and in turn fails to offer a viable critical project for criminology, intellectually or politically.[15]

But Hughes' is a flawed critique. We would readily acknowledge that many in criminology would accept the ills are a product of an unequal and divided world. In addition, nowhere do we parody the plural forms of contemporary criminological work. Crucially, and here Hughes totally misunderstands our argument, we certainly do not wish to

---

11    Hughes, 'Book Review of Beyond Criminology: Taking Harm Seriously ', 2006.
12    Hughes *The Politics of Crime and Community* ,2007: 197.
13    Ibid.
14    Ibid, 198.
15    Ibid.

offer a viable critical project for criminology, either intellectually or politically, as we want to abandon criminology because it can never escape the dictatorial definitions of crime and criminality set by the State. Nor can it escape from the discursive functions of words such as crime, criminal justice and criminology. The discursive power can be clearly seen in the thousands of young people who sign up to the burgeoning criminology courses.

## Imperialists

Imperialists support a policy of extending their authority over foreign countries. Like colonialists they are eager to expand the discipline of criminology notwithstanding any problems with it. They are happy to sweep up every new area of social harm and embrace it in their own territory. But unlike colonialists they are aware of the criticisms which are made of their own nation State and acknowledge the positive elements of the nation State of zemiology.

There are a number of people in this camp. Hil and Robertson, two Australian academics, were the first to comment upon zemiology in a paper in *Crime, Law and Social Change* in 2003. They argued for a critical criminology, which was more mindful of the growing number of critiques of its general epistemological direction. They were specifically harsh on critical criminology's focus on crime and penalty and argued that the harm approach provided the space for a much broader approach.

> Zemiological analysis seems far better placed than much critical criminological analysis in the sense of being able to more fully grasp the nature and significance of current world formations and their effects on various aspects of contemporary social meaning.[16]

---

[16]   Hil and Robertson, 'What sort of future for critical criminology?', 2003: 97.

In particular, they argued that the zemiological perspective is better able to draw upon a human rights approach, which takes the attention beyond the confines of criminal law or cultures of crime control. Moreover, they argue that a zemiological approach is able to engage more actively with "the big questions such as inequality, poverty, disadvantage, racism and sexism." However, they argue that all of this can be done within critical criminology.

## Nationalists

Nationalists believe in the integrity of their nation State and they write their blue books to lay out their values. A good example is the work of Ian Loader and Richard Sparks in their book entitled *Public Criminology*. They spend two and a half pages discussing zemiology and they present perhaps one of the best précis of our ideas to date. They rightly pick up on our contradictory analysis where we argue that zemiology does not have a necessary superiority over criminology and then a little later argue for the long term strategy of abandoning criminology. In fact, this contradiction reflected a difference in view between the two authors of the piece.

They describe zemiology as 'harm science' because the discipline 'becomes at times surprisingly positivistic'. This is to confuse positivism with the use of statistics in presenting an analysis of harm. Harms can be counted. They have a material and ontological reality. In any event, to compare the zemiological perspective alongside 'crime science' distorts and trivialises the otherwise fair analysis of our position.

Like Hughes, nowhere do they, however, present a critique of our main arguments against criminology. Instead they present two unrelated criticisms. First, they criticise the disproportionate amount of effort that is devoted to the critique of criminology rather than building what is going to replace it. This is a bit rich coming from two authors who spend a whole book navel-gazing at the current state of criminology and asking what is the role and value of criminology in a demo-cratic society arguing the case for a 'public criminology'.

> We think that there is some worth in being cautiously friendly to criminology, in seeking to value and defend its pluralism, and in thinking anew about the public purpose and how that might be best understood and realized.[17]

Their second criticism, like that of Hughes, is that we produce 'a scarcely recognisable caricature of the fragmented and diverse field that is being trashed and left behind'.[18] But it was not our intention to describe the diverse field. Instead, we wished to bring together all the criticisms and problems of the discipline to encourage others to move beyond it.

## Reluctant nationalists

Reluctant nationalists are people who agree with the main arguments put forward by zemiology but wish to remain within the nation State of criminology. For example, Eugene McLaughlin is particularly worried about the state of critical criminology. In the edited book '*What is Criminology*' he writes:

> Not surprisingly, an age-old question continues to unsettle twenty-first century Critical Criminology – should it abandon what it deems to be the compromised discipline of criminology to the managerial criminologists and the crime scientists?[19]

He argues that "Crime must continue to be problema-tised because it has no ontological reality and dominant

---

[17]  Loader, I & Sparks, R. *Publish Criminology*,) 2010: 26.

[18]  Loader, I & Sparks, R. *Publish Criminology*, (London: Routledge) 2010: 25.

[19]  McLoughlin, 'Critical Criminology', 2011: 53.

constructions misrepresent and distort the real problem of crime".[20] But while referring to the zemiological approach, he was not prepared to leave the shores of critical criminology.

Robert Reiner also appears to be a reluctant nationalist. In his book *Law and Order* he notes that many critical voices have argued for 'the abandonment of criminology' because of its ties with the notion of crime. He acknowledges that "the pains inflicted by officially defined crime, and by criminal justice, are relatively minor compared to the even more severe and extensive harms done by the criminal and legitimate activities of the powerful."[21] But then he goes to say:

> Nonetheless the focus of the rest of this book will be on analysing the trends and patterns of crime conceived of in this ultimately *indefensible* (Italics added) way... A plea in mitigation is that my analysis will show that the most damaging trends in crime and crime control can best be explained by the same neo-liberal political economy that is also the source of those broader harms not dealt with by criminal justice.[22]

## Misguided nationalists

Finally, there is a strange group of scholars who have been focusing on various types of social harm for many years who have considered it necessary to apply for citizenship within criminology and, of course, they have been welcomed with open arms. Rob White fits into this category. He has done more than anyone to establish the sub-discipline of environmental criminology. But it is unclear why he wishes to shoe-horn environmental harms into a criminological framework. He admits in *Crimes Against Nature* that:

---

[20]    Ibid: 55.
[21]    Robert Reiner. *Law and Order,* 2007: 43.
[22]    Ibid.

the 'conundrum of definition' is exacerbated in the specific area of environmental harm in that many of the most serious forms of such harms in fact constitute 'normal social practice' and are quite legal even if environmentally disastrous.[23]

In short, zemiology has had a respectable but diverse reception within criminology. While many are sympathetic to some of the arguments, most want to incorporate the ideas within critical criminology. No-one within criminology has come out in support of moving beyond criminology.

## CONCLUSIONS

A number of points can be made in conclusion. The first is that criminology will always remain a mythical discipline which perpetuates the bias that crime harms are by far the most serious. Second, however radical it becomes it will never be able to rid itself of the cast iron State defined frame of selected behaviours and responses. Third, the notion of harm embraced by zemiology is very different from the notion of social harm embraced by criminology and critical criminology.

The riots in Britain in August 2011, for which many of our Members of Parliament had to give up their sun loungers and return to Parliament to discuss the events, provide an excellent illustration of these points. The behaviour was quickly defined within the criminological paradigm: gangs, lawless youth, criminal scrum, and feral rats. The response was repressive criminalisation. The discourse inevitably has been about responsibility.

For me [David Cameron, on the Steps of Downing Street, 10.8.11], the root cause of this mindless selfishness is the same thing that I have spoken about for years. It is the complete lack of responsibility in

---
[23]    White, *Crimes against Nature*, 2009: 88.

> parts of our society, people are allowed to feel that the
> world owes them something, that their rights outweigh
> their responsibilities, and their actions do not have
> consequences. Well they do have consequences.

Needless to say his comments set the tone for all subsequent commentary. It foreclosed other discourses. As with criminal justice, it was all about the individual and their irresponsibility, which needs to be punished hard. While critical criminologists will attempt to present a more progressive discourse, the events and responses have already been defined within the criminological paradigm. Even the progressive British paper the *Guardian* joined in the criminalization of those involved by publishing all their names on the web. While riots are a fairly irregular occurrence, the attention which these riots received served a useful purpose in further disguising the regular and more destructive physical and financial harm which kills us and robs us on a daily basis.

To develop the discipline of zemiology we need to do a number of things. First, we need continue the work of Copson, Pemberton and others on the conceptualisation of harm. Second, we need to analyse systematically the many harms which restrict and damage our lives from the cradle to the grave on a daily basis and bring this work within the boundary of zemiology. Third, we need, in honour of Louk Hulsman, to stop using the word 'crime', 'criminal justice' and 'criminology'. Finally, we need to develop ideas and plans for a new social order based on justice, fairness and equality.

Foucault reminded us that the power of discourses lies in their ability to determine who can says things, what can be said and what is counted as the truth.[24] In all his work he made it clear that we can only escape the power of criminology by crossing borders and starting another discipline. This is why I believe that we need to use the word Zemiology to name the new discipline. Social harm does not capture the notion of a

---

[24]    Foucault, *Power/Knowledge* 1980.

discipline and moreover social harm is already, as has been shown, a strand within critical criminology. Only in these ways will be able to challenge the power of the criminological discourse.

## Bibliography

Burke, R.H. *An introduction to criminological theory*, (Cullompton, Devon: Willan), 2nd edn., 2005.

Foucault, M. *Power/Knowledge: Selected Interviews and Other Writings, 1972-1977* (Pantheon Books) 1980.

Hil, R. and Robertson, R. 'What sort of future for critical criminology?' *Crime, Law and Social Change*, 39, pp 91-115. 2003.

Hillyard, P. Pantazis, C. Tombs, S. and Gordon, D. *Beyond Criminology: Taking Harm Seriously*, (London: Pluto Press), 2004.

Hillyard, P. and Tombs, S. 'Beyond Criminology?' in Hillyard, P. Pantazis, C. Tombs, S. and Gordon, D. *Beyond Criminology: Taking Harm Seriously*, (London: Pluto Press), pp 10-29, 2004.

Hughes, G. 'Book Review of Beyond Criminology: Taking Harm Seriously, *Social & Legal Studies: An International Journal*, 15(1), pp 157-159. .2006.

Hughes, G. *The Politics of Crime and Community*. (London, Palgrave Macmillan), 2007.

Linklater, A. *The problem of harm in world politics* (Cambridge: Cambridge University Press) 2011

Loader, I. and Sparks, R. *Public Criminology*. (London, Routledge), 2010.

McLaughlin, E. 'Critical Criminology'. in *The Sage Handbook of Criminological Theory*. E. McLaughlin and T. Newburn. (eds) London, Sage: 153-174. 2010.

Naughton, M. *Rethinking Miscarriages of Justice: Beyond the Tip of the Iceberg*, (Basingstoke: Palgrave Macmillan), 2007.

Nutt, D.J., King, L.A. and Phillips, L.D. 'Drug harms in the UK: a multicriteria decision analysis', *Lancet*, 376:9752, pp 1558-1565. 2010.

Pemberton, S.A. 'Social harm future(s): exploring the potential of the social harm approach', *Crime, Law and Social Change*, 48(1-2), pp 27-41. 2007.

Reiner, R. Law *and Order: an honest citizen's guide to crime and control*, (Cambridge: Polity Press), 2007.

Whatuni.com    http://www.whatuni.com/degrees/university-uk/University-Of-Sunderland-ranking/3764/page.html    [Accessed    23.08.11], 2011. Whatuni.com [accessed 2.1.13], 2013.

White, R., Ed. *Environmental Crime: A Reader*. (Cullompton, Devon, Willan) 2009.

# SECTION C

DISSENT

during the strike. At the fortieth Annual Conference in Cyprus in 2012, delegates joined striking hotel workers on picket lines and passed resolutions of solidarity to support their campaign for fair pay and welfare rights. In recent years, European Group conferences have passed motions condemning the violent policing of anti- 'austerity' protests and racist immigration policies across Europe.

This section brings together six papers delivered at European Group conferences during the last forty years. As Phil Scraton notes in his paper in *Section A* of this anthology, the formation of the Group represented a break from the positivist orientations within mainstream criminology and their translation into State policy and institutional practice. The Group's founders sought to resist the predominance of what Nils Christie later termed 'useful knowledge' - useful only to institutions of the State. The papers showcased in this section reflect the group's commitment to break away from dominant analytical frameworks for understanding deviancy and social control and offer a critical, emancipatory criminology.

In the first paper in this section, Karl Schumann considers the relationship between mainstream criminology and State policy and institutional practice. Describing the production of criminological knowledge in Germany, Schumann notes that the German State draws a distinction between 'proper' criminologists – who advocate a 'pseudo-science' of criminology; and 'deviant' criminologists – who examine law in its social context. Schumann suggests that the former category plays a central role in legitimising the repressive practices of criminal justice institutions. Schumann dismisses claims to scientific objectivity prevalent within the positivist orientations of mainstream criminology as the work of 'charlatan scientists'. In doing so, he identifies various 'deceptive practices' adopted by criminologists in order to demonstrate legitimation. First, there is a claim that criminology is a unique and coherent subject which is able to explain 'crime'. Noting that the only consistent feature of all 'crimes' is that they are labelled as such by actors within the criminal justice system, Schumann dismisses these claims as an 'illusion' designed to obscure the partial application of criminal law by the State. Second, there is the claim that 'legitimate' criminological research adopts the highest standards in research methodology. Schumann suggests that this has resulted in a 'fetishistic' attachment to scientific research standards and the rejection of critical research which falls foul of the scientific model. Schumann also considers the prevalence of 'embedded' research and the growing patronage of criminological research by the State in terms of research funding. These developments have led to what Schumann describes as an 'access for loyalty bargain' – an understanding that the researcher will not report on his or her observations in a way that will harm the institution studied. The impact of disloyalty by 'deviant' criminologists' is the rejection of research findings and the incompatibility of future research possibilities.

The (ab)use of social-scientific research to legitimise repressive State practices is also the focus of Olli Stalstrom's paper in chapter twenty one. Writing in the context of the Finnish gay rights movement, Stalstrom highlights the role of scientific 'experts' in manufacturing stereotypes of homosexuality that led directly to discriminatory State practices and the widespread suffering of gay people. Stalstrom notes that the application of the 'sickness' label, which became the prevailing psychiatric school of thought about homosexuality in Finland in the 1970s and 1980s, legitimised the introduction of broad censorship laws to prohibit open and positive discussion about homosexuality. These developments, together with the widespread attack on gay people during the AIDS panic of the 1980s, triggered a significant demoralisation within the gay liberation movement and a rapid deterioration of the living conditions of gay people in Finland. Stalstrom considers the emancipatory potential of critical research and the role of academic researchers within emancipatory movements. Describing himself as both 'gay rights fighter' and 'sociological researcher', Stalstrom charts his involvement in a participatory action research project at Helsinki University and the strategies by which the research was used to expose State-sanctioned stereotypes of gay people as both scientifically unfounded and homophobic.

In Chapter twenty two the Welsh Campaign for Civil and Political Liberties consider the role of women during the 1984-5 miners' strike in Britain. Drawing on interviews conducted with women in the mining communities of South Wales at the height of the strike, the chapter describes the dual struggle faced by the women in both standing up for their communities against the onslaught of Thatcherism and also claiming their right to take an active part in the struggle in the face of hostile attitudes towards women's involvement in the strike from within the trade union movement. The article describes the strength and remarkable resilience of the women, whose various acts of solidarity sustained the strike in spite of the extreme hardship faced by mining communities. With the removal of wages, reduction of welfare benefits and the lack of an adequate strike fund, women in these communities developed an 'alternative welfare State' in order to support the striking miners and their families. This included the formation of support groups, arranging food collections and distributing resources. The chapter concludes that although the strike was eventually defeated, the lives of these women were changed dramatically through struggle, not only as individuals, but in terms of their relationships with men in the communities in which they lived. Their active participation in the strike also played an essential part in changing attitudes towards women within the trade union movement.

The themes of solidarity and survival are developed in chapter twenty three. Writing in the context of long-term imprisonment in Northern Ireland, Bill Rolston and Mike Tomlinson consider the impact of imprisonment on prisoners and their families. At the time the paper was written, Northern Ireland had an unusually high proportion of prisoners serving long sentences of imprisonment, many of whom were incarcerated as a direct result of policing techniques and a criminal justice system specifically adapted for the eradication of 'political violence'. Although a body of social scientific research had begun to consider the impact of imprisonment on the general long-term prison population, there were significant gaps in the literature regarding the experiences of political prisoners in Northern Ireland. Rolston and Tomlinson's research was an attempt to begin to fill this lacuna. Drawing on interviews with prisoners and their relatives, the researchers found that whilst there were similarities in how 'political' and 'non-political' prisoners and their families survived long-term imprisonment, such as breaking down the sentences into manageable periods, the former category invoked additional dimensions of survival. In particular, they found that the central role played by prisoners in the political situation in Northern Ireland, the involvement of relatives in prisoners' support groups and the collective struggle which led to their incarceration, played an important role in the prisoners' psychological survival. Rolston and Tomlinson found that this broader political context translated into the ongoing processes of survival inside the prison. Through engaging in acts of collective solidarity such as protest and education, prisoners were able to establish a 'collective identity' which enabled them to withstand even the most extreme privations. Rolston and Tomlinson conclude that for many political prisoners and their families, prison was not merely an individual experience but was rather a matter of 'collective survival'.

The impact of imprisonment is also the focus of Susan Smith's paper in chapter twenty four. Here, Smith analyses the experiences of prisoners' wives and girlfriends, highlighting the dichotomy between the construction of prisoners' families as a potential source of rehabilitation, and the isolation, neglect and lack of basic civil rights that prisoners' families experience. Smith argues that despite not being the sentenced party, prisoners' families suffer a punishment at least as profound as that of their imprisoned partner. Moreover, although prisoners' families constitute a category 'victims of crime' in a very real sense, they are excluded from the financial and other forms of support available to those upon whom a 'crime' is perpetrated.

Smith argues that this neglect of prisoners' families should be understood in the context of the withdrawal of the welfare State and the reassertion of individualistic free market values. With some of the State's welfare functions passed on to the family, prisoners' families are expected to uphold current expectations of familism within a set of circumstances that renders this an impossible task. Prisoners' families thus deviate from the accepted norm of the ideal nuclear family, attracting additional formal and informal policing of their activities. Smith suggests the neglect of prisoners' families has a punitive motive. She argues that the State relies on their non-vocality and inability to construct a cohesive and cogent set of demands which stems from their isolation and vulnerability. In order to challenge the State's punitive control over their lives, prisoners' families must develop a 'political voice', discarding their isolation and control and expressing their own 'unique strength'.

In addition to analysing the violent practices of criminal justice institutions, European Group conferences have considered the development of radical alternatives to the criminal justice system. In the final chapter in the book, Karen Leander, former Coordinator of the European Group and a long-time advocate of women's rights, considers the regulation of rape beyond the criminal justice system. Leander's chapter powerfully exposes the inability of the criminal justice system to adequately deal with cases of sexual violence. Describing legal reforms in Sweden to improve attrition rates in rape cases, including changes in statutory definitions of rape, Leander notes that although the reforms did lead to some increase in the number of reported rapes, they did not lead to a corresponding increase in convictions. Leander traced the flow of reported rape cases through the criminal justice system, finding that three-quarters of reported rapes were dropped during the police and prosecutorial stages. These statistics, Leander suggests, highlight the limitation in relying on the 'blunt instrument' of criminal law to deal with sexual violence, with the majority of cases unable to reach beyond the 'glass ceiling' of prosecution. Leander thus advocates the consideration of radical alternatives to criminalisation in rape cases. One suggestion considered by Leander is the use of civil rather than criminal law to allow rape victims to gain some degree of redress. Although accepting that such a move may appear to amount to the 'decriminalisation' of sexual violence, Leander suggests that given that the burden of proof is lower in civil cases, there is a higher possibility of holding rape perpetrators responsible. Until worthy alternatives within the State's apparatus begin to emerge, Leander argues that it is necessary to consider 'complements' to the criminal law that could give the victims of sexual violence a strengthened sense of empowerment, redress and emancipation.

# ON PROPER AND DEVIANT CRIMINOLOGY

## VARIETIES IN THE PRODUCTION OF LEGITIMATION FOR PENAL LAW

**Karl F. Schumann**

*This is an abridged version of a paper delivered at the Bremen conference in 1978 and originally published in 'Working Papers in European Criminology, State Control on Information in the Field of Deviance and Social Control'.*

## TWO TYPES OF CRIMINOLOGY

Criminology is an intellectual effort to produce legitimation for penal law in general and the practices of agencies within the criminal justice system. This general assessment of the discipline's function seems to be true for all States working under the condition of capitalist economy. However, there may be minor differences in the relationship between agencies of social control and educational institutions due to the particular historical development of the State apparatus.

States, therefore, may differ in respect to:
1. the importance of criminology for the professional training of lawyers, sociologists and social workers;
2. the policies of recruitment to faculties in law schools and universities;
3. the legal provisions for cooperation between criminologists and staff of social control agencies;
4. the law governing the access to documents and files of the criminal justice system for researchers from the outside.

Let me give a sketchy description of the situation in Germany. (1) For law students criminology is an optional field like, for example, canonical law, chosen by rather few people mostly for humanistic reasons. Completely independent from law schools, there is some teaching of deviance and social control in sociology departments. (2) Criminologists who teach in law schools have to be lawyers by training because they are expected to contribute also to the teaching of penal law. (3) Traditionally criminologists are asked to serve as expert witnesses in trials; some are also part-time judges; and all criminologists to a larger or lesser degree work with current legislation. (4) Access to court files and to information from the General Register (Bundeszentralregister) in Berlin (on all convictions and sentences of any German citizen) may be granted if the importance of the research justifies it. The decision on 'importance' is at the discretion of the president of the court or the Attorney General.

Recruitment patterns separate the criminologists in law-schools from those working in sociology departments or schools for social work. The criminal justice people trust the law-school-criminologists because they used to be prosecutors and judges themselves during their education. They are considered, so to speak, as of the same breed. The sociologist-criminologist on the other side may gain trust if they cooperate with the needs of the State apparatus for crime control. Thus there are two ranks of criminologists. The first, consisting more or less of lawyers, tries to advance the pseudo-science of criminology. They are the proper criminologists. The other, very often sociologists, but also critical lawyers, work toward the 'sociology of law'. For this rank the access-for-loyalty-bargain is of utmost importance - the first rank gets access to all available data because these criminologists contribute to the legitimation of social control by the State on a primary level and produce the scientific rationalisation for penal law. Sociologists usually have problems with such a task. They are, however, able to cooperate on a second level - the rationalisation of particular features of the criminal justice system. We will look at each of these levels more closely, but before that it may be useful to describe briefly the functions of penal law in capitalist societies and to specify the legitimation problems involved in its use.

# THE RATIONALE FOR THE USE OF PENAL LAW

The democratic State needs legitimation for its activities. A minimum level of legitimacy is granted by the independence of the State from the fate of particular parties through period-ical elections and the principle of representation. They relieve the State of the necessity to strive permanently for actual legit-imacy.[1] The effort of the State, however, to grant a normatively defined identity to society may be threatened by side-effects of economic crises. The State has bound itself (1) to prove that the capability of capitalist economy allows for the optimal fulfilment of public needs and (2) to keep the dysfunctional side-effects within acceptable limits.[2] The effort of the State, however, to eliminate short comings without interfering with the autonomy of economic forces and thus itself being part of the economic system, constitutes a set of contradictory tasks. Moreover, the State, being a tax-State, relies completely on the amount of money available through taxes to avoid interfering

---

[1]    C. Offe, Berufsbildungsreform. (Frankfurt: Suhrkamp, 1975), 288.
[2]    J. Habermas, Zur Rekonstruktion des Historischen Materialismus. (Frankfurt: Suhrkamp, 1976), 288.

too much with the economy. In many cases the State has the option to act in terms of social investments or in terms of social costs.[3] For example, to cope with the problem of youth unemployment the State may offer vocational training and jobs (social investments) or it may hire social workers to get the unemployed youth off the streets (social costs). It is always cheaper to spend money for a small group with manifest problems rather than spending it for a large group where problems might emerge. Therefore the State tends to turn to reactive instead of preventive measures, to social costs rather than to social investments.

The same is true for deviance. The function of criminal law is to react, because prevention failed. But no real crime-prevention exists, at least not in terms of equal rights and equal opportunities for all members of society. Rather a structural inequality is granted by various laws other than penal law and the penal law prohibits protest against those laws. For example, unequal and unsocial housing laws constitute an exploitation scheme between landlords and tenants. If a tenant wants to attack a given exploitative condition of his contract they may sue the landlord but will fail, given the unequal rights within housing law. Or they may try to argue their case personally with the landlord - and will also fail because if they protest too loudly and actively the landlord may call the police, relying on trespassing laws. Trespassing is thus the legal provision to criminalise protest.

Let us take another example, divorce laws, which generally determine for one partner the duty to support the other who has custody of their children. Very often lower class fathers cannot afford to split their funds between two households. Failing to support the family may be (and in Germany is) a crime. Thus the penal law is the backbone for a civil law which discriminates against the poor. Family law makes sense only for the entrepreneur. To raise your own kids means to invest into a cheap labour force and an

---

[3]    J. O'Connor, The Fiscal Crises of the State. (German transl, Suhrkamp: Verlag, 1974).

equivalent to a pension.[4] Public funding for working class families who raise children and who have costs, and no material benefits, would be much too costly. It is cheaper to punish a few people for non-support and force the rest into the hardship of complying with the family law. The same function, as a backbone of civil law, may be demonstrated for the criminalisation of petty theft for it forces men and women to sign exploitative labour contracts and thus enforces labour law. A similar relationship has been described for vagrancy law by William Chambliss.[5]

The function of penal law is to strengthen civil law provisions which establish and perpetuate inequality. The exemplary punishment of a few deviants demonstrates to the remaining members of society that they had better discipline themselves and obey civil law even if it constitutes a cage of regulations around their existence. Acts which essentially are a protest against discriminatory regulations will be distorted in their social meaning: they will be treated as crimes. For a juvenile to run away from home and survive on small property theft may be his or her way to protest against unlimited parental authority. Abortions, where they are still illegal, are simply a kind of protest against inequality in that the one who gives birth to a child has to raise it without getting help from the public.

If penal law distorts the meaning of acts which are meant to protest again legal norms or morals, then criminology makes sure that the structural and legal reasons for deviance get completely ignored. Crimes are explained completely as individual events to be understood only from biographical information. If crimes were in fact considered as collective responses to unequal legal status of a particular kind, it would be the most logical thing to ask the State to change the laws so that the principle of equality would be actually realized. Such a reform, however, would change

---

4       Heinsohn and Knieper, Theorie des Familuenrechts (Frankfurt: Suhrkamp, 1974).
5       W. Chambliss, "A sociological Analysis of the Law of Vagrancy." Social Problems 12 (1964): 46-67.

the relations of production and thus interfere with the State's role to grant conditions of production which allow for making substantial profits.

A significant piece of evidence for that is to be found in the miserable state of knowledge on crime prevention. If one forgets about advice like street-lighting, which divert but do not prevent crimes, there is no exact knowledge available to guide political action. Criminology simply looks in the wrong direction: into biographies, personalities, motives. There cannot be any valid approach to crime prevention unless criminology changes its topic to the sociology of penal law. But to study and explain the way the law covers up all types of damaging behaviour, excluding those subsumed by penal law, would be to abandon the major function of criminology: to provide rational legitimation for the State's priority-scheme of substituting crime control for social policy.

## FIRST-ORDER-LOYALTY: THE CHARLATAN-SCIENTIST

In addition to the production of rational legitimation for penal law, criminology produces an abundance of ideas to be available for agencies of special control if they wish to defend their practices against criticism. By various tricks of scholarly trade the criminological insights are granted a touch of science. That criminology is not much of a science may be even the opinion of legal practitioners within the criminal justice system, who know next to nothing about criminological findings. If this field has had any influence on the daily routines of enforcement of penal law at all, it must be in the area of penology. The essential categories in penal law however, intent or negligence, complicity, error, attempt and so forth are, at least in German law, without any reference to criminological or social science knowledge. If criminology has almost no impact on the actual practice of penal law, what might be its function then? And of what use are criminologists if their effect on legislation is as minimal as Platt and Skolnick[6] have argued?

It seems to me that the task of the science criminology boils down to exactly that - pretending to be a science. This charlatanry is being accomplished by two deceptive practices (1) by claiming a unique and coherent subject and (2) by demanding the highest standards in respect to theory and methodology. Since many scholars have demonstrated the lack of scholarship in criminology.[7] I will abbreviate my argument.

## CLAIMING A UNIQUE AND COHERENT SUBJECT

The fiction of a unique and coherent subject is produced by the main task of criminology: to explain crime. Crimes include such a variety of behaviour that takes place in so many different situations that it is not imaginable that one theory might explain all crime. If one looks at the penal code there are provisions against lying (perjury) and against being honest (if it is insulting), running away (escape) and not leaving when asked to (trespassing), taking things away (theft) and depositing things (loitering), touching (assault) and not touching persons (failing to render assistance) and so forth, depending on the circumstances. Each provision in the penal code may be violated by a variety of activities. The courts rather unpredictably decide if particular types of behaviour are subsumed under the code or not and with the possibility of being changed from day to day. There is nothing that divergent types of behaviour have in common that can be subsumed under all provisions of a penal code, besides the fact that they are called a crime. The fact that the only common denominator is the legal evaluation by judges will,

---

6     A. Platt and J. Skolnick, The Politics of Riot Commissions, 1961-1970 (New York, 1971).
7     I. Taylor, P. Walton and K. Young, The New Criminology. (London: Routledge and Kegan Paul, 1973); M. Phillipson, "Critical Theorizing and the New Criminology." British Journal of-Criminology 13 (1973); F. Sack, "Probleme der Kriminalsoziologie", in Handbuch der empirischen. (Sozialforschung, Stuttgart Enke), 1978.

however, be distorted through the assumption in penal law that in all criminal behaviour there is a specific quantum of guilt. This particular portion of responsibility for not choosing the legally appropriate reaction to a given situation seems to provide enough common ground for criminology to go on and systemise the chaos of subsumed behaviour. The pretention of communality between the various crimes thus perpetuates the illusion that the penal law is based on common morals shared by the community as a whole, rather than representing particularistic interests.[8]

# DEMANDING HIGHEST STANDARDS IN RESPECT TO THEORY AND METHODOLOGY

Criminology strives for one good theory that can explain all crimes. Notwithstanding the impossibility of such an undertaking, many theories have been developed in the past and even enlightened sociologists have been cheated by the tricky 'rules of the game'. The most important rule is that a theory that cannot explain all crimes is not a good one. If anomie theory cannot explain white-collar crimes, then look for a better theory. If the theory of differential association cannot come to grips with a simple family-killing, do away with it and get a new one. This rule ensures that it is impossible to ever fully explain crime. However, if no theory is able to explain all crimes completely, then maybe every theory has some value. This is rule two - whatever the theory, it can explain some crimes. To be comprehensive therefore you have take every theory into consideration and use a multi-multi-factor-approach. The larger the list of variables, the better. Both rules together establish the message crimes are not fully explainable. No one theory can do it. For a comprehensive explanation of all crime a list of variables is necessary that is too long to serve its purpose. There will be always unexplained variance

---

[8]    D. Matza, D. Becoming Deviant. (Englewood Cliffs: Prentice Hall, 1969), 15.

left, and this is of course due to the freedom of will involved in criminal acts. Proper criminology fails to explain crime, and yet its failure is in fact its success. If even multi-factor-approaches of high complexity cannot account completely for the occurrence of crime, the free will, the axiom of penal law, must be a realistic assumption. As long as the scientific efforts of criminology fail, it fulfils an ideological function. That is, it produces a rational for the adequacy of penal law.

Any criminologist, who accepts those two rules for their work, may do whatever he wants in research or writing - nobody will bother them. A criminologist, however, who denies the assumption of internal communality of criminal acts and who looks for explanations without pre-course to individual irrationality, may get into trouble. This is the case with many sociologists who try to grasp the totality of social control and who tend to understand penal law as one of many instruments to establish order in society and argue that it may be invalid, inhuman or ineffective when compared to other measures.

A scholar who lacks 'first-order-loyalty' may, however, still be allowed access to data or funds if he or she shows loyalty to the agencies of social control. This entails adherence to what I refer to as 'second-order-loyalty'.

## SECOND-ORDER-LOYALTY: NEVER CRITICISE WHAT YOU HAVE SEEN

Besides the production of legitimation for penal law, criminology is also obliged to produce handy rationalisations for particular trends and policies within the criminal justice system. For usefulness the scientific results must be impeccable, that is they must comply with the highest of methodological standards. However, in order to be trustworthy these results should have been produced by free (not hired) research. Or, if the research has been funded by agencies like police or prison authorities, the results should at least survive possible criticism. Thus a good criminology has to offer the State agencies the best possible reservoir of insights to be of use for legitimation of particular activities of the system. The State agencies may tolerate a considerable number of controversies so long as the State-funded research findings survive most of it. Consequently, State-funded research should advance standards of research methods such as large samples, control groups, and of course advanced techniques of data analysis. In particular, the fetishistic 'large representative samples' creates a strong dependency between criminal justice agencies and researchers. While small samples may occasionally be conceded even to an outsider, large samples usually can be drawn only with consent of high ranking officials. Only a loyal researcher merits that level of access and the notoriously scarce resources of a criminal justice agency may be misused by helping to draw a sample of some size. On one side high methodological standards stress the access-for-loyalty-bargain. On the other side they make sure that many small-scale research projects which produce results with some critical potential for crime control practices don't have to be taken seriously. And the loyal researcher will be the first to stress exactly that - that his (sic) findings are tentative, that more research IS necessary and that he has done only a pilot-study.

In order to establish the illusion of a science there have to be controversies of some magnitude. The critical potential of the labelling approach was hugely welcomed in this respect. Controversies produce new insights; prevent the field from sterility; demonstrate fantasy; and invite young social scientists to join the battle who can be tamed later on by the access-for-loyalty bargain. The labelling approach has helped to open the criminal justice system for evaluative research and to improve effectiveness. Second-order loyalty means that the rules of the scientific game are obeyed and not criticised as being not appropriate or not feasible. Moreover, the research carried through must not ignore the interests of the practice. Gunther Kaiser, a leading criminologist in Germany, puts it its way:

To follow only positions which criticise norms and

agencies of control, as the new, critical or radical criminology does, would not only result in a narrow and impoverished criminology, but would also cause a criminal policy ignorant to reality, which would lack, being left alone, any criminological foundation. Moreover the practice in its multitude of needs and the Victims of crime would be ignored and abandoned.[9]

The cooperation between agencies of social control and criminology is founded on the conviction that both work on the same important social task: the reduction of crime. In this battle the police, the courts and correctional system constitute the front while criminologists work safely at remote military bases. From this division of labour the minimal expectation is that criminologists do not attack in the rear. Small criticisms may be allowed. Indeed they may even contribute to greater efficiency. But if a criminologist criticises the prison system, the modes of police interrogations or the discretion used by Judges and prosecutors, and proves that they are illegal or discriminatory in general (not in a few cases of black sheep) then the relationship is broken at once and most probably for all times. The control apparatus cannot afford being criticised for acting illegally, for that would contradict the legitimation for the State's monopoly to use coercion against people - a monopoly legitimized by the promise to act within the limits of law. However, power corrupts. Extra legal coercion occurs daily. If a criminologist is allowed to see the daily routine, he is expected to report about it only in a way that does no harm to the institution studied. Actually, most codes of ethics of research demand exactly this. This then is the essence of the access-for-loyalty-bargain. The one who violates the silent promise to keep their mouth shut will get no further access.

---

[9]   G. Kaiser, Professorenstreitfall. In Kaiser/Schoch Kriminologie, Jugendstrafrecht, Strafvollzug, Munchen, 13-.

# REACTIONS OF THE STATE APPARATUS AGAINST PERSONS LACKING LOYALTY

The thesis of this paper is that the hidden, second code[10] for criminologists is compliance with expected loyalty of the first or second order. I know of very few cases of first-order-disloyalty. I am familiar with two cases in which scholars criticised penal law for its contributing to the perpetuation of capitalist society. Both were blocked from working in a law school. The first person was a harsh critic of penal law and a Judge who used to give lectures to law students at Bielefeld for some years until the faculty terminated his contract in 1977. He introduced the students to psychoanalysis and to the psychoanalytic understanding of penal law and tried to raise awareness about their own suppressed wishes to punish other persons. This was apparently not tolerable for the conservative faculty. The second case involved a member of the European Group, well known as a co-author of a Marxist critique of criminology, including the labelling approach. He became victim of the Berufsverbot-policy when he applied for jobs in Berlin and Hannover Law School.

Lack of first-order-loyalty will have dramatic consequences for the persons involved, and will draw rebuttals from researchers who are loyal to the State, while lack of second-order-loyalty will hamper research possibilities. If research is threatening to the legitimation of the use of penal law by the State it will be rejected with much publicity. Let me give two examples. The first happened in 1977 when some scholars argued that unemployment of youth causes juvenile delinquency.[11] They demanded that the State should change the legal and structural conditions of youth unemployment, especially the law which leaves vocational training almost

---

[10]   P. MacNaughton-Smith, "The second Code". In Journal of Research in Crime and Delinquency 5 (1968): 189-197.

[11]   A. Wacker, "Arbeitslos und agressiv? Zum Verhaltnis von Arbeitslosigkeit, Agression und Kriminalitatsentwicklung, in Soziale Welt, 1977: 364-381.

completely in the hands of private capital.[12] In particular they demanded more jobs and apprenticeships for youth. Thus, they challenged the mechanisms of the reproduction of the national labour force in advanced capitalism through the currently existing selective processes in schools and vocational training. In such processes the whole pattern of job qualifications, ranging from experts to unqualified workers, is reproduced and the unqualified persons are forced into unsatisfying jobs through the real threat of being otherwise unemployed. This use of an industrial reserve army would be restricted if these demands for qualified training for everybody were fulfilled; a policy option that is impossible for the State. Thus a scientific campaign was launched to refute the suggested correlation.

It started early in 1978 when the current head of the justice department of Lower Saxonia published a book with a chapter on unemployment[13] where he found that 35 per cent of the juveniles suspected of a crime are unemployed while the unemployment rate among juveniles amounts only to 5 per cent. He pointed at the importance of social policy but then he warned the reader of any mono-causal interpretation, lacking ability to spend leisure time in a proper way, looking for cheap thrills and adventures and making friends with bad guys are suggested as additional reasons which cause unemployed youth to commit crimes.[14]

Later Martens published a study, funded by the Bundeskriminalamt and directed by the leading criminologist of Germany, Gunther Kaiser, who again found a high proportion of unemployed youth among delinquents, but concluded that unemployed and criminal juveniles may come from the same group of persons characterised by poor family and living conditions.[15] The highly publicised message was it is not unemployment that causes criminality, but some third

---

[12]   C. Offe, Berufsbildungsreform. (Frankfurt: Suhrkamp, 1975), 288.
[13]   Schwindt, Ahlhorn and Weiss, Empirische Kriminalgeographie (Wiesbaden: BKA, 1978).
[14]   Ibid., 292.
[15]   Ibid., 146.

factors that causes unemployment as well as criminality. G. Steinhilper, of the funding agency BKA, wrote along similar lines in the introduction.[16] And the leading criminologist Kaiser wrote that unemployment hits in most cases already delinquency-prone persons.[17] Steinhilper and Kaiser issued press-statements to this effect and managed to argue away the structural relationship between features of the economy and juvenile crime, as well as to legitimate the State intervention that took place not in terms of social policy but in terms of increased criminalization. This example demonstrates how criminologists help in times of legitimation crises.

Another case is the debate on rising crime rates among juveniles. In 1979 two young sociologists published a study on juvenile delinquency which rejected two favourite arguments of functionaries of social control: (1) Juvenile delinquency rises steadily and (2) it becomes more brutal. Albrecht and Lamnek presented data for the period between 1971 and 1977 showing that while according to the police-statistics there was an increase of crimes committed by juveniles, according to the court statistics the convictions of juveniles decreased during the same period.[18] Thus many cases apparently were dropped for triviality before getting to the judge. Lamnek and Albrecht argued moreover that the crimes committed by juveniles tended to be less and less serious, most of them were playful acts which even the juvenile victims would understand. When reported to the police by angry parents, rather than being dismissed as they would have been twenty years ago when nobody would have taken such cases seriously, in the mid-1970s they were prosecuted as aggravated assault-cases.[19] Apparently, these results hit a nerve of the legitimation efforts of the criminal justice system. Year by year, the police get important attention when the Secretary of the Interior presents the annual

---

[16]  Ibid., XI.
[17]  G. Kaiser, Jugendkriminalitat. (Weinheim: Beltz, 1978), 167.
[18]  Ibid. 67.
[19]  Ibid. 116.

crime statistics, where the Secretary points to the rising crime rates and falling rates of successful police work. The almost natural suggestion follows from this that more money and more personnel should go to police. To invest into the police seems to be logical for a State who substitutes criminalization for social policy. If general deterrence depends on quick arrests and a high police presence in the city there must be more police. That more police does not mean less crime, as the deterrence-doctrine will have it, but more crime, is another matter. The police tend to illustrate their importance by reporting more and more acts as serious crimes. Criminologists generally will not look critically into this relationship because their research money depends likewise on rising crime rates. Albrecht and Lamnek behaved deviantly, by any criminological standard, when they explained the crime rate as a fake, as a consequence of the rising investment in the police force. But they also broke the silent law of loyalty.

Furious critique of their work followed. The research division of the Bavarian Police issued a report to prove that the crime rate rose, especially among children[20] and that the drop of the conviction rate was due to a drop of convictions in theft cases but not in assault cases. They claimed also that there would be no evidence available for the contention that assault cases tended to be of lesser gravity. Thus it was demonstrated that juvenile criminality becomes more and more dangerous. Next, in a detailed methodological critique, the criminologist Kreutzer tried to destroy almost every argument of Albrecht's and Lamnek's as being derived from poor science and based on tricky categorisation. He offered a general statement for the benevolent criminology that Albrecht and Lamnek lied with statistical tools to show what is contrary to the truth.[21] The truth, of course, is what the BKA and almost all heads of State police aggressively stressed in the media after the

---

[20] W. Steffen, Kinder- und Jugendkriminalitat in Bayern, Munchen Bayerisches-LK, 1979, 14.

[21] A. Kreutzer, Anstieg der Jugendkriminalitat - ein Mythos ? 1n Kriminalistik 2 (1980): 67-73, 68f.

publication of Albrecht and Lamnek's book: that crime rises as regularly as the prizes.

Turning to cases involving lack of second-order-loyalty we have various examples of a type rather familiar to any sociologist-criminologist; the negative versions of the access-for-loyalty principle. One criminologist was denied access to court files by a District Attorney because he was considered to be an enemy of police and one of those 'who want to change society'. A research group, working in a prison that learned about the construction of a maximum security unit and subsequently informed the public, were thrown out of the prison and subjected to a libel suit. Another criminologist and critic of prison conditions was denied access to prison files and even asked by the Department of Education to report about his research and explain if the research might have something to do with activities for benefit of the members of Red Army Faction (RAF). Apparently the criminal justice system acts similarly against the known or suspected deviant criminologist as it does act against the known or suspected deviant person without discrimination.[22]

## FUTURE TRENDS

Let me close with a brief speculation on the future. In West Germany many State ministries of justice, the BKA (the German FBI) and the police training centre at Hiltrup have created research divisions in the last few years.[23] These research units are in charge of rebuttals of critical findings, they also carry through more and more evaluative research of State control agencies. Some years ago the State agencies gave away money to trustworthy researchers to do evaluations so that now the evaluations are home-made. If a free researcher wants to do a study about an

---

[22]   see Brusten, Eberwein, Feltes, Gollner, and Schumann, "Freiheit der Wissenschaft - Mythos oder Realitat." (Frankfurt Campus, 1981).

[23]   see M. Brusten, M. "Social Control of Criminology and Criminologists", paper presented to the European Group for the Study of Deviance and Social Control Annual Conference, 1979, at Kopenhagen.

institution or about the police there is a strong tendency to reject such requests on the grounds that that agency or that topic has already recently been studied so that all knowledge is available.[24] The access-monopoly which such research units have created is used to push aside outside researchers.

It is not too probable however that all free research which lacks first or even second order loyalty will come to an end in the near future. There are a number of reasons for this. First, home-made or hired research is not a good resource for purposes of legitimation as long as it is not respected in the scientific community. Those research results may be suspected to be self-serving even by the liberal media if they cannot refer to similar findings by independent scholars. Second, in the context of fiscal crisis the State cannot afford to get only self-serving research findings because they do not help too much as a guide for determining priorities for investments. Evaluations must have an objective kernel and to allow for that the researcher must be able to look for sensitive areas without being blinded by loyalty. Third, given the unpredictable topics of legitimation crisis the State wants to have a reservoir of data available to choose what may help in a given situation. State-initiated research tends to be reactive - it produces arguments with a time lag only after the need for legitimation has already occurred. Free research may have produced handy findings before the need for legitimation comes up: some serendipity is quite useful. Fourth, the control apparatus wants to produce an image of modernity and of progressiveness. It is always in need of new ideas. Since persons working in the penal apparatus tend to become narrow-minded because they have to defend the present situation, they tend to be conservative. Consequently innovations must be looked for from the outside. Free research will help.

In as much as State-organised research depends on acceptance by free researchers, even those who lack loyalty to the

---

[24]    cf Malinowski, Munch and Schwielick, "Monopolisierte Polizeiforschung." In Kriminologisches Journal 2 (1973): 126-130.

criminal justice system will have a chance to do research. Strict criticism of research findings produced by hired hands on methodological grounds, especially with respect to the validity of data and analysis, will help them to keep a niche open for free research. It will be a small one but given the tendency of social control to move into the community[25] the practices of control may become more observable in future.

On the other side the tendency to soften control goes along with improvements of data banks used by the criminal justice system. Instead of keeping persons in prisons they are put on probation or community treatment but their behaviour is kept track by comprehensive record keeping and large computer systems. In fact, the head of Germany's FBI, the well known BKA, is convinced that the computer facilities of the BKA provide the largest data-storing and processing capacity available in any German administration.[26]

One of the various data-processing systems covers criminological literature.[27] Thus in principle it is possible to have files on the publications of every German criminologist including a rating of his deviancy according to the first- and second-order-loyalty. And this makes a check possible before he gets access or money or invitations to cooperate. The future of the control of criminologists will be linked to the future of social control in general. Based on centralised and comprehensive data-systems it will be possible to calculate the risks involved for the State if a given person is granted or denied some degree of freedom.

25   S. Cohen, S., "The Punitive City." In Contemporary Crises 3 (1979): 339-363.
26   H. Herold, "Kriminologisch-kriminalitische Forschung im Bundeskriminalamt", In BKA-Kriminologentreffen, Wiesbaden, 2-17, 3.
27   Ibid., 14.

# Bibliography

Albrecht, P. 'Viel Larm um (fast) nitchs.' In Kriminalistik 3 (1980): 116.

Albrecht, P. and Lamnek Jugendkriminalitat in Zerrbild der Statistik, Munchen Juventa, 1979.

Brusten, M. 'Social Control of Criminology and Criminologists.' Paper presented to the European Group for the Study of Deviance and Social Control Annual Conference at Kopenhagen, 1979.

Brusten, Eberwein, Feltes, Gollner, and Schumann 'Freiheit der Wissenschaft - Mythos oder Realitat' Frankfurt Campus, 1981.

Chambliss, W. 'A sociological Analysis of the Law of Vagrancy.' In Social Problems 12 (1964): 46-67.

Cohen, S. 'The Punitive City.' In Contemporary Crises 3: 339-363, 1979.

Habermas, J. Zur Rekonstruktion des Historischen Materialismus. Frankfurt: Suhrkamp, 1976.

Heinsohn and Knieper. Theorie des Familuenrechts. Frankfurt: Suhrkamp, 1974.

Herold, H. Kriminologisch-kriminalitische Forschung im Bundeskriminalamt, in BKA-Kriminologentreffen, Wiesbaden: 2-17, 1973.

Kaiser, G. Jugendkriminalitat. Weinheim: Beltz, 1978.

Kaiser, G. Professorenstreitfall, in Kaiser/Schoch Kriminologie, Jugendstrafrecht, Strafvollzug, Munchen: 13-16, 1979.

Kreutzer, A. Anstieg der Jugendkriminalitat - ein Mythos?' Kriminalistik 2: 67-73, 1980.

Malinowski, M. and Schwielick. 'Monopolisierte Polizeiforschung.' Kriminologisches Journal 2: 126-130, 1973.

MacNaughton - Smith, P. 'The second Code.' Journal of Research in Crime and Delinquency 5: 189-197, 1968.

Martens, U. Wirtschaftliche Krise, Arbeitslosigkeit und Kriminalitatsbewegung. Wiesbaden: BKA, 1978.

Matza, D. Becoming Deviant. Englewood Cliffs: Prentice Hall, 1979.

O'Connor, J. The Fiscal Crises of the State, German transl. Suhrkamp: Verlag, 1974.

Offe, C. Strukturprobleme des kapitalistischen Staates. Frankfurt: Suhrkamp, 1973.

Offe, C. Berufsbildungsreform. Frankfurt: Suhrkamp, 1975.

Phillipson, M. 'Critical Theorizing and the New Criminology.' British Journal of Criminology 13, 1973.

Platt and Skolnick. The Politics of Riot Commissions, 1961-1970. New York, 1971.

Sack, F. Probleme der Kriminalsoziologie, in Handbuch der empirischen Sozialforschung, Stuttgart Enke, 1978.

Steffen, W. Kinder- und Jugendkriminalitat in Bayern, Munchen Bayerisches-LKA, 1979.

Schwindt, Ahlhorn and Weiss. Empirische Kriminalgeographie. Wiesbaden: BKA, 1978.

Steinhilper, G. Vorbemerkung, in Martens 1978: V-XI.

Taylor, I., Walton, P. and Young, J. The New Criminology. London: Routledge and Kegan Paul, 1973.

Wacker, A. Arbeitslos und agressiv ? Zum Verhaltnis von Arbeitslosigkeit, Agression und Kriminalitatsentwicklung, in Soziale Welt, 364-381, 1977.

Werkentin, Hoffer, Eert, and Baurmann. 'Criminology as Police Science or 'How Old is the New Criminology?'' Crime and Social Justice 2: 22-4, 1974.

# PROFILES IN COURAGE

## PROBLEMS OF ACTION OF THE FINNISH GAY MOVEMENT IN CRISIS

### Olli Stalstrom

*This chapter was originally delivered at the 1983 Finnish conference and published in Working Papers in European Criminology, Volume 5, 'Social Movements and Social Conflicts', pp. 49-61*

Genocide is defined in United Nations Conventions not only as 'killing members of a group' but also as 'causing serious bodily or mental harm to members of a group' and 'deliberately inflicting on the group conditions of life calculated to bring about its physical destruction in whole or in part'.[1] If this extended definition of genocide may be applied to other than racial groups, Finland is at this very moment witnessing the attempted destruction of a whole social movement and the beginning of State-imposed genocide. The gay liberation movement in Finland, SETA,

---

[1]  United Nations, Human Rights: A compilation of international instruments. (New York: United Nations, 1978), 31.

is being wiped out in its present form by what may be the worst backlash against gay people in the history of Finland.

# THE STATE AGAINST ITS CITIZENS

The well-known critic of psychiatry, Thomas Szasz[2], has argued that the 'sickness' label and traditional stereotypes of gays have been 'manufactured' by the medical profession and the State without any solid scientific basis. Two general observations can be made about the current position of gays in Finland in line with Szasz's reasoning: (1) the actual crisis, which is discussed in this paper, is a creation on the part of the medical profession, the press and the Finnish State, and (2) the discrimination and suffering imposed on gay people in Finland is the direct result of an explicitly stated policy by the highest legal authorities of the State.

Homosexuality between consenting adults of either sex was labelled a crime in Finland until 1971; formally classified as a mental disease until 1981; and has been traditionally labelled a sin, a disease and a contagious condition by the politically powerful Lutheran State church. Homosexuality has been under a blanket of silence in Finland longer than in any other Nordic country. There has been an almost complete lack of information, and still today, partly because of the censorship law (see below) there are no books in Finnish about gay people. In 1969, when the decriminalisation of homosexuality was proposed by a State committee, the Supreme Court of Finland argued in its statement to the Finnish government that such 'pathological deviance' should not be given the status of minority behaviour and that homosexuals should 'be made to feel sick', because this would encourage them to seek 'treatment'.[3] Is this not a declaration of a policy of genocide as defined above? Does it not make the State of Finland directly comparable with the apartheid systems?

The statement by the Supreme Court resulted in what is

---

[2]  T. Szasz, The manufacture of madness. (St Albans: Paladin, 1973).
[3]  Statement by the Supreme Court to the Finnish Government, June 13 1969.

now the main legal instrument of oppression, a censorship law enacted in 1971 in connection with the decriminalisation of homosexuality. The law prohibits 'public encouragement of indecent behaviour between members of the same sex'.[4]

According to Fitzgerald [5]the law is 'in essence, a censorship law that prohibits open and positive discussion about homosexuality'. In 1976 a radio programme had legal action taken against it because the editors mentioned that the American Psychiatric Association had removed the sickness label of homosexuality. After another case of legal action against the Finnish State monopoly broadcasting company, full censorship of homosexual topics became the unofficial policy for Finnish radio and television for a number of years at the end of the seventies, although in both cases the journalists charged with 'public encouragement' were acquitted. As one of the editors of the forthcoming first book in Finnish about homosexuality, I face the risk of a jail sentence in the event that the Finnish courts find any part of the book an 'encouragement' of homosexuality. While the censorship law has impeded in practice the production and dissemination of factual and scientific information in the mass media and secondary schools, stereotypes and fears about homosexuality have been produced at an increasing rate by the gutter press and members of the medical profession.

Certain professors of psychiatry have been important in creating the discrimination. One of the early psychiatric 'authorities' - a priest and professor of psychiatry - combined the repression of homosexuality with a general moral crusade to clean up the world. In the forties he called for cooperation with Hitler's troops to 'annihilate' the 'arch enemy', the Russian forces[6]; in the fifties he called

---

4   RL 20:9:2.
5   T. Fitzgerald, "Gay self-help groups in Sweden and Finland", International Review of Modern Sociology, 10(July-December, 1980), 191-200, 197.
6   A. Stenback, "We and Greater Finland", Ad Lucem, 5 (1941): 5-7.

for the castration of homosexuals[7]; and in the sixties, as the psychiatrist 'expert' of the State church, he called for a censorship law against information about homosexuality. This latter call resulted in a statement from the State church to the government, demanding the enactment of a censorship law.[8] A typical cultural lag can be seen in subsequent Finnish psychiatry. What Fitzgerald calls the 'outmoded, psychoanalytic, anti-gay' movement of American psychoanalysis of the McCarthyan fifties reached Finland over a decade later, after homosexuality was declassified by the American Psychiatric Association. The stereotype of 'homosexual' as a sick, pathetic person, who actually wants to be a member of the opposite sex, became the essence of the prevailing psychiatric school of thought in Finland about homosexuality and the main source of stereotypes in the seventies and eighties.[9] A formal complaint against this type of labelling, in which homosexuality was also compared to the copulation of rats to prove that it is substitute behaviour, was submitted by the gay liberation movement, SETA, to the Finnish National Board of Health in 1982. A formal communication was also submitted by SETA to the United Nations Human Rights Committee in that the censorship law violates freedom of expression. Neither complaint has achieved any results.

This official oppression of homosexuality, together with the peripheral 'backwoods' cultural climate of Finland and the fears of 'contagion' upheld by scientific 'experts', have created and maintained an underlying, irrational fear of homosexuality which has remained very deep-seated in spite of apparent liberalisation during the seventies. This homophobia has only been covered up by apparent tolerance, ready to explode into repressive action in deteriorating societal conditions.

---

[7]   A. Stenback and L. Pautola, Sexual Development and Education in Childhood and Adolescence, Helsinki: Otava, 1952), 290.

[8]   Statement by the Committee of Family Affairs of the Finnish State Church (in reply to the request by the Ministry of Justice for a Statement), 1968.

[9]   K. Achte et al, *Psychiatry* (Porvoo: WSOY, 1981).

# DREAMS OF A BETTER WORLD

The Finnish gay liberation movement has a history similar to that in other Western countries, although there has always been a time lag of many years, typical of Finland. The roots of the gay liberation movement are in the so-called 'November movement', a protest movement of the late sixties against all types of authoritarianism and State control. There was a working group within this organisation demanding decriminalisation and complete equality for gays. Out of this group emerged Psyke, the first gay rights organisation, in 1969. The organisation had a radical charter demanding not only decriminalisation but also total equality in all legal and social fields and the integration of homosexuality into society. Psyke was a factor in speeding up decriminalisation.

However, after this most visible form of oppression was removed, the partial improvement, together with the increasing exploitation of homosexuality by the scandal press, rapidly diluted all radicalism. The original organisation changed into a social club, with its only function that of organising dances and publishing a semi-pornographic magazine. The leader of the organisation even sent a letter to the Members of Parliament thanking them for changing the law and promising that homosexuals would never again disturb the public with further demands. After a period of disagreement on strategy, a splinter group sprang up in May 1974 under the name SETA (meaning 'sexual equality').

The founding members of SETA saw decriminalisation only as a first step. Old ideals of complete equality and integration were taken up again. Most important, the ideological leaders of SETA did not see the increasing growth of the so-called 'gay subculture' (commercial discos, porno magazines and a network of separate meeting institutions) as a step towards equality. On the contrary, a separate 'gay subculture' was seen as an obstacle to genuine equality, at least to the extent that commercial discos and publications were an exploitation of gays and run solely on the terms of individual businessmen's commercial interests. The working methods and problems of the movement have been similar in some respects to those in other Western countries[10] and the leading ideology was influenced by the English Gay Liberation Front Manifesto, published in 1971.

The main fields of action have been social work (telephone counselling , service and a social worker); organising consciousness raising groups, discussions, and discos; producing, translating and publishing information; and political lobbying for the removal of the remaining forms of inequality (removal of the sickness label, equalisation of age limits for gays and straights, removal of the censorship law, etc.)

The same pressures of commercial exploitation that effectively finished Psyke were felt from the beginning in SETA. During its whole life, up to the current crisis, there have been two competing schools of thought within the movement about the role of the so-called 'men's magazines' and the commercial 'gay subculture'. Some have seen these mainly as exploitation to which SETA should provide an alternative and refrain from supporting. Others have welcomed new commercial discos and porno magazines. The question of whether SETA should cooperate with the 'men's magazines' and provide material to them or whether this press should be left alone has become complicated because the censorship law has kept the general press and the Finnish broadcasting company very quiet, helping the 'men's magazines' become the most widely-spread media dealing with homosexuality. The circulation of the 'men's magazines' is several hundred thousand, and because they deal with both straight and gay pornography and scandals, they can be easily be bought even by closet gays, people who hide their homosexuality. This type

---

[10]  See L. Stanley, "Male Needs and the Problems of Working with Gay men." In On the Problem of Men, edited by S. Friedman and E. Sarah, 190-213. London: the Women's Press, 1982; L. Humphreys, Out of the Closets: The Sociology of Homosexual Liberation. (Englewood Cliffs: Prentice-Hall, 1972); K. Jay and A. Young, Out of the Closets: Voices of Gay Liberation. (New York: Jove/HBJ, 1972); R. Tielman. Homoseksualiteit in Nederland. (Meppel: Boom, 1982).

of magazine, however, usually presents all sexuality in a sensational manner and the message of even some factual articles tends to get lost in that context. The business men behind the 'men's magazines' have expanded into other areas as well: attempts to start sauna clubs in Finland, the production and sales of pornography, 'counselling services', gay travel tours and contact services. Some of these activities are sheer abuse of young homosexual men. According to the evidence gathered by SETA, the telephone 'counselling services' of the 'men's magazines' have often been used for the sexual and commercial gains of private businessmen. However, up to the current crisis there was an uneasy but peaceful coexistence between the gay rights movement and the 'men's magazines', because the activists tried to avoid wasting energy on internal policy struggles. A number of men and women from SETA have supplied material and appeared personally in the 'men's magazines'.

The question of whether the SETA magazine itself should become a pornographic magazine with erotic articles or be a more culturally and socially oriented high-standard paper was argued over the early years and nearly finished SETA before it got off the ground. Another pressure which has been felt from the beginning in SETA is that as a result of small steps of liberalisation of attitudes there has been a decrease in the radical drive to change society and a growing emphasis on internal 'social-clubs' activities. The movement itself was becoming a kind of 'gay subculture'. SETA's magazine changed from its radical 'fighting' image to a rather unprofessionally made hobby publication. The magazine contained items written by gays to gays. As a result of this trend, SETA lost in 1982 a large proportion of the financial support it had received from Ministry of Education funds for alternative magazines. The reason was stated very clearly: 'loss of quality'. The radical opposition within SETA grew more and more vocal and led to a series of crises in the summer of 1982. A split within the organisation and the formation of a new protest movement were discussed.

The loss of the Ministry of Education support, the growing fears generated by news about the AIDS panic in the United States, as well as the growing protests within the movement, finally changed the image and strategy of SETA during 1982/83 and several new radical members joined the organisation. The magazine now again aims at high journalistic standards. It has been quoted in the general press again for the first time in years and it seems to have regained respect as a magazine worth reading. The editors define SETA magazine not as a gay magazine produced for gays, but as a culturally and socially oriented forum for dialogue between different majorities and minorities. The unifying and radicalising effect of external pressure has rapidly improved the intensity, quality and seriousness of the work done within the movement. Predictably, there has been some criticism of the recent image of SETA as being too radical and moralising. In any case, the old deals of complete equality and integration have been taken up again only to be threatened by financial collapse, as will be explained shortly.

An interesting aspect of the Finnish gay rights movement has been the great emphasis on the integration of people in the movement regardless of age, gender, sexual orientation or political opinion. SETA is one of the few gay rights organisations where women work side by side with men in spite of occasional differences of opinion about the strategies and structure of the organisation. A large number of active members have been women and women form almost half of the clientele of the disco. SETA's women are internationally very active, the headquarters of ILIS (International Lesbian Information Service) being in the hands of SETA women.

A unique aspect of SETA is that it always actively welcomed straight people to support its cause and to work in it. Several of its board members have been straight and one of its chairpersons has been a straight woman Member of Parliament. SETA may be the only gay movement in the world where two-thirds of its paid workers are straight. This has not been intended as an attempt at a 'respectable' front, but rather as an expression of the underlying ideology that homosexuality should not be separated into a subculture and that people should not be differentiated because of their age, gender, sexual orientation or political belief but rather according to their attitude towards social justice and equality in general. A practical effect of this policy is that it has given SETA a broader base. Active members range in age from under 20 to over 70, and in the political spectrum from conservative to communist. This also made it easier to get support from outside groups and individuals who think along the same lines about sexual equality, regardless of sexual orientation. SETA is receiving increasing support from university professors, researchers, politicians, political parties and social movements, and the more responsible sector of the press.

## THE CRISIS: THE MANUFACTURE OF MADNESS

The basic conditions for the present crisis have been created by the information vacuum caused by the censorship law; the sharply increased competition between the two afternoon papers in Finland; and the growing number of pornographic and sensation magazines. These have published, since the late sixties, an increasing number of more or less fabricated articles about homosexuality, usually presented in a way that creates more stereotypes and feeds on the stereotypes and fears already existing. The actual crisis was triggered by the first case of a sexually transmitted disease, Acquired Immune Deficiency Syndrome (AIDS), being found in Finland on June 22, 1983. It is important to keep in mind that from an epidemiological point of view, the disease is not a national problem. In spite of extensive screening projects only two cases have been confirmed so far (dated September 1983). The 'fast lane gay lifestyle of certain large American cities, with sauna clubs and backrooms providing possibilities for instant sex with a high number of different partners is virtually non-existent in Finland.

In a study currently underway here in Finland,[11] and in a previous cross-cultural study,[12] the researchers have been surprised to find that the majority of Finnish gay males (and two-thirds of lesbians) have a regular partner relationship and that the number of sexual contacts with different partners are very low, the lowest of all the societies studied (Australia, Ireland, Sweden, and Finland). Research data indicate that the stereotypes commonly held by certain Finnish medical 'experts',[13] portraying Finnish gay men as 'extremely promiscuous' and 'terribly infested with diseases transmitted in homosexual rituals', are not only scientifically unfounded but also contain irrational and homophobic elements. By the time the first Finnish case of AIDS was announced in June 1983, already more than 50 scare articles had appeared in the press. Following the first Finnish AIDS case, a wave of fear and panic swept the country in what persons interviewed by me described as a 'nightmare'. The afternoon press created a national alarm by presenting the disease in extremely sensational and biased coverage at the beginning of July 1983. A large number of the articles concocted by the press contained errors and false information, or were simply irrational: some of them were intentionally (as my interviews with the editors and journalists revealed) designed to create panic and hatred against gay men by screaming headlines and fear-provoking pictures of dying people whose eyes had been eaten out by cancer. Even government officials privately expressed their concern about the effects of the sensations created by the afternoon press.

There was a wave of extremely hostile articles, some of them expressing joy that homosexuals are dying out and that nature has invented this method of cleaning up human kind.[14] For a week, the sensations were on the front pages. A

---

11   M. Gronfors et al, "Results of a Survey of Finnish Homosexuals." In The Many Faces of Love, edited by K. Sievers and O. Stalstrom. Espoo: Weilin and Göös, 1984.

12   M. Ross and O. Stalstrom. "Attitudes to Venereal Disease Clinics in Finnish Homosexual Men." European Journal of Sexually Transmitted Diseases 1 (1984): 169-171.

13   e.g. T. Rostila. "New Diseases of Homosexual Men." Duodecim 3 (1983): 190-193; Lassus 1983: Interview with Professor Lassus in Iltalehti, 28.3.1983.

14   e.g. A. Alhainen. "Without Belittling the Matter." Riihimaen Sanomat, 3 July 1983.

number of gay men went into a state of panic, fear and despair - from my interviews, it seems not so much because of fear of the disease itself but because of feeling and seeing the moral climate turning back years and seeing the slow progress made in the seventies crumble in a matter of days. The disease was falsely labelled a 'homosexual disease, although the disease has been found mainly in the subgroup of gay males who have had an extremely high number of different partners, in Haitian immigrants in the United States, and in intravenous drug users of either sex or sexual orientation, although no cases of AIDS have been found among lesbians.

Gradually the fear of the heterosexual majority was transformed into ridicule: AIDS and people dying of it were made the butt of dozens of different jokes printed in newspapers and spreading rapidly around the country. Many Finnish heterosexuals are actually having a lot of fun cracking jokes about people dying of this leukaemia-related disease![15] One can even buy T-shirts with AIDS jokes printed on them. While the Finnish heterosexual public was amusing itself with AIDS jokes, SETA's crisis task force tried to protect the patients from the gutter press. We did this by warning them in advance of the motives of the press, by misleading sensation-seeking journalists, and by motivating the patients not to allow themselves to be exploited by literally holding their hands, pledging solidarity, collecting money to send them away from Helsinki and out of the reach of the gutter press. These protective manoeuvres have been completely successful up to now, although several of the frustrated journalists promised to cause a lot of trouble for us.

A sharp increase in threats of violence and discrimination against gays was immediately noticed. Paul[16] has also noted a sharp increase in physical violence and discrimination after 'organized campaigns of vilification against gay people'. One

---

[15]   The editors would like to note here that there is no evidence connecting Leukaemia and Acquired Immune Deficiency Syndrome.

[16]   W. Paul (1982) "Minority status for gay people. Majority reaction and social context," in Homosexuality: Social, Psychological and Biological Issues, edited by W. Paul. Beverly Hills: Sage, 1982.

of the factors that aggravated the crisis was that medical staff did not react in time, although they were approached already at the end of 1982 when the first danger signs were seen. Some of the statements in early 1983 by medical 'experts' were unscientific and even irrational and fuelled the panic. When the medical screening project of possible AIDS cases in Finland was begun in May, 1983, SETA organised gay volunteers for the project and appealed to the sense of social responsibility of the medical staff involved. They were asked to influence the news coverage and to take extreme care in preventing sensational writing and panic. Although there has been an increase in responsible attitudes among the medical staff, SETA failed to make them realise their responsibility and the responsibilities of influencing the press and acting in time. Basic education about homosexuality and the social responsibility of physicians is almost non-existent in the medical field in Finland. At the beginning of the crisis, more time was wasted on arguing with the gay rights activists and dismissing their concerns than was spent in correcting the biased press coverage. News about the first case of AIDS was unexpectedly leaked to the public by the medical staff before any preventive strategies or proper press releases could be formulated. From what I saw, every mistake that could have been made was made. Only after the full impact of the gutter press was felt did the medical staff react rapidly and in a responsible way. However, the damage was already done.

The 'peaceful coexistence' between SETA and the 'men's magazines' turned into hot war literally overnight when the role of the gutter press became clear in the creation of fear and panic during the AIDS crisis. Members of SETA's crisis task force confronted the editors and journalists of the 'men's magazines' and the afternoon papers. The shady activities of the businessmen behind the 'men's magazines' were publicly exposed by SETA in the general media. The dirty and old sex club kept by the same businessmen was literally raided by the women and men in SETA's task force in order to have it closed as a preventive measure against the spread of venereal disease. This was accomplished in one attack and SETA is now preparing a report on the abuse of young men by the 'counselling services' of the 'men's magazines', to be presented to the authorities. More than ten thousand leaflets were printed by SETA in the summer of 1983 and distributed around the country at intervals of two weeks to combat rumours and fear and to give accurate information about medical risks in the present situation. For the first time, SETA has publicly criticised the exploitative aspects of the 'men's press' and the afternoon papers and has demanded professional standards for all 'counselling services'.

SETA itself has suffered a massive blow from the backlash. The organisation lost its disco, which had provided 90% of its income. The owners of the disco are a student organisation, which has remained impervious to appeals to reverse its decision. With SETA's financial foundation abruptly removed, all its employees have been given notice and most of its activities, including the publication of the magazine, will have to be discontinued, at a time when the movement is most urgently needed. On October 1, 1982, there will be no money to pay the social worker, at a time when the number of people contacting SETA's crisis line is up roughly 1200% from the previous summer. On October 1, 1983, there will be no money to pay the salary of the editor or the cost of printing SETA magazine, at a time when factual information is needed more urgently than ever to combat mounting irrational fears. The general press has published more articles attacking gays in the past six months (literally hundreds of articles) than during the whole ten years in which the organisation has existed. There will be no money to pay the office staff or the counselling service at a time when it has been necessary to recruit a dozen new volunteer physicians, counsellors and nurses from mental hospitals to take care of the growing number of gay men in panic or suicide crisis.

The largest and best social meeting place for gays has been lost at the very time when the few other existing meeting places are closing down or are in danger or being closed down – one because of physical threats against the owner, one because the waiters are reluctant to handle money received from homosexuals – and at a time when the newspapers report physical attacks against gay men. There will be no money to continue supporting scientific research at a time when new research data is most urgently needed to combat a sudden wave of new stereotypes and fears about homosexuality. Not only is the whole social movement crumbling, but most of its activists who work in outside jobs have become targets of pressure from their employers and a number of activists have received bomb threats or become targets of physical violence. The chairman of the organisation has not only been told by his employer to stop his SETA activities but also told not to use his company toilet.

SETA's integrated approach and broad base of support may be the critical factor in keeping some kind of gay movement alive in Finland after SETA has collapsed financially. During the worst days of attack by the gutter press there was strong and spontaneous solidarity among Finnish opinion leaders. A number of university professors called to ask what they could do, several important columnists immediately criticised the sensational press: two newspapers in their editorials defended gays against the sensational press, many people simply walked into SETA's office and reported for voluntary work: one of the more responsible government ministers postponed her summer holiday in order to be available for SETA. Several leading artists are now planning solidarity events to save the gay rights movement. All of SETA's employees have decided to stay in their jobs even if the organisation collapses financially, they will earn their living by taking outside work.

From a sociological point of view it is interesting - but frightening - to follow the collapse of a whole social movement and the rapid deterioration in the life conditions of one of the largest minorities in Finland. As a gay rights fighter and a sociological researcher, I have personally participated in the events for several months; together with the activists of the movement I was already involved in a qualitative research project at Helsinki University, a study of the lifestyles of and discrimination against lesbians and gay men. The first stage of the project, a survey of 1051 women and men, was carried out at the beginning of 1983 and its results will be published soon.[17] With the AIDS crisis, the research project became suddenly action-oriented and participatory in the extreme, involving alternately handling incoming death-threat calls and counselling suicidal callers, in addition to the everyday work of confronting the wave of sensational reporting and discrimination. During early July my home was used as a shelter for SETA's office staff after they had started receiving death-threats not only at the office but also at their homes. The most serious bomb and murder threats, six during July, were reported to the police.

All actions and daily reports have been recorded on tape, including, for instance, interviews with the chief editors of the scandal press, the journalists writing the most sensational articles, meetings with government and medical officials, as well as live recordings of some of the actual confrontations and personal interviews with gay men.

# TWO STEPS FORWARD, ONE STEP BACK

Some of the problems of action of the Finnish gay rights movement in respect to the State and society are illustrated by the current crisis. Some of the major difficulties have always been the negative and condescending attitudes of 'experts' within the medical field as well as the cynicism and lack of moral courage of politicians. SETA has met several consecutive Ministers of Justice (the present one twice) and demanded the removal of the censorship law; a Private Members' Bill was introduced in Parliament for the removal of the law already in 1977 and is now signed by 19 MPs from different parties; several demonstrations have

---

17    M. Gronfors et al, "Results of a Survey of Finnish Homosexuals." In The Many Faces of Love, edited by K. Sievers & O. Stålstrom. (Espoo: Weilin and Göös, 1984).

been held outside Finnish embassies in all Nordic countries; the treatment of gays in Finland has received wide international attention in scientific journals: the International Commission of Jurists has recently criticised both the Finnish government and the United Nations Human Rights Committee for giving 'blanket approval for censorship'.[18] The removal of the censorship law has not taken place in spite of ten years of intensive domestic and international pressure. Some leading politicians admit in private that the law violates basic human rights but that they refuse to abolish it for fear of losing votes to the extremely reactionary and vocal Christian party. All existing means have now been exhausted. The current crisis and the financial collapse of the gay rights give a new sense of urgency to getting the State policy of oppression changed.

Several simultaneous and dialectical trends seem to be emerging. There is a clear polarisation: those who have hated homosexuals and wanted them to be wiped out now feel they have reason to say it aloud; those who have given passive support to the struggle for equality have felt compelled to state it openly. There may be a growing feeling of fear and hatred of homosexuality among the heterosexuals and an escalation feeling of despair, panic and hatred of the oppressive system within the gay community. The afternoon press has constantly attacked SETA and fabricated front-page sensations about AIDS. It is impossible to estimate at this moment how widespread these trends are. However, the sheer number of individuals in crisis and feeling they have no future is alarming. The mood of the gay community has changed within recent months. On the one hand there is at least a temporary feeling of hopelessness and bitterness growing. It is difficult to assess the negative long-term effects of the silent and persistent fears of violence, of the future and one's health, and the fear of when the sensational press will decide to create 'the next wave of hatred'.

---

[18]   Freedom of expression. (1982) The Review 28, 44-46.

On the other hand, there is a strong process of unification and solidarity, both within the gay community and among the general public. New volunteers are still coming in. A new, dedicated movement may be emerging from the crisis. It seems that gay rights fighters and their straight supporters have never before worked so intensely and effectively. Fitzgerald[19] in his study of Finnish and Swedish gay liberation movements summarises neatly the function and moral effect of the gay rights movement:

> when a self-help organisation takes on primarily a political role, it in effect becomes the ombudsman for the minority in question ... The gay self-help group have made positive and tangible contributions to gay people, as well as, I believe, to the societies in which they occur. Not only in terms of personal growth and change (providing more social alternatives, community and identity) but also as a vehicle of change. Ultimately such grass-roots activity is what participatory democracy is all about - people in action on their own behalf.

The crucial question now is: is there still time and are there enough individuals to keep up the fight and mobilise sufficient support within Finland and to bring international pressure against the Finnish government to prevent fear, panic and destruction? Can the surge of emotions within the gay community be channelled in a constructive way? How long can individual citizens be motivated to act as grass-roots ombudsmen when the real ombudsmen and government ministers show no sign of responsibility? A new solidarity, a healthier, more open and integrated lifestyle and gay pride may emerge from the crisis. If not, will the violation of human rights by the State of Finland, irresponsible reporting by the gutter press and the prejudices of the public lead to violence towards gays or by gays? Who will then be held responsible?

---

[19]   T. Fitzgerald. "Gay Self-Help Groups in Sweden and Finland." International Review of Modern Sociology 10 (July-December 1980), 15-24, 199.

## Bibliography

Achte, K. et al, Psychiatry (Porvoo: WSOY) 1981.

Alhainen, A. 'Without Belittling the Matter.' Riihimaen Sanomat, 3 July 1983.

Fitzgerald, T. 'Gay Self-Help Groups in Sweden and Finland.' International Review of Modern Sociology 10, (July-December 1980): 15-24, 199.

Freedom of expression. The Review 28: 44-46. 1982

Gronfors, M. et al, 'Results of a Survey of Finnish Homosexuals.' In The Many Faces of Love, edited by *K. Sievers & O. Stålstrom*. Espoo: Weilin and Göös, 1984.

Humphreys, L. Out of the Closets: The Sociology of Homosexual Liberation. (Englewood Cliffs: Prentice-Hall) 1972.

Jay, K. and Young, A. Out of the Closets: Voices of Gay Liberation. (New York: Jove/HBJ) 1972.

Paul, W. 'Minority status for gay people: Majority reaction and social context,' in Homosexuality: Social, Psychological and Biological Issues, edited by W. Paul. (Beverly Hills: Sage) 1982

Ross, M. and Stalstrom, O. 'Attitudes to Venereal Disease Clinics in Finnish Homosexual Men.' European Journal of Sexually Transmitted Diseases 1 (1984): 169-171.

Rostila, T. 'New Diseases of Homosexual Men.' Duodecim 3 190-193; Lassus 1983:

Interview with Professor Lassus in Iltalehti, 28.3.1983.

Stanley, L. 'Male Needs and the Problems of Working with Gay men.' In On the Problem of Men, edited by S. Friedman and E. Sarah, 190-213. (London: the Women's Press) 1982.

Stenback, A. 'We and Greater Finland', Ad Lucem, 5 (1941): 5-7.

Stenback, A. and Pautola, L. Sexual Development and Education in Childhood and Adolescence, (Helsinki: Otava) 1952

Szasz, T. The manufacture of madness. (St Albans: Paladin) 1973

Tielman, R., Homoseksualiteit in Nederland. (Meppel: Boom) 1982

United Nations, Human Rights: A compilation of international instruments. (New York: United Nations) 1978 p.31

# WOMEN AND THE STRIKE

## IT'S A WHOLE WAY OF LIFE

### *Welsh Campaign for Civil and Political Liberties*

*At the 1984 conference in Cardiff the women of the mining communities spoke passionately about their struggle. This article, based on interviews with the women, was published in Working Papers in European Criminology, volume 6, 'The State of Information' (1984), pp. 11-27*

> My attitudes have changed through the strike. I
> thought I was a socialist before. Now I know what
> socialism is – it's a whole way of life, and we're living
> it in our valley right now.

The National Union of Mineworkers strike, which lasted
over a year, was in full swing when the conference of the European Group took place in Cardiff in September 1984. The
strike is now over, but not the long analysis of this historical
confrontation between militant organised labour and Thatcherism. The following piece is not a 'post-mortem', but an article
based on interviews conducted with women in the mining
communities of South Wales at the height of the strike. It

therefore captures many of the things which the women of the mining communities themselves told us in September 1984 of their food collections, of their 'alternative welfare State', as well as of their determination, having once stood up, not to kneel down again.

In the tradition of their foremothers, women living in the South Wales mining communities have, from the very start of the 1984 strike, taken up the struggle as their own. That has meant battling on two fronts: standing up for their communities, their menfolk and their children's future, but also claiming their right to take an active part, to define the struggle as being as much theirs as their menfolk's and the NUM's:

> If I want to go, I'll go (picketing). After all, it's my money. If he doesn't have a job to go on we're not taking that lying down.

There is an understandable reticence on the part of the women in the strike to voice at this time their anger and frustration at attempts by some individual miners and certain union officials to undermine their independence and muffle their voices. The women are dealing with it as they have to - speaking out against some of it, keeping quiet about the rest. When many of the women speak about this strike they may be treading a tightrope between their solidarity with and their grievances against the men in their communities. Union officials who in public applaud these 'heroines' sometimes in private do their damnedest to prevent them gaining any political ground. The women are often gagged by their loyalty and their entirely justifiable fear of dividing communities and households which are already up against a rich, powerful and sometimes violent enemy. But many of the women believe their part in this strike is changing attitudes in the union:

> We're overcoming the problem slowly, but it is slow because the NUM is a male dominated industry. But attitudes are changing. The younger miners

are better than the older ones. But there are a lot of older miners in the group and we do get a bit of hassle, but in the end they give in.

# FOOD COLLECTIONS

Women's groups in most areas become involved initially through organising food collection and distribution, organising fund raising events such as galas and sponsored walks. That was, and is, vital work - not just because of what was collected but because food collection and fund-raising are the first points of contact between those on strike and the rest of the community. The most fundamental act of solidarity is to give food or money to a family on strike - and fund-raising events have become an important focal point for communities to show their support for the struggle. Food collection and distribution is a full-time operation for many women and men involved in the strike. Maerdy Lodge, for instance, distributes 700 food parcels a week to miners' families all the way down the valley as far as Porth. The support group pays £600 a week, which it has to collect itself, to the NUM headquarters at Pontypridd. After a food-buying run to a cash and carry store, £1,400 worth of food is then delivered to Maerdy. There, volunteers divide it into parcels.

> We can only afford to put in the basics: eight pounds of potatoes, a tin of veg, rice pudding, fruit, sometimes sugar, tea bags, tins of beans or spaghetti and so on. We have to raise the money ourselves through raffles and socials, and going away to speak at meetings. We did well last week - from meetings in Birmingham and Oxford we brought back 1,000 pounds. If someone's in real need, they can ask for more food - single men are the worst off. They're never turned away if they come and ask.

Children are getting free school dinners which helps to take some of the pressure off families. The women are amazed at the generosity of many people:

> There's an unemployed centre in the Midlands that regularly collects and sends us money. They're poor themselves - yet they give to us. And two Germans came over to visit us recently - now they've opened a second-hand bookshop and they're sending us all the proceeds on a regular basis.

In Gwent the food distribution is handled independently of Pontypridd. The Gwent Food Fund covers 14 NUM areas, including the Rhymney Valley. They collect 10,000 pounds a week, buy all the food from a wholesaler and deliver 5,000 food parcels to 10% of the people in the areas they cover (between 25,000 and 30,000 people). The local councils have been helpful: Islwyn has let the Fund have a room equipped with freezers to store the food, and both Islwyn and Blaenau Gwent loan vans for the massive distribution operation to local collect on points around the county.

Collecting money has been both heartening and depressing:

> I've been out collecting and taken the most terrible abuse I have ever heard in my life, and I am 58 years of age and I never thought I'd hear that.

> We get a lot of support from the pensioners around here. They're always giving what they can. Most people seem to support us. We've had letters from people who were on strike in 1926 and in Australia now and they've sent us donations. It's overwhelming.

# ALTERNATIVE WELFARE STATE

What the women have done, in effect, is to set up an alternative welfare system. In conjunction with the NUM strike committees at each lodge they are supporting over 100,000 people in the South Wales valleys. They provide both moral support and practical help, and they are prepared to deal with any situation that arises. In Maerdy, for instance, any family short of food could go to the miner's welfare institute and get another food parcel. They try to ensure that no one suffers exceptional hardship if they can find a way to help. The history of their own communities obviously has influenced the success of the support groups, but the women have also travelled the length and breadth of Britain speaking at meetings and rallies to win support. The fact that the strike is still on is evidence of their success. Despite the government's attempts to undermine them financially, the women have ensured that the strike will not fail through overpowering financial pressures. Their organisational skills and the speed with which they have mobilised their resources from the start is practical evidence of their determination.

# WOMEN PICKETING

Women began to go on picket lines a couple of months into the strike - and by July they had organised themselves on an area basis, with regular meetings where groups from all over South Wales could meet and plan and share experiences. Abertillery women organised a huge and highly successful rally in July, and the same week saw the first mass women's picket at Port Talbot steelworks. Some women from the support groups have travelled all over Wales, England and Scotland to speak to public meetings, and make contact with other women from mining communities. For some women, the full horror of what was happening on the picket line was brought home to them when their husbands returned home from Orgreave:

The string vest was ripped to pieces, the strap of the watch was broken, his gym shoes were split all the way round where the dogs had caught him, his jeans were ripped at the bottom and he had a big mark where the shield had caught him. He was covered in bruises, and all marks and cuts. And he was only doing his duty.

After going on picket lines themselves, many of the women said they began to understand how easily anger can flare up in that situation:

We hadn't been on the picket line before. Our men had come back with all these stories of police violence and provocation, and we thought maybe it was an exaggeration. But we found out that it wasn't. You see a convoy coming out and you're seething with rage. I did a V sign at one of the drivers and a policeman told me I could be taken away for that. So I just turned my fingers round the other way. But the drivers made signs like that at us - and no one threatens to arrest them.

I was surprised at how aggressive I felt that day. Your fuse is shorter than usual. I could feel it bubbling up inside me.

I'm beginning to see how the violence happens. Coming back from Birmingham we were on the motorway and we ended up in the middle of the coke convoy from Port Talbot. Lots of the drivers saw us and made rude signs at us, they showed us their union card and waved money at us. It drove us mad in the back of our bus. We regard ourselves as law-abiding people but we were really furious. I can see why our boys get so angry on the picket line and sometimes lose their self control. When you've been

out for nearly five months and someone taunts you
like that, it drives you wild.

Now many of the women see picketing as an integral part
of their involvement in the strike:

> Now the women in our valley would go on any picket
> anywhere they were needed. Not at the beginning
> of the strike - we wouldn't. Now it's all changed.

There are still a number of support groups, however, which
don't go on any picket lines. This often seems to be because
the men put their foot down, saying it's too dangerous and
several of the women said they wouldn't want to go after what
they'd seen of Orgreave on television. Some were deterred
by the worry that if they were arrested they wouldn't get the
NUM's legal backing if their local lodge hadn't approved
them picketing. Others were too worried about their children.

## WOMEN AND THE POLICE

For many of the police, it has been the first time they've had
to deal with women on the picket line. The women we talked
to had very differing impressions of how that affected police
behaviour:

> The police were surprised because we were women.
> They didn't know where to put their hands, because
> when they touched us we gave them abuse. They
> didn't know how to react.

> The police treated us all with contempt. They didn't
> care if it was a woman or a man they were dealing with.

Disillusionment with the police is almost universal among
the women who talked with us - their anger reflects a growing
rift between the police and the communities they work in:

The wounds left in this community will go on for a long time. Some time ago they took away our local copper who lived in the village – before the strike this was – so there was already some bitterness about the police round here. Now the way the local men are being treated on the picket line makes us very angry. We didn't have a lot of faith in the police before. We have none now.

The government's policy in this strike is to 'criminalise' the miners by mass arrests and the use of charges such as breach of the peace and obstruct on of a police officer. The women are well aware of this process. Mary Coombes from Maerdy was arrested at Port Talbot for throwing an egg at a coke lorry, and she was charged with breach of the peace:

I said (to the police) I didn't see why I should be treated differently to a farmer's wife who a month previously had thrown an egg at Mrs. Thatcher, and that day nobody was charged, but when a miner's wife throws an egg at a lorry you're charged with a breach of the peace and locked in a cell.

Another woman who took part in a demonstration at Thatcher's visit to Porthcawl was furious at the police attitude to her and her friends:

We were waiting outside for Thatcher to arrive. I wanted to go across the road - the police wouldn't let me. I said to them, 'Why am I not allowed to go across the road? Is it because I am not a Tory? (There were a lot of very posh women across the road). Because I'm a socialist? A miner's wife?' The policeman said, 'You need to be policed'. But if we'd been wearing nice frocks and carrying handbags they would have let us go there. Yet it was quite obvious it was a peaceful demonstration.

What concerned and saddened many mothers was the effect the strike was having on their children's attitudes to the police. In Ystrad Hynach the children played 'police and pickets' instead of 'cowboys and indians', and another mother reported:

> What's sad is that my children boo the police through the car windows. And when we went to the demonstration in Cardiff, my two - one's three and one's six - were asking, 'Are the police going to arrest us here today, Mam? Are they nice police or nasty police?'

## THE EFFECTS ON FAMILY LIFE

The strike has put whole families under tremendous emotional strain. Relationships between men and women where both are involved in the strike are difficult, and when the men are at home all day - sometimes because of their bail conditions - there is added tension. In some cases other members of the family don't agree with the strike, or the striking families have relatives in the police force which has led to bad feeling, but the difficulties at home have reinforced their determination to ensure a victory. The women and families of the mining communities have experienced through this strike the equivalent effects of unemployment, and are now even more determined to fight for jobs. The relatively short-term hardship has been borne in the knowledge of how much worse their circumstances would be if they lost, and all hope was gone. And despite the tensions, the overriding factor has been that husbands and wives have been united in their common struggle for a victory.

The women have only two regrets. The first is that their children have had to go without, even though this strike has been for their children's futures. Explaining to their children why they can't have all the things they've been used to has been difficult. They knew that Christmas would be very different, and many mothers feared their children wouldn't understand. The contradictions in fighting for their children's future while denying their immediate needs has really hurt. However, on the whole the children - especially the younger ones - have been very good and have accepted the situation, and parents and friends have helped tremendously:

> My parents and my husband's parents have been good, otherwise they were wearing slippers to school before the summer holidays, but they've bought them shoes now.

The second regret is that they have had to depend on their relatives, often on retired parents living on State pensions. Coupled with the gratitude they feel towards their families who have helped them through this very difficult period is the feeling expressed by a women in Ferndale:

> Our families are being pretty good. I have lost my independence during this strike. I never had to borrow money off my mother until now. Having to rely on relatives for financial help is not easy, but elderly parents have paid their bills for food, HP (Hire-Purchase), and other basic necessities. In some families, of course, the parents themselves have been on strike. One family in Beddau had ten members working in the pit, and could offer each other very little help. But again, the longer-term prospects if the miners lose would be much bleaker: There would be ten in our family out of work, if the Cwm shut. I've got a son and a daughter on the dole now. Our sons can't even get into the pits. There's nothing for them.

# WELFARE BENEFITS

> I have lived through the '72 and the '74 strikes and
> it was tough but it was a picnic compared to this
> strike. Believe me, this is a tough one.

Striking families have not only the media and the police
to contend with but also the Department of Health and Social
Security (DHSS). The deduction of fifteen pounds and now
sixteen pounds per week from the Supplementary Benefit (to
counterbalance the theoretical strike pay which the NUM cannot
afford) has caused particular bitterness and anger because this
is a new measure introduced since the '72 and '74 strikes. But
this attempt to 'starve them back to work', while intensifying
their financial problems, has not weakened their resolve. But it
is mainly the women who are having to make ends meet at home
and deal with a largely unsympathetic and unhelpful DHSS staff:

> We went to our office at the beginning of the strike
> and there were lots of people there and one woman
> to deal with them all. I got to the counter and
> she said there was nothing they could do. I asked
> if there was somewhere else we could go because
> we couldn't live on three pounds odd a week - we
> couldn't keep the little boy on that - and she said
> there was nowhere at all we could go. They just
> didn't want to help.

> There are many miners we know who have supported
> their families for years and now for the first time
> they have to go hand in hand to the Social Security.
> They hate having to do it. And all they get there is
> officialdom, no real help.

Many of the DHSS staff have implied that the problems are
self-induced. A woman in Ystrad Mynach was refused Maternity
Benefit on the grounds that her husband could go back to work

at any time, and a woman in Oakdale had to wait three weeks with several costly bus trips to the DHSS offices before she was sent a Giro for a mere ten pounds fifty. Even in cases of particular difficulty, families have had to survive as best they could:

> One woman had a boy in hospital, and she asked the DHSS for help to buy him pyjamas and slippers and also with the fares for visiting him because she didn't have a penny, but they said they were very sorry but they couldn't help.

Although household incomes have varied according to individual circumstances, such as women working in part-time jobs while their husbands have been on strike, some women received £28, £31, £37 per week, including their Family Allowance of £6.50 to keep up to five people. Some received less:

> I work in the (National Coal Board) canteen, so I'm on strike as well. We receive £3.28 for myself, my husband and our son, £6.50 Family Allowance, so we get about £10.00 per week.

In response to the reduction of the Supplementary Benefit and the difficulties in extracting any information from the DHSS on their entitlements, women have formed their own groups to give advice and provide practical help. For example:

> One of the women on our committee, her daughter fell off her bike and broke her jaw, so all her food had to be liquidised. The DHSS looked into the case and said they were very sorry but it wasn't an illness so there was nothing they could do. We felt as a group we should do something, and so we bought her a liquidiser. But then someone from Social Services came to the hall and said they could buy her a liquidiser. We won't lose out because we can raffle the first liquidiser.

Shared experiences and information passed from group to group have enabled the women to learn from one another and also support each other in their claims for benefits. Besides looking after their immediate families, they have supported unmarried miners who are not entitled to any State benefit at all. There was a sit-in in Cwmbran to try and force the DHSS to allow payments to single miners, but this tactic failed. A street blockade was planned in Aberdare, where an unmarried miner had been threatened with disconnection of his gas and electricity. But in the end the NUM intervened with the Electricity Board and Wales Gas, and his debts have been frozen until after the strike.

## LIFE IN THE LONG TERM

The women's anticipation of victory and a longing to get back to normal is counter-balanced by their dread of the end of the strike. Banks and local companies may have been more lenient than HP companies, because they rely on local goodwill to keep their customers, but the women anticipate an 'avalanche' of bills from creditors all expecting payment in the first week:

> I know with my two mortgages now I'm about £1,500 in arrears. It's about £60 a month. So I don't know what we'll owe when it's over. There is no way I'm going to be able to find that kind of money when he goes back, because everyone is going to want payment.

> After the strikes over we are all going to have big problems. And there will be interest to pay on many of our debts – like to the bank and so on.

> It's going to take years. But we all knew this in the beginning anyhow. We were told by our union that it's going to be a hard fight and a hard slog, and

we knew we wouldn't have the strike money and we knew a lot of these things, so we didn't go into it with our eyes closed.

So the financial problems will be far from over. The end of the strike will mean starting from minus square one. Savings have been spent, home comforts which have taken years to build up are gone. Striking families have witnessed the quick collapse and devaluation of things they've worked for over the years. It has been hard to keep up the spirited defiance for which the women of the South Wales mining communities are famous:

> I get depressed every other day. One day I'm happy and I think, 'Right, I'm going to have to fight now, and fight all the way'. Then another day I'm very depressed and I think the opposite way. But I still turn out on rallies, and I still try to do my little bit of collecting and picketing and things like that because I think that although I'm depressed I put those things behind me because three quarters of me wants to win anyhow … But that depression is bound to come in because we haven't got money to live, and there's pressures coming on you all the time.

There are a number of reasons why some women have to deal with the depression on their own: sometimes husbands discourage their wives from involvement with the local group, sometimes women lack confidence to make the initial contact. Women in support groups feel under pressure themselves but also feel sorry for those women who have to manage in isolation at home. The support groups have not only been a source of practical help, but have also provided a forum for discussing mutual problems, for sharing fears and hopes, and have given women a confidence and resolution that will long outlast the strike.

There's no way I'm going to sit down in the house
after this is over, after being so active. We've been
so strong now that it would be pointless not to stay
together. And many of the women's support groups
will stay together.

Some women will be pressing for recognition and representation within the NUM:

I know we're brought in as a women's support group,
that's the idea and we don't mind that, but it's nice
sometimes that we have more of a say, which we
don't have really.

But they will also be campaigning on other fronts, and
returning the support that people have offered them:

We've got a strong pressure group which we can
use to protect our communities and fight for what
it needs in all sorts of ways. Some of us have made
friends and contacts in coalfields all over Britain.
The latter support group has begun to establish a
co-operative to make and sell crafts as a long-term
proposition.

The women have changed through giving up financial
security and a normal family life in the present to fight for
those very things in the future. They have changed not only
as individuals, but their relationships with the men in the
mining communities have altered, and they have changed
the communities in which they live. The strike has changed
the whole nature of politics. Although they don't think of
themselves as being special, the strength and resolve of the
women can be felt by all those who have spoken with them.
Their endurance seems to know no limits; their energy
is boundless; their imagination and cheerfulness has
touched people far and wide. For the people of the mining

communities life has changed: through this struggle they have ensured that their lives will never by the same again. As a woman from Neath said:

> This strike had extraordinary effects. Out of something that is terrible, something very good has grown. We know we have the strength to do a lot of things.

# LONG-TERM IMPRISONMENT IN NORTHERN IRELAND

## PSYCHOLOGICAL OR POLITICAL SURVIVAL?

**Bill Rolston and Mike Tomlinson**

*This chapter is a paper originally presented at the Hamburg conference in 1985 and published in Working papers in European criminology, volume 7, 'The Expansion of European Penal Systems', pp. 162-183*

## INTRODUCTION

This paper is a report on an ongoing project. What we are seeking to do is to open up a series of questions concerning the population of long-term prisoners in Northern Ireland (NI). Our interest in the position of long termers is triggered by a number of factors:

1.  In a European context, NI's prisons contain an unusually high proportion of persons serving long sentences and particularly life sentences. This situation is of recent origin.

2. Many of these prisoners find themselves incarcerated as a result of policing techniques and a criminal system specially adapted for the eradication of political violence. For the foreseeable future there is no reason to expect that the prisons will be short on new recruits to the long-term population.

3. There are some signs of public disquiet over long-term imprisonment from people and groups other than the prisoners themselves or their relatives and friends.[1]

4. The Northern Ireland Office (NIO), at about the same time as we became involved in researching the subject, issued an 'explanatory memorandum' on 'lifers', which, if taken as a statement of policy, does little more than formalise practices and procedures which have long been criticised by penal reformers in Britain.

The first section of the paper reviews the published statistics on prison reception and discharges and suggests that the large long-term population raises a number of problems both for policy and for the sociology of the prison. The second section looks at some of the social scientific work which has sought to tackle the question of how people survive long spells of incarceration and what effects it has on them. As we shall see, the evidence is still very contradictory and open-ended, but there are a number of insights which seem applicable to the NI situation, equally, there are significant gaps in the literature revealed by that same situation. In the third section we put forward some tentative ideas regarding the uniqueness or otherwise of long-term imprisonment in NI, based on interviews with some prisoners and their relatives.

---

[1]   In particular, see Northern Ireland Association for the Care and Resettlement of Offenders (NIACRO), *Detention at the Secretary of State's Pleasure.* (Belfast: NIACRO) 1984; Northern Ireland Office, *Life Sentence Prisoners in Northern Ireland: An Explanatory Memorandum.* (Belfast: NIO) 1985; Northern Ireland Assembly, *Official Report*, No 15, col. 583, June 20th, 1984.

# LONG-TERM IMPRISONMENT: TRENDS IN NORTHERN IRELAND

Long-term imprisonment is a social construct. There is no general agreement from one country to another as to the definition of 'short' or 'long' prison sentences. We can observe, though, that in countries where penal policy is such that the State attempts to dispose of convicted persons in ways other than sending them to prison, the dividing line tends to be low, 'long-term' comes to mean sentences of, for example, more than one year. In contrast, countries with a strong propensity to imprison, and, more specifically, with judiciaries keen on long sentences, such as Britain and West Germany, have a much higher cut-off point. Even within the United Kingdom, conventions vary. As Fitzgerald and Sim[2] write:

> In England and Wales, a long-termer is a man serving over four years, or a woman serving over three years. In Scotland it is anybody serving over eighteen months.

These conventions also change over time. In the case of NI, prisoners used to be categorised in the manner explained in the Report on the Administration of Home Office Services for 1961:

> The principle categories are short-term prisoners, who are serving sentences of less than two years imprisonment, long-term prisoners, who are serving two years and above, corrective trainees, preventive detainees and young prisoners.[3]

---

[2]  M. Fitzgerald and J. Sim, *British Prisons* (London: Blackwell (1979), 20.

[3]  Under the Criminal Justice Act (NI) 1953, 'persistent offenders' of either sex could be sentenced to 'corrective training' or 'preventive detention'. The former meant a sentence of two to seven years, and was applied only to those over 21 years and, in practice, those under 30. In theory, 'trainees' worked an eight hour day on a range of manual trades which would provide them with a livelihood on release. Such prisoners were normally eligible for release on license after serving two-thirds of their sentence. Preventive detention was intended for those over 30 years of age 'from whose persistent criminal activities the public requires protection'. Release on license was considered after serving two years or one-half of the sentence, whichever was the greater.

But during the 1970s the prison administration adopted the British standard, now a long-termer is someone serving a sentence of four years or more, if male, three years if female. Even with this relatively high cut-off point, however, there is no disguising the fact that the numbers of long termers in NI's prisons has risen dramatically in the last fifteen years. It should be noted also that while the description 'long-termer' is reserved in the official statistics to sentenced prisoners, some of those held on remand as a result of 'supergrass evidence' have served the equivalent of a long-term sentence with 50% remission, that is, two years.[4]

50% remission was introduced in 1976[5] as part of the 'criminalisation' strategy of the NIO. The end result of this policy has been a major change in prison regime since 1976, whereby lifers are subjected to 'normal' prison conditions in the H Blocks as opposed to the 'special category' conditions in the compounds. Consequently, where there were 1,476 special category prisoners in the compounds in February 1976 - 895 of them Republicans and 581 Loyalists[6] - there are now less than 175 such prisoners.[7] The numbers will continue to decline.

---

[4]    See Belfast Bulletin, *Supergrasses*, Bulletin No II. (Belfast) 1984.

[5]    Under the Treatment of Offenders (NI) Order 1976, anyone granted remission who is convicted of an imprisonable offence subsequently can be returned to prison to serve all or part of the balance of their sentence remaining at the time the court makes the order.

[6]    K. Kelley, *The Longest War Northern Ireland and the IRA*. (Dingle: Brandon Book Publishers) 1982, 251.

[7]    Belfast Telegraph 5(1): 85.

**Table 1** Length of Sentences of Male Prisoners Committed in Each Year 1960-69

|  | SHORT-TERM | LONG-TERM | | | | TOTAL |
|---|---|---|---|---|---|---|
|  | Less than 4 years | 4 to less than 8 years | 8 years or more | Life | Total |  |
| 1960 | 1385 | 14 | 6 | 0 | 20 | 1405 |
| 1961 | 1381 | 21 | 3 | 3 | 17 | 1408 |
| 1962 | 1336 | 13 | 3 | 0 | 16 | 1552 |
| 1963 | 1439 | 20 | 4 | 0 | 24 | 1463 |
| 1964 | 1560 | 8 | 2 | 0 | 10 | 1570 |
| 1965 | 1528 | 8 | 1 | 0 | 9 | 1537 |
| 1966 | 1849 | 24 | 5 | 4 | 33 | 1882 |
| 1967 | 2221 | 11 | 0 | 2 | 13 | 2234 |
| 1968 | 1911 | 33 | 8 | 0 | 41 | 1952 |
| 1969 | 2115 | 15 | 2 | 0 | 17 | 2132 |

*Source* Annual Reports on the Administration of Home Office Services

**Table 2** Length of Sentences of Female Prisoners Committed in Each Year 1960-69

|  | SHORT-TERM | LONG-TERM | | | | TOTAL |
|---|---|---|---|---|---|---|
|  | Less than 3 years | 3 to less than 8 years | 8 years or more | Life | Total |  |
| 1960 | 120 | 2 | 0 | 0 | 2 | 122 |
| 1961 | 105 | 0 | 0 | 0 | 0 | 105 |
| 1962 | 123 | 1 | 0 | 0 | 1 | 124 |
| 1963 | 100 | 0 | 0 | 0 | 0 | 100 |
| 1964 | 111 | 0 | 0 | 0 | 0 | 111 |
| 1965 | 79 | 0 | 0 | 0 | 0 | 79 |
| 1966 | 82 | 2 | 0 | 0 | 2 | 84 |
| 1967 | 82 | 0 | 0 | 1 | 1 | 83 |
| 1968 | 47 | 1 | 0 | 0 | 1 | 48 |
| 1969 | 37 | 0 | 0 | 0 | 0 | 37 |

*Source* Annual Reports on the Administration of Home Office Services

Applying the current 'four years or more' definition of long-term to the 1960s, we can see from Tables 1 and 2 that long-termers committed in any one year ranged from nine (in 1965) to 42 (in 1968).[8] Expressed as a percentage of total committals, long-termers were consistently below 2%, except in 1968 (2.1%) Only seven women received long sentences, and only one of these was 'life'. Nine life sentences were given to men in the same period.

The picture changes markedly after 1972, as revealed by tables 3 and 4. Long-termers increase to more than a quarter of all committals by 1975, and a similar trend is observable for women. The tables also highlight a bulge which occurred in the mid-1970s and in the second half of the 1970s with respect to lifers.

**Table 3** Length of Sentences of Male Prisoners Committed in Each Year 1970-79

|  | SHORT-TERM | LONG-TERM |  |  |  | TOTAL | LONG TERM SENTENCES AS PERCENTAGE OF ALL COMMITTALS |
|---|---|---|---|---|---|---|---|
|  | Less than 4 years | 4 to less than 8 years | 8 years or more | Life | Total |  |  |
| 1970 | 2148 | 34 | 0 | 0 | 34 | 2182 | 1.4% |
| 1971 | 2189 | 12 | 1 | 4 | 17 | 2206 | 0.8% |
| 1972 | 1906 | 11 | 4 | 3 | 18 | 1924 | 0.9% |
| 1973 | 1672 | 151 | 62 | 14 | 227 | 1899 | 12.0% |
| 1974 | 1475 | 274 | 161 | 26 | 461 | 1936 | 23.8% |
| 1975 | 1442 | 281 | 167 | 65 | 513 | 1955 | 26.2% |
| 1976 | 1465 | 221 | 204 | 57 | 482 | 1947 | 24.8% |
| 1977 | 1599 | 263 | 304 | 80 | 647 | 2246 | 28.8% |
| 1978 | 1558 | 175 | 150 | 46 | 371 | 1929 | 19.2% |
| 1979 | 1551 | 157 | 139 | 58 | 354 | 1905 | 18.6% |

*Source* Annual Reports on the Administration of Home Office Services 1970-71; Annual Reports on the Administration of the Prison Service 1976-79

---

[8]   It must be stressed that the vast majority of 'short-term' sentences were for periods of less than one year.

Tables 1 to 4 reveal the intake figures for sentenced prisoners in specific years Table 5, on the other hand, shows the distribution of the sentenced prison population at a fixed point in time, mid-December 1983.

**Table 4** Length of Sentences of Male Prisoners Committed in Each Year 1980-83

|  | SHORT-TERM | LONG-TERM | | | | TOTAL | LONG TERM SENTENCES AS % OF ALL COMMITTALS |
|---|---|---|---|---|---|---|---|
|  | Less than 4 years | 4 to less than 8 years | 8 years or more | Life | Total |  |  |
| 1980 | 977 | 110 | 78 | 25 | 213 | 1190 | 17.9% |
| 1981 | 1253 | 128 | 81 | 33 | 242 | 1495 | 16.2% |
| 1982 | 1346 | 154 | 91 | 22 | 267 | 1613 | 16.6% |
| 1983 | 1541 | 150 | 71 | 14 | 235 | 1776 | 13.2% |

*Source* Annual Reports on the Administration of the Prison Service 1980-83

Two points are of note in relation to this table. Firstly, the size of the lifer population has grown from 13 in 1969, through 181 in 1976 and 377 in 1980, to 421 in 1983. Secondly, there are distinct differences between the sentence profiles of scheduled (political) and non-scheduled prisoners. Only 13% of scheduled prisoners are serving short-term sentences, while only 16% of non-scheduled prisoners are serving long-term sentences.

More than one-fifth of the sentenced population currently in prison is made up of lifers. The question arises as to whether these trends are likely to continue. Two factors must be taken account of here firstly, any changes which may occur in the levels of political violence and the State's response, and secondly, the policy regarding the release of lifers. It is not the business of this paper to detail the policies adopted to contain political violence, but suffice to say that special powers, inter-rogation methods, the Diplock courts and latterly the use of informers have all contribute to the capability to put people behind bars for 'life'. There is no reason to believe that the State will run out of the means or the will to continue to do the same in the immediate future.

**Table 5** Sentenced Prison Population mid-December 1983

| SENTENCE LENGTH | SCHEDULED (Political) | NON-SCHEDULED | TOTAL |
|---|---|---|---|
| Less than 4 yrs | 187 | 494 | 681 |
| 4 to less than 8 yrs | 242 | 74 | 316 |
| 8 yrs or more (excludes life) | 624 | 21 | 645 |
| Life | 420 | 1 | 421 |
| Totals | 1473 | 590 | 2063 |

*Source* NIO statistics, cited in MacNiallais, 1984

On the other hand, we do need to examine the proce-dures for releasing lifers. The formal position is set out in a paper issued by the NIO in January 1985, a paper which was a response to the detailed submission of the NI Associa-tion for the Care and Resettlement of Offenders (NIACRO) on the problems surrounding 'detention at the Secretary of State's pleasure'. Around 60 persons are currently held for an indefinite period because they were found guilty of murder committed when under the age of eighteen. As Caul[9] shows, the vast majority of SOSPs (as they are called) were convicted between 1974 and 1979, and in this sense, SOSPs are a 'once-off' population who could be subject to a 'once-off' solution. However, just as the Baker review of the Emergency Provisions Act begged the question as to whether SOSPs should be treated any differently from lifers, so too

---

9    B. Caul. 'Juvenile Offending in Northern Ireland a Statistical Overview'. In The Juvenile Justice System in Northern Ireland, edited by B. Caul, J. Pinkerton and F. Powell. (Ulster Polytechnic, 1983), 62.

the present government has decided to treat the two categories of prisoners under a similar review procedure.

As the NIO memorandum explains, a life sentence gives
the State the power to detain someone for the whole of their
life. Lifers can be, and are, however, released on a conditional
license. These conditions – such as the requirement to see
a probation officer periodically – may be changed and even
cancelled providing the licensee 'has shown that he has settled
down in the community and his behaviour has not given
any cause for concern'. A license may also be revoked, with
the consequence that the licensee is recalled to prison. Any
offences or a breach of the license conditions can result in the
license being revoked, it can also be revoked '*where there are
grounds for believing* that the licensee might again be a danger
to the public' (our emphasis).

Life sentence prisoners have their cases reviewed regularly, according to the NIO memorandum. There are annual
reports furnished by prison officers which discuss the behaviour and attitude of the prisoners, his or her relationships,
family, work performance and education.

After three years the Life Sentence Unit of the NIO reviews
the case. Further reviews are held six and ten years into the
sentence. Prisoners are now informed when their cases are
being examined by the Life Sentence Review Board and are
invited to make a written statement. They may also petition
the Secretary of State. This is the extent of their 'rights', they
may not appear before the Board, or be represented, and they
are given no indication as to why the Board makes its recommendations. Thus they have no basis from which to adapt their
attitude or behaviour (if they so choose) to measure up to
the Board's standards these are invisible.[10] The memorandum
does indicate in a very general way what is required, but it is
clear that the main concern is to use the review procedure

---

[10] On the secrecy surrounding the British parole system, see S. Cohen and L. Taylor, *Prison Secrets*. (London: Radical Alternatives to Prison/NCCL) 1978; I. Cameron, 'Life in the Balance the Case of Frank Marritt.' In Causes for Concern British Criminal Justice on Trial? edited by P. Scraton and P. Gordon (eds), (Harmondsworth, Penguin) 1984.

to control prisoners, particularly non-conforming or political prisoners. As stated, reports on prisoners:

> cannot be completed in any meaningful way where the prisoner refuses to cooperate in the reporting procedure, and will necessarily be fuller and generally more informative where a prisoner is taking part in a normal prison regime.

In fact, those prisoners who are converted to conformity cannot be fully trusted:

> even where a prisoner may clam, or indicate by his behaviour and attitude in custody, that he has given up his paramilitary associations, the question must arise whether this can be relied upon in view of the pressures which he may face if and when he returns to his former environment.

The reader of the memorandum might be forgiven for wondering if any lifers are ever released. Statistics on the numbers discharged from prison were published for the first time in 1977. In that year, four lifers, all men, were released, along with 281 other long-termers. Table 6 details the more recent releases of lifers. Long-termers as a whole would appear to be being released at a rate of approximately 300 per year (which is above the current committal rate for long-termers), but it remains the case that lifers are being committed at three or four times the rate at which they are being released.

**Table 6** Number of Lifers Released 1981-3

| YEAR | MEN | WOMEN |
|------|-----|-------|
| 1981 | 6 | 2 |
| 1982 | 7 | 0 |
| 1983 | 3 | 2 |

*Source* Annual Reports on the Administration of the Prison Service, 1981-3

Perhaps the most striking feature of the NIO memorandum is the determination it reveals to apply the policies developed in Britain in response to the renewed calls for retribution. It squashes the notion, widely held by British lifers[11] that 'life' means serving around ten years, a 'misconception' said to be based on commuted sentences of capital punishment (the death sentence was finally abolished in Britain in 1965, and in NI in 1973 under the Emergency Provisions Act). Under new guidelines for England and Wales announced by the Home Secretary in October 1983, certain categories of murder, 'including terrorist-type murder', will mean serving a minimum of twenty years.[12] The mid-to-late-1970s 'bulge' referred to earlier, might, under the ten year notion, have been expected to lead to a similar bulge of releases in the mid-1980s, but there are no indications of this as yet.

One final point in the memorandum is worth noting. Reference is made to preparation for release of lifers, because 'the prisoner is likely to need help to readjust to outside conditions after a long period in custody'. This is the only hint of official concern at the possible effects of long sentences, but it is only a hint. It is unclear whether or not this suggestion is informed by the available research on the social and psychological consequences of long-term imprisonment, which we review in the next section, but our contention is that policy

---

[11]  See P. Sapsford, *Life Sentence Prisoners Reaction, Response and Change.* (Milton Keynes, Open University Press) 1983.

[12]  For a view arguing instead for lower sentences, see L. Blom-Cooper, 'The Penalty for Murder.' *The Howard Journal* 21 (1982): 129-132.

towards long-termers, especially lifers, is more wrapped up in politics and problems of control than in concerns about the welfare of the prisoner.

The main issues arising from this section can be summarised as follows. The consequences of the massive build-up of the long-term prison population in NI have been the subject of very little research.[13] It is inevitable that there have been major consequences for the administration of the prison system, as well as for the State, although the latter seems remarkably unconcerned – if the NIO memorandum is anything to go by – about the fact that it is sitting on what might well be a 'time bomb'. Moreover, it would seem logical to expect that severe stresses result from the discretionary and indeterminate nature of life sentences; stresses not only for individual prisoners, but also for their relatives and the political movements which support them. It is to this latter point that we turn our attention in the rest of the paper.

## THE EFFECTS OF IMPRISONMENT: A REVIEW OF THE LITERATURE

Studies of the effects of imprisonment fall into a number of categories which reflect both the distinctive concerns of different academic disciplines and the variety of approaches

---

[13] Although there has been a considerable amount written on NI's criminal justice system, the focus has tended to be on issues such as interrogation, the courts, policing, emergency law, etc. Particularly since the end of internment, prison has received somewhat less attention than might have been expected and what literature there is has tended to be Journalistic (see T. P. Coogan, *On the Blanket.* (Dublin: Ward River Press) 1980; N. McCafferty, *The Armagh Women.* (Dublin: Co-op Books) 1981), autobiographical (see M. Darcy, *Tell them Everything.* (London: Pluto Press) 1981; B. Sands, *The Diary of Bobby Sands.* (Dublin: Sinn Fein Publicity Department) 1981 or polemical (see D. Faul and R. Murray, R, *H Blocks: British Jail for Irish Political Prisoners.* (Dungannon: Authors) 1979; P. Robinson, *Self-Inflicted an Exposure of the H Block Issue.* (Belfast: Democratic Unionist Party) 1980). For the few items which attempt to go further, see C. Crawford, *Long Kesh: An Alternative Perspective.* (Cranfield Institute of Technology) 1979; P. Heatley and M. Tomlinson 'The Politics of Imprisonment in Ireland: Some Historical Notes.' in *Securing the State: Politics of Internal Security in Europe,* edited by P. Hillyard and P. Squires. (Bristol: European Group for the Study of Deviance and Social Control) 1982; P. Hillyard, 'Police and Penal Services.' in Violence and the Social Services in Northern Ireland, edited by J. Darby and A. Williamson. (London: Heinemann) 1978.

within particular disciplines. There are studies, such as Clemmer's pioneering Prison Community,[14] which tackle the subject by exploring traditional sociological concepts - the relationship of individuals to groups, conflicting roles, norms and values, problems of social integration and organization. More recently, two further approaches can be identified in the sociological literature. Firstly, there is the 'structural' approach, seeking to establish links between the broad historical developments of capitalist societies and forms of punishment.[15] The politics of imprisonment are often to the forefront here.[16] Secondly, there is the more social-psychological approach (sometimes loosely referred to as 'phenomenological'), of which the influential *Psychological Survival*[17] is the prime example. This particular work also directly engages penal policy. Psychologists, particularly 'experimentalists' and 'behaviouralists' have made a substantial contribution to the literature.[18]

In part, the different theories and methods that have been applied to the problem of how prison affects people can be related to historical developments in penal policy. According to Flanagan[19], many early studies assumed that the 'pains of imprisonment' were ubiquitous, they failed to be sensitive to the notion that 'facing and serving a term of life or twenty years may be fundamentally different from facing and serving a term of two, three or four years'[20]. Another common assumption was that prisoners, particularly long-term prisoners, like

14    D. Clemmer, *The Prison Community*. (New York: Holt, Rinehart and Winston) 1940.
15    M. Foucault, *Discipline and Punish the Birth of the Prison*. (London: Allen Lane) 1977; A. Ignatieff, *A Just Measure of Pain*. (London: MacMillan) 1978; D. Melossi and M. Pavarini, *The Prison and the Factory*. (London: MacMillan) 1981.
16    M. Fitzgerald, *Prisoners in Revolt*. (Harmondsworth: Penguin) 1977.
17    S. Cohen and L. Taylor, Psychological Survival. (Harmondsworth: Penguin) 1977.
18    P. Banister et al, 'Psychological Correlates of Long-term Imprisonment.' *British Journal of Criminology*,13(4 1973): 312-330; K. Heskin et al, 'Psychological Correlates of Long-term Imprisonment Attitudinal Variables.' *British Journal of Criminology* 14(2 1976): 150-7; N. Bolton et al, 'Psychological Correlates of Long-term Imprisonment a Longitudinal Analysts', *British Journal of Criminology* 16(1 1976): 38-47.
19    T. Flanagan, 'Lifers and Long-termers Doing Big Time.' in The Pains of imprisonment, edited by R. Johnson and H. Toch. (London: Sage) 1982.
20    *Ibid, 115.*

inmates of other 'total institutions', were subject to progressive deterioration and dependence. Whether one calls the process one of 'institutionalisation'[21] or 'prisonisation'[22], there was the general belief that long spells in prison inevitably led to withdrawal and depression, or what Seligman[23] has called 'learned helplessness'.

Certainly in the British context, the abolition of the death penalty resulted in a resurgence of research. Setting aside the debate over the extent to which abolition contributed to the increase in long-term imprisonment, the historical trend towards longer sentences has given a very contemporary urgency to the problem of effects, especially psychological and physical damage. As Cohen and Taylor[24] remark

> In the absence of the death penalty, transportation
> or deliberate physical torture, the only way our
> society can think of dealing with certain offenders
> is to send them to prison for very long periods.

The same authors make the point that psychologists have tended to dominate officially sponsored research into long-termers. They attack such research for its WDP - 'window dressing potential' - on the grounds that

> a principal function of official research into crime
> and punishment is to reassure the public that the
> problem is being scientifically tackled.[25]

In particular, those responsible for penal policy and the custody of prisoners need the scientific resources from which to fend off criticisms of the prison system. Prisoners have thus been subjected to batteries of tests, such as the MMPI

21    E. Goffman, *Asylums*. (New York: Doubleday) 1961.
22    D. Clemmer, *The Prison Community*. (New York: Holt, Rinehart and Winston) 1940.
23    M. Seligman, *Helplessness*. (San Francisco: W H Freeman) 1975.
24    S. Cohen and L. Taylor, Psychological Survival. (Harmondsworth: Penguin) 1977, 188.
25    S. Cohen and L. Taylor, Psychological Survival. (Harmondsworth: Penguin) 1977, 205.

(Minnesota Multiphasic Personality Inventory) and other personality tests, intelligence tests, semantic differential tests, cognitive reasoning tests and so on, not to mention lengthy questionnaires, in-depth interviews and medical examinations. As Sapsford[26] reports, however, the results of all this investigation are inconclusive. On the one hand, many authors have found signs of deterioration ranging from disturbed comprehension, impoverished ability to relate and increased introversion, to clinical depression and hypochondria. A number of authors identify, in particular, similarities between long-term prisoners and schizophrenics. On the other hand, other researchers have found little evidence of deterioration, even among prisoners serving very long terms, or indeterminate sentences such as 'life'. Chief among these studies in a British context is the research of the Durham University team in the 1970s, which found evidence of increases in hostility and decreases in self-esteem among two hundred long-term prisoners. However, none of these changes was highly significant, and in two aspects at least, those of measured intelligence and verbal reasoning, there was actually some evidence of improvement over time'.

In summary, Sapsford[27] concludes

> Some studies find psychological and behavioural deficits which they identify as effects of time spent in prison, others fail to identify such changes. On the whole, the second group are more convincing by their scope and methodology, and at best the case must be considered not proven.

In his own research of sixty 'lifers', Sapsford hoped for some clearer results. He identified twelve areas for examination depression and hopelessness, anxiety, introversion, neuroticism and emotionality, apathy, dependence on staff

---

26    P. Sapsford, *Life Sentence Prisoners Reaction, Response and Change.* (Milton Keynes: Open University Press) 1983.
27    Ibid., *23.*

and routine, motivation to do one's best, sociability, interest in the outside world and outside contacts, concern with release, 'orientation' in time and lack of future time perspective, and general psychiatric state.[28]

The conclusions of his study are clear

> All of the lifers in the sample showed considerable emotional disturbance during the year or so following their reception into prison. This dies down in most people, however, as they settle into the new life.[29]

After the initial 'emotional floundering', prisoners tested showed some signs of increased social introversion over time, but

> the tests of depression, apathy, motivation and dependence on staff or routine do not show any marked loss of competence during the sentence.[30]

Indeed, hopelessness, an essential element of the 'learned helplessness' model of Seligman, decreased significantly. There was no evidence of 'psychosis, personality disorders, sexual abnormality or immaturity of thinking, and no loss of interest in the outside world'.[31] However, longer serving men did have a reduced future time perspective and tended to talk more of the past than the future.

Sapsford was inspired by these findings to reject the whole notion of 'learned helplessness' and indeed of 'institutionalisation', at least in the context of life sentence prisoners. In doing so, he turned from the deterministic psychology of systematic personality destruction to what he terms a 'humanistic psychology'. Thus, he interprets long-term imprisonment in terms which would be familiar to interactionists in sociology. People adapt to circumstances. They engage in many strategies to do so,

---

28   *Ibid., 45.*
29   *Ibid., 62.*
30   *Ibid., 52.*
31   *Ibid., 60.*

whether it is acquiring one's own set of personal belongings, no matter how meagre - a point stressed by Goffman in relation to other 'total institutions'- or in terms of mapping out their own personal territory. In addition, Sapsford's prisoners knew the average life sentence, give or take a year[32], and did their time by literally breaking the sentence down into 'manageable periods'; so many months in a hostel, so many years in an open prison, and so on. Moreover, within the general chore of surviving day to day, of 'just coping', Sapsford looked for evidence of Goffman's four styles of coping - 'colonisation', 'conversion', 'intransigence' and 'situational withdrawal' - and found little. He identified a fifth style, namely, 'escape'. That is, the prisoners he studied often donned specific roles of which they were highly conscious, the prisoner is no longer merely a prisoner, but a student, an orderly, a craftsman, etc. Conforming to these legitimate roles thus becomes the lifeline to continued sanity and lack of deterioration. As Sapsford concludes

> People adapt to even the most extraordinary privations, even concentration camps are situations which have rules and those become to some extent predictable after a while, it is possible to some extent to survive under them.[33]

There are some 'coping' and 'adaptive' strategies reported in the literature which Sapsford does not mention. In a useful summary of the American research, Parisi[34] draws attention to the use of grievance mechanisms and litigation. She suggests that such strategies not only keep prisoners occupied, but also 'help to relieve the tension generated by the degradation of being a prisoner'.[35] Litigation is a popular means of

---

[32]  *Ibid., 78.*
[33]  *Ibid., 62.*
[34]  N. Parisi, *Coping with Imprisonment.* (London: Sage) 1982.
[35]  Sapsford is much more dismissive of litigation. 'A small group may also be distinguished - among the newly-received men - who are still preoccupied with appeals and have not yet come to terms with prison as an inescapable reality'. (P. Sapsford, *Life Sentence Prisoners Reaction, Response and Change.* (Milton Keynes: Open University Press) 1983 p. 88).

addressing individual and collective problems (in that the latter may involve prison conditions generally), though clearly the scope for such action is very dependent on legal resources and a country's constitution[36] Parisi also looks at involvement in non violent and violent collective action by prisoners. This interest in the more collective aspects of survival strategies is absent from Sapsford's study. He thereby misses one of the central functions of prisons, namely, social isolation and individualisation. Prison individualises prisoners, and staff encourage that individualisation by directing it into acceptable (in the prison's terms) channels. The Open University student and the craftsman are ordinarily no threat. But what prison systems discourage and actively suppress is collective consciousness and action among prisoners. Moreover, the prisoner is wrested from a social milieu outside the prison in which he or she had routines and activities, only a few of which in all likelihood could be labelled criminal. The prisoner had family and friends, but being in prison now puts all sorts of obstacles - material and otherwise - in the path of continuing these relationships. Indeed, Sapsford himself points out that while prisoners in his sample maintained good contacts with their 'natal' families (parents, siblings and children),

> wives and girlfriends, on the other hand, had nearly all lost contact by the end of the fifth year, and most dropped off early in sentence.

If the optimistic conclusion about people adapting to even the most extraordinary privations is not to be misunderstood as some sort of justification for regimes administering these privations, then we must put the problem of coping in its full social context. Such a context allows us to include the necessary point that it is not just prisoners who are doing time, it is 'wives and girlfriends' who do not survive the course, it is

---

[36]   in the Irish context see R. Byrne, G. Hogan and P. McDermott, *Prisoners' Rights a Study in Irish Prison Law.* (Dublin: Co-op Books) 1981.

families who do, but at great emotional and financial cost. Prisoners may survive as individuals, as Sapsford aptly shows, by narrowing the gap between their expectations and the reality of their present lives. But much needs to be added to this. Firstly, those who are connected to the prisoner by bonds of kin or friendship have to make similar radical adaptations. Secondly, there is much in the whole experience of imprisonment that is, deliberately or otherwise, individualising for both the prisoners and their families and friends, so what needs to be examined is the potential, if any, for collective survival by both prisoners and their families and friends. Without these additions, the investigation of deterioration in prison is too narrow, and runs the risk of lending legitimacy to penal policy as it stands.

Since the abolition of the death penalty in Britain, some sociologists have been counted among those who have critically examined the prison system. In addition, some have lobbied for alternatives to prison, whether it be in terms of prison reform (such as lessening of overcrowding, liberalisation of prison regime, etc) or, more widely, for the abolition of prison altogether. But, while such approaches have been strong on structural analysis and indeed on political commitment (there is no chance of them being misunderstood as legitimising penal policy as it stands), they may be criticised for over-concentration on long-term structural change at the expense of 'short-term' concern with collective survival.

It is now widely recognised that a number of factors, relating specifically to sentencing and the indeterminacy of sentences, are responsible for major stresses on prisoners and their social contacts outside the prison. Sentencing disparity is a major source of frustration amongst prisoners.[37] The vagaries of the parole system and other review procedures have been under attack in Britain and America for well over a decade.[38] The apparent inconsistency of decisions flowing

---

[37]  Toch, *Living in Prison the Ecology of Prison Survival.* 1977.
[38]  Flanagan, 'Explaining the Parole Decision' 1982.

from such procedures is perceived to be related to prisoners' willingness to surrender their identity to the correctional ideology of penal policy. 'Trouble-makers', those who protest, write to politicians, etc, are obvious candidates for continued incarceration. However, it is also the case that prisoners who appear to conform to the correctional ideology and who fulfil the requirements of rehabilitation - a place to go to on release, secure relationships outside the 'criminal world', work or good prospects of a job - are likewise at risk of failing to gain release. Shirley and Peter Adams put it like this

> Shirley: 'They (the Home Office) like to be in a very controlling situation with people in their charge, or their care. I think that applies to the welfare, and to the Home Office and to the prison in general'

> Peter: 'If somebody has got the very things that the Parole Board say they require in order to release a man, at the same time they resent it. They don't like independence. And if you display any kind of independence at all in a prison, you force them to see you as an individual, and they can't cope with that. They only want to talk about a case, or the population, they don't want to talk about individuals'[39]

Independence, however expressed, is not a recipe for release.

The failings of perspectives which see prisoners in isolation from social relationships external to the prison have been recognised in a recently published study by the Nottingham Prisoners' Families Project. As they point out, nothing substantial had been published in Britain on the subject of 'throughcare' with prisoners' families (that is, working with the entire family during the imprisonment of one member

---

[39]   Abolitionist, 'Interview with Shirley and Peter Adams.' 1983. See also Adams, *Knockback*, 1983; Boyle, *A Sense of Freedom*, 1977; McVicar, *By Himself*, 1974.

of it) since Pauline Morris' classic *Prisoners and their Families*[40], almost twenty years earlier. In addition, they criticised the Probation Service because they

> had not, in the normal course, seen the family as a client, but rather as an influence on the behaviour of the offender - important, but to some degree secondary.

While the above concern may be criticised for extending the client status to prisoners' families, it does at least reflect a growing concern with how the families of prisoners adapt to prison. Jean Craig's research[41] provides an interesting footnote on this in the NI context. She found that respondents who had served more than five years reported fewer problems of adjustment to life outside prison than those who had served one to five years. This is explained as follows

> The marked drop in reported difficulties amongst respondents whose sentence was over five years is a function of the fact that those whose sentence was more than eight years (all 'terrorist-type' offenders) had no reported difficulties. This is possibly an indication of the high levels of family and community support 'terrorist-type' offenders are known to enjoy'[42].

## LIFE-SENTENCE PRISONERS AND THEIR FAMILIES IN NI

It is clear that most long-term prisoners in NI would not be in prison were it not for the political situation. Indeed, prisoners have at times been central to the political situation. Thus, historically relatives have featured prominently in prisoners' support groups, in the recent 'troubles'

---

40   Morris, *Prisoners and their Families. 1965.*
41   Craig, *The Probation Throughcare Services*, 1984.
42   *Ibid., 38.*

alone these have included the Political Hostages Release Committee (during internment), the Relatives' Action Committee (in the early days of 'criminalisation') and the H Blocks and Armagh Committees (during the no-wash protest and the hunger strike). The question of how prisoners and their families survive imprisonment, therefore, must be answered within the notion of collective survival. For many political prisoners and their relatives prison is not merely an individual experience.

Of course, it is also an individual experience for both prisoner and relative. So the further question arises of whether what is recorded in the literature about the problems and techniques of individual survival is relevant to the NI experience. In the course of interviewing a number of prisoners and their relatives, we found that many of the points from the literature did fit, but with some qualifications. In addition, there is also scope to apply some of the conclusions of the literature to relatives.

As we noted earlier, prisoners in Britain seem to be highly aware of what 'life' means on average. In this sense, what is an indeterminate sentence becomes, at least psychologically, somewhat determinable. In NI the position of 'lifers' is more precarious. Not enough of them have been released to allow for the calculation of a realistic average, except to say that it looks like it is more than ten or eleven years.

The indeterminacy of the life sentence is in stark contrast to the determinacy of other sentences, with their 50% remission. In short, the initial problem facing lifers and their relatives in NI is that of indeterminacy. As one prisoner's wife put it

> I was hoping he would get an 18 or 20 year sentence rather than a life sentence, the reason being you would get a date and see a light at the end of the tunnel.

For prisoner and relative alike depression in the face of such indeterminacy is always a possibility. However, there does seem to come a point where both can settle down. One wife says of her husband[43]

> At first I noticed he was always saying to me 'What's happening?' and always looking for information. He still does, but not with maybe the same enthusiasm. He seems to have settled down just a wee bit.

Another woman recounted that she too had settled down

> Before he went in, if I had have thought I would have had to face a life sentence, I wouldn't have thought I'd have been able to cope. At the time I went through a bad patch. All I could do was walk about thinking 'How's he going to survive in jail?'. Until the day I realised, I've three kids who've lost their father and they need a very strong mother.

Seven years after his arrest she could look back and say

> It was harder before the trial because you didn't know what was in front of you I really didn't think in terms of him getting a life sentence. But once he got it, you just had to accept reality. It was easy after the sentence, because you knew what was happening. Looking back on the seven years the time I would hate most to go through again was the time before the trial.

---

[43] Not all long-term prisoners in NI are married. There is little statistical information available on this point. However, MacNiallais, using the records of Green Cross - an organisation which raises money for the support of Republican prisoners' relatives - calculated that of the 445 Republican prisoners from the Belfast area, 271 (or 61%) were single (T. MacNiallais, Prisoners' Families: *Who Serves the Sentence? A Dissertation.* (Ulster Polytechnic, 1984).

The tactics used by prisoners and relatives we have spoken to in coming to terms with 'life' are similar to those noted in the literature. One such tactic is the breaking down of the sentence into manageable periods. However, given the absence of open prison, half-way hostels, etc in NI, and the occurrence of very long periods of remand and often almost equally long trials, it would seem that this tactic is more useful in relation to the beginning of the process rather than the end. We asked one woman if her husband had expected a life sentence when arrested

> He thought maybe it would go to court, that he would be held for a year or so, especially when the remand went on for so long. But by the time they were actually sentenced, he had conditioned himself.

In almost identical terms another woman says of her brother

> By the time he actually got around to being given the sentence, the shock had passed.

Even in the long stretch after the sentencing, there are still landmarks of time. In particular, there is the weekly visit

> You sort of come to a stage on a Wednesday night that you're getting all ready for the visit on a Thursday and you do come to a high. When I come home, I be very bad-tempered because I know I have away to next week to wait.

A second tactic of individual survival is the preservation of some sense of personal privacy. One woman pointed out that her husband does not like to share a cell because he likes to be alone with his thoughts at the end of the day. She and he were married some years before his arrest, so he has a lot of memories which keep him going. He can think back. He himself thinks that he's better off than the younger ones are because he's got all those memories.

For her part, she is also on her own with the children and the home has become her private domain. She realises that she will not easily give that up

I know it's going to be very hard, but I know he's going to have to make the adjustments. I made my adjustments in that I've had to be a one-parent family. So, I do think that when he comes out I'll expect him to suit me. I'll not pamper him.

A third tactic is not to dwell too much on the privations imprisonment brings, whether present or future

I want to wait for him because he's my husband and we had a good relationship, and I have two children belonging to him and I'm determined these people, the Brits, are not going to smash that. But at the same time, I don't like giving up eighteen years of my life and then, when my husband comes home, that all falls through. Where would I go from there? I'll be forty-odd, shit! That depresses me. That's the kind of thing that I have to put out of my mind as soon as it comes in, but it does come into my mind an awful lot.

Another woman recounts how she and her husband differ in their views of one of the privations of the present

He's wanting to be more lovey-dovey than what I would be, even in his letters I'm more like writing to a friend. I don't think about the sex side of our marriage because it's not there and there's no point thinking about it.

Of course, prisoners also have to block things out of their consciousness

> He tells me that whenever he goes back (to the H Blocks after a visit), although he misses us and loves us, he tries not to think about us too much.

Other prisoners cope with the privations of the present in a way reminiscent of long-term hospital cases

> He sometimes would say to me 'God, you think you're bad- there's a fellow in here and he's doing thirty years recommended', or 'There's a wee lad in here and he signed a Statement and he was only sixteen'. Whether that's the only thing that keeps him going, I don't know, but he is always looking at somebody who is worse off than he is.

A further important technique of individual survival is the creation of some social distance between prisoner and relatives. There are certain things which are taboo subjects in visits and letters, prominent among them being finance and health. One wife, now in paid employment, remarks

> We were always very open about money, but now, if he asks me if I'm all right, I don't want to talk about it. That's my business.

A lifer told us that his wife had been in hospital for three days with 'a woman's problem' and it was months later before this came up in conversation between them. Another woman had had a miscarriage and a stillborn baby and was pregnant when her husband was arrested. When the baby was born, it had severe breathing difficulties and was rushed to intensive care. Although depressed, she did not want her husband to be told what had happened.

Both prisoners and relatives realise that this distancing is going on, but neither challenges it because each is doing it

> Maybe he is holding himself up for me on the visits. He could do that. I mean, I do it. Sometimes I'm not feeling the best, but I would go down and let on everything's fine.

Another relative spoke in similar terms

> I would never tell him anything that I thought he would worry unduly about. I wouldn't tell him anything unless I was absolutely sure, in other words, I would be very conscious of not passing on rumour to him. If you've got to wait a full week to confirm whether or not it's true, it must be heartbreaking.

She adds that her husband behaves similarly

> If it was something minor that I could do nothing about, I don't think he'd tell me.

Despite such distancing, it is important to note the extent to which relationships are maintained despite a life sentence

> There may be things we don't talk about, but it's important to remember that we do talk. Being in prison means you're forced to talk, outside you could just walk away from a discussion.

Visits are an essential element in maintaining the relationship

> There's never enough time. The half-hour just flies by. We've had a few visits in which the talking wasn't easy, but those were special visits, say, after the death of my father. It wasn't easy, but then it wouldn't have been easy even at home.

Another woman told us

> To tell you the truth, the only time that I could say
> that I'm relaxed, really and truly relaxed, is when
> I'm on the visit for half an hour. I could fall asleep
> on my visits, I mean, that sounds ridiculous.

The importance of the continuance of the relationship, especially for the prisoner, is expressed well by one wife

> Now and again he probably wonders if I'm going to
> wait on him. He has said to me that as long as he
> has me and the kids there, he can do his time, but
> he couldn't do it on his own. That must be the fear
> of nearly every man who's inside.

It is significant that a great many relationships between prisoners and their families in NI do survive against apparently overwhelming odds. Prisoners can even have close relationships with their children born around the time of their own imprisonment.

> I've kept him as part of the family. The youngest
> talks of his daddy as if he was at home.

One other woman has not been so lucky. Despite two and a half years of effort, her son, when he comes home after a visit to the prison, calls his grandfather 'daddy'.

There are a number of reasons for the maintenance of relationships, including the high status of the political prisoners in the community, especially in Republican communities. When one wife was asked why she had stuck by her husband- doing life for murder- unlike many British long-term prisoners' wives, she said 'Ach, but they're criminals! If he'd stolen something, I'd have died'. The suspicion must be that the position on the Loyalist side is less clear-cut and that ambivalence towards political prisoners causes specific problems, especially for relatives.

Prison systems view the maintenance of strong social ties with the outside world with suspicion. On the one hand, these ties can be one sign of the 'rehabilitation' of the prisoner. On the other hand, they are a potential magnet drawing the prisoner away from the individualisation and social control of the prison system. This ambivalence is enhanced in the NI case, where at least one element in the maintenance of strong social ties with the outside world is political ideology.

All of which must lead to a qualification of Sapsford's notion of prisoners 'escaping' into new and legitimate individual roles. There is of course evidence of prisoners doing just that in NI, for example, one compound prisoner writes of two principles which underlie his (and by extension others') commitment to education

> The first has been that I have never been naive enough to regard education as a 'quicker way out'. My second principle is that it has been a point to refuse to regard education as a substitute for prison work, or especially, an aid to something so vague as rehabilitation.

At the same time, his commitment to education is one factor in his being favourably considered for parole at present. So, education has become his ticket to individual escape.

But education in a less formal sense can become a badge of collective solidarity within the prisons of NI. Republican prisoners, for example, teach themselves and each other Irish history and the Irish language. During the 'no-wash' protest Irish was as much a symbol of defiance as was the blanket. Even though, as one wife joked, 'it's their Irish, I don't think it's an Irish anyone else could understand', it is still one major factor in the preservation of a collective identity.

Similarly, the role of craftsman becomes slightly more dubious (within the prison system's definitions) when the products being produced are Celtic harps and even imitation armalites. Craft work thus becomes a means of proclaiming one's cultural identity and in doing so, strengthening that identity collectively. It is for this reason that it is threatening to the prison system and is frequently controlled, or even curtailed, as it has been in Long Kesh since the mass escape of 1983.

What makes these roles 'dangerous' is that they are imbued with a political motivation and collective solidarity. Even the role of relative, which one had before entering the prison system, can take on the same connotations for both prisoners and those left outside prison can increase the political commitment and solidarity of both prisoners and relatives. As one woman put it

> There's no way it's changed his convictions, if anything, it's hardened them.

And another

> It's not as if you're going in as a single person to face something on your own.

And a third

> He's definitely become more political since he went in. He wants to know what's going on. I can't really keep him up to date because I'm not really up to date myself. He talks about social things outside to the other fellows. I think he's more like a communist than anything else - a Catholic communist - he goes to chapel, like.

Nor is this experience of enhanced political awareness and solidarity confined to prisoners. Relatives outside, especially women, many of whom may have been politically inactive until their partner's imprisonment, become resolute in their opposition to the State

> The thing that keeps me going, to be quite honest, is that I am determined to fight against this.

In doing this, they can find individual strength

> I had to look for some way that I could help him, and having found some way that I thought would help him, that in turn helped me survive.

More importantly, they find themselves part of a movement in which they were either not involved or only marginally involved before, or, if they were involved before, they now have a renewed motivation to belong.

The end result of all this can be a prisoner incorporated into a strong and rewarding collective identity inside the prison, with his or her relatives having the same experience outside. The visit, finally, becomes the interface where the two aspects of this solidarity meet

> The remarkable thing is that a lot of people go up to visit someone in prison and they think that they are going to comfort the prisoner, but the reverse is often true. You go up and maybe you're quite pessimistic about things, and just his attitude, his positive attitude about things, you come away cheered up by the person, the sense of comradeship and the feeling there is of solidarity there with each other in prison. I think that solidarity and that comradeship in a way, because it helps them cope, when they come out to face a visitor, they in fact quite often cheer them up, maybe give them strength, some hope. You often come away feeling that you can face things and that you know what to do.

## CONCLUSION

We would not be foolish enough to believe that everyone survives equally well, even though it is in the interests of the survival of prisoners and relatives to maintain that that is so. There are prisoners who do not make it, who succumb to the individualisation of prison and turn, for example, to drugs. There are relatives who end up isolated and make what can be judged as the ultimate 'betrayal' of 'deserting' the high-status prisoner and living with someone else

> It wouldn't be so bad if your husband wasn't in prison, say, and you were seeing another man. But because your husband's in prison, I mean, that would stay with you forever. That's the kind of stigma that I would imagine would be left the children too, especially in these nationalist areas where the prisoners really get the support. And the wives have got the support, and the children, but when it comes to the end of the day, the men will have the support, because they're inside and the people see it as being a war.

Being on a pedestal as a prisoner's wife can bring its own form of isolation

> They wouldn't understand if I said 'I'm fed up being on my own'. Maybe some night thinking I'd love to go out, but you're always aware you're on your own even if you go out in company. They can't understand that I miss him as a man. Funny enough, my brother, the one who would be very much against my husband's political feelings, he can understand my feelings as a person maybe more than what the rest can, because he doesn't have the political involvement.

At the same time, we would conclude that collective solidarity and political ideology is a major element in the survival of prisoners and their relatives in the NI case. As one woman put it to us

> There's no isolation. You can isolate a political prisoner in the sense that you can put him by himself, but I don't think he'll ever feel he's on his own.

## Bibliography

Abolitionist, No 14, 'Interview with Shirley and Peter Adams.' (London: Radical Alternatives to Prison) 1983

Adams, P. and Knockback, S. London: Duckworth, 1983.

Annual Reports on the Administration of Home Office Services, 1960-71.

Annual Reports on the Administration of the Prison Service, 1976-1983.

Baker Report, Review *of the Northern Ireland (Emergency Provisions) Act 1978,* Cmnd 9222. London: HMSO.

Banister, P. et al. 'Psychological Correlates of Long-term Imprisonment.' *British Journal of Criminology 13*(4 1973): 312-330.

Belfast Bulletin. *Supergrasses*, Bulletin No II. Belfast, 1984.

Blom-Cooper, L. 'The Penalty for Murder.' *The Howard Journal 21* (1982): 129-132.

Bolton, N. et al. 'Psychological Correlates of Long-term Imprisonment: A Longitudinal Analysis.' *British Journal of Criminology 16* (1 1976): 38-47.

Boyle, J. *A Sense of Freedom.* London: Pan Books, 1977.

Byrne, R., Hogan, G. and McDermott, P. *Prisoners' Rights: A Study in Irish Prison Law.* Dublin: Co-op Books, 1981.

Cameron, I. 'Life in the Balance: The Case of Frank Marritt.' In Causes for Concern British Criminal Justice on Trial?, edited by P. Scraton and P. Gordon, P. Harmondsworth: Penguin, 1984.

Caul, B. 'Juvenile Offending in Northern Ireland a Statistical Overview.' In The Juvenile Justice System in Northern Ireland, edited by B. Caul, J. Pinkerton and F. Powell. Ulster Polytechnic, 1983.

Clemmer, D. *The Prison Community.* New York: Holt, Rinehart and Winston, 1940.

Cohen, S. and Taylor, L. *Psychological Survival.* Harmondsworth: Penguin, 1977.

Cohen, S. and Taylor, L. *Prison Secrets.* London: Radical Alternatives to Prison/NCCL, 1978.

Coogan, T. P. *On the Blanket*. Dublin: Ward River Press, 1980.

Craig, J. *The Probation Throughcare Services: A Report on a Consumer Survey*. Belfast: Policy, Planning and Research Unit, 1984.

Crawford, C. *Long Kesh: An Alternative Perspective*, in MSc Thesis. Cranfield Institute of Technology, 1979.

Darcy, M. *Tell them Everything*. London: Pluto Press, 1981.

Faul, D. and Murray, R. *H Blocks: British Jail for Irish Political Prisoners*. Dungannon: Authors, 1979.

Fitzgerald, M. *Prisoners in Revolt*. Harmondsworth: Penguin, 1977.

Fitzgerald, M. and Sim, J. *British Prisons*. Oxford: Basil Blackwell, 1979.

Flanagan, T. 'Lifers and Long-termers Doing Big Time.' In The Pains of Imprisonment, edited by R. Johnson and H. Toch. London: Sage, 1982(a).

Flanagan, T. 'Explaining the Parole Decision.' In Coping with Imprisonment, edited by N. Parisi. London: Sage, 1982(b).

Foucault, M. *Discipline and Punish the Birth of the Prison*. London: Allen Lane, 1977.

Goffman, E. *Asylums*. New York: Doubleday, 1961.

Heatley, P. and Tomlinson, M. 'The Politics of Imprisonment in Ireland: Some Historical Notes.' In Securing the State: Politics of Internal Security in Europe, edited by P Hillyard and P. Squires. Bristol: European Group for the Study of Deviance and Social Control, 1982.

Heskin, K. et al. 'Psychological Correlates of Long-term Imprisonment: Attitudinal Variables.' *British Journal of Criminology 14* (2 1976): 150-7.

Hillyard, P. 'Police and Penal Services.' In Violence and the Social Services in Northern Ireland, edited by J. Darby and A. Williamson. London: Heinemann, 1978.

Ignatieff, M. *A Just Measure of Pain*. London: MacMillan, 1978.

Kelley, K. *The Longest War Northern Ireland and the IRA*. Dingle: Brandon Book Publishers, 1982.

MacNiallais, T. *Prisoners' Families: Who Serves the Sentence?* A Dissertation. Ulster Polytechnic, 1984.

McCafferty, N. *The Armagh Women*. Dublin: Co-op Books, 1981.

McVicar, J. *By Himself*. London: Hutchinson, 1974.

Melossi, D. and Pavarini, M. *The Prison and the Factory*. London: MacMillan, 1981.

Monger, M. et al. *Throughcare with Prisoners' Families*. Nottingham: Department of Social Administration and Social Work, University of Nottingham, 1983.

Northern Ireland Assembly, *Official Report*, No 15, col 583, June 20th, 1984.

Northern Ireland Association for the Care and Resettlement of Offenders (NIACRO). *Detention at the Secretary of State's Pleasure*. Belfast: NIACRO, 1984.

Northern Ireland Office, *Life Sentence Prisoners in Northern Ireland an Explanatory Memorandum.* Belfast, 1985.

Parisi, N. *Coping with Imprisonment.* London: Sage, 1982.

Robinson, P. *Self-Inflicted: An Exposure of the H Block Issue.* Belfast: Democratic Unionist Party, 1980.

Sands, B. *The Diary of Bobby Sands.* Dublin: Sinn Fein Publicity Department, 1981.

Sapsford, P. *Life Sentence: Prisoners Reaction, Response and Change.* Milton Keynes: Open University Press, 1983.

Seligman, *Helplessness.* San Francisco: W H Freeman, 1975.

Smith, D. *Life Sentence Prisoners.* London: Home Office Research Unit, Report No 51.

Toch, H. *Living in Prison: The Ecology of Prison Survival.* New York: The Free Press, 1977.

# NEGLECT AS CONTROL

## PRISONERS' FAMILIES

### Susan Smith

*This chapter is based on a paper presented at the Madrid conference in 1986 and originally published in working papers in European criminology, volume 8, 'Civil Rights, Public Opinion and the State', pp. 42-51*

It is now some 200 years since Cesare Beccaria wrote of European penal systems:

> Confiscations put a price on the heads of the weak, cause the innocent to suffer the punishments of the guilty. What spectacle can be sadder than that of a family dragged into infamy and misery by the crimes of its head which the submission ordained by the law would hinder the family from preventing even it if it had the means to do so?[1]

---

[1]   Beccaria, *On Crime and Punishments*, 1963.

In 1986, the situation of the legally innocent families of prisoners' remains little changed. It is this paradox which I intend to explore within this paper and to demonstrate how the theme of this conference, 'Civil Rights, Public Opinion and the State', applies to their particular situation.

There is a marked lack of public or academic awareness of the very profound and peculiar problems facing prisoners' families, problems over and above those of other one-parent families, problems of stigma, demoralisation, public hostility, and a lack of basic civil rights. Existing research which does include the families of prisoners is usually directed primarily at the rehabilitation of the prisoner, with the family being seen as a potentially valuable treatment agent in the rehabilitative process, or at the welfare of the children of imprisoned fathers, thus denying the existence of the many childless partners of prisoners. The needs of the families themselves, and especially the wives and girlfriends, who bear the main responsibility for ensuring the survival of the family unit and the marital relationship, are relegated to a secondary and peripheral importance. The main thrust of the research is oriented towards the prisoner, with scant concern for the families per se.

Few of the studies have incorporated into their analyses any open questioning of the assumptions regarding gender divisions which underpin penal philosophy, nor do they state or challenge the inherent masculinity of penal policy. Most significantly, few studies confront the principle of specificity of punishment, or how this is being violated by contemporary imprisonment policies and in particular the very considerable hidden costs to women of this violation. The domestic sphere of the prisoner's family has been ignored by both feminist critiques and radical criminology. There appears in this instance to be an unusually general acceptance of traditional assumptions regarding the role of women in the home and family as being essentially nurturing, supportive, and above all else, dependent, without any corresponding analysts of the ways in which these assumptions contribute to the implementation of imprisonment policies. Whilst radical criminology and feminist critiques have indeed begun to examine the criminal woman, they have offered no insights into the experiences of the female dependents of criminal men, or the ways in which they perform a central, yet unstated, role in imprisonment policies.

My research into the experiences of prisoners' wives and girlfriends demonstrates that they and their families suffer a punishment at least as profound as that of their imprisoned partner, yet they are not the sentenced party. For the most part, they are innocent and often ignorant of their partner's offence. My findings reveal a group of women marginalised into silence and invisibility, and subject to a wide range of pressures from the penal and welfare systems, public attitudes, their partners, and to a certain extent, from themselves since they too internalise the expectation that the norm is a dependent woman rooted firmly within a conventional family structure headed by a working male. They are in a double bind of suffering a general oppression as women, and a particular oppression as the partners of prisoners. They appear to defy all the assumptions which constitute a 'normal' family, and so attract the suspicion and hostility which attaches to anyone who deviates from the norm (especially a woman) and who is seen to erode the monopoly which the virtuous hold in being the 'deserving' claimants of benefits. That they are suddenly thrust into independence, irrespective of their desire or ability to cope, is seen as irrelevant. That they are largely unable to prevent their partner's offence is also seen as irrelevant. They are 'guilty by association' and treated accordingly.

The imagery of the deviant woman presented by the media (i.e. as failing to conform to gender expectations and family values), not only reinforces their lack of self-esteem and further heightens their vulnerability, it also serves to bolster and justify their marginalisation. The role played by the press in identifying offenders has certain historical justifications[2] but is nevertheless devastating to the families. For a sentenced

---

[2]   Jones, *Justice and Journalism*. 1974; Jones, *Crime, Punishment and the Press*. 1980.

man, the publicity and notoriety accompanying his trial can be ego-boosting and can help establish a credible reputation with other inmates. For his partner left outside, there can be a more negative effect. With the actual offender out of reach, the ill-defined hostility of the public can focus on the woman and children so easily identifiable from the press reports. The family is immediately set apart from other one-parent families and ostracised from normal community life. The woman does not fit into the social categories of married, single or divorced. They are independent in one way but extremely dependent in another. As a result they have very unclear role expectations, and this fact also shapes the responses of others to prisoners' wives and girlfriends.

This marginalisation is in turn emphasised and deepened by the women's dealings with penal and welfare authorities. My findings also shed light on the lack of positive and effective interaction between these two systems. Penality does not include any family policy, and despite Beveridge's universalism (but due partly to his lack of provision for single parents), the Welfare State also fails to recognise the existence of this group of families, thus their needs are not catered for by either system. The women become caught up in a tangle of bureaucratic procedures which serve to confuse, intimidate, and degrade those who, for lack of information, do not understand them, even though they shape their existence. This reinforces their feelings of isolation and powerlessness. They feel trapped, manipulated, and controlled.

An analysis of prisoners' families can also serve to penetrate the ideology of a benevolent State and to bring into the open the latent and punitive motives behind the persistent neglect of prisoners' families. It is more usual to criticise existing policies than it is to recommend policy innovations, but that is what I intend. The 'how' and 'why' criticisms must be replaced with the 'why not' question, since non-policy can be as indicative of motives as existing policies. I do not suggest that either the penal or welfare system overtly set out to dismantle the family relationship of prisoners and their dependents, but I do maintain that in practice they do little to sustain such relationships, to the detriment of all concerned. However, before outlining policy recommendations, we must consider the 'why not' question. This entails unpicking the image of compassion and benevolence with which the apparently minimalist State surrounds itself, but which in practice can be systematically punitive and destructive.

If we extend our vision of the effects of crime to prisoners' families, it becomes apparent that they constitute a category of victims of crime in a very real sense, parallel to victims in the more conventional sense of a victim being the person(s) upon whom a crime is perpetrated. But for prisoners' dependents there is no Victim Support Scheme, no Criminal Injuries Compensation Board, no Reparation and Mediation Scheme. The existence of such schemes suggests that the Home Office can and does extend its vision of crime beyond the immediate area of the offender and his/her punishment/treatment, and in so doing helps bolster the paternalistic and benevolent image it tries to propagate in order to gain credibility and public allegiance. So why are prisoners' families, who are also victims, not included? For them there is no one statutory agency responsible for their welfare, no comprehensive source of information on the penal and welfare systems, little public recognition or understanding, and a corresponding lack of professional awareness. Why not?

Is the lack of any family policy from the Home Office a deference to public opinion which is hostile to crime? I think not, since the Home Office must also play a part in shaping the very media representations which contribute to public opinion. Or is it a shortage of cash which prevents them from mitigating a family policy? Possibly, but the new prison building programme suggests that priorities be in a more punitive and short-sighted direction.

Could the reason be that as women (and women lacking more than most the status, power, income, protection and support which a male partner signifies), these prisoners' dependents simply do not enter into the predominantly masculine arena of penality? This gender issue is certainly important and is a partial explanation, but it is not sufficient explanation for such a prolonged and persistent neglect. If the Home Office has widened its horizons to include victims of crime, why the glaring omission of prisoners' families, who are also victims, unless the omission serves a purpose?

As to the welfare system, there appears to be virtually no awareness of the unique difficulties facing these families who do not match up to the nuclear family norm, and hence there is little specific provision for them in a supposedly universalist welfare philosophy. Constituting a 'hybrid' class of claimants, prisoners' families are often ignorant of the discretionary benefits which might apply to their situation and so consistently fail to receive benefits which might aid their passage through the shadow of imprisonment. The DHSS produce and publicise leaflets for other particular categories of claimants, for example, the disabled, but not for prisoners' families. Why not?

Recent research[3] has shown that most female supplementary benefit claimants are lone mothers and that their activities are doubly regulated formally by the DHSS and informally by the community. Their status is problematic since they are mothers but are not wives, and are dependent upon the State and not a traditional breadwinner-husband, therefore, they are regarded as deviant. Prisoners' dependants further complicate the issue, deviating even from the accepted norm of the ideal nuclear family and thus attracting even more formal and informal policing of their activities. Following the re-assertion of individualistic free market values, the welfare State is attempting to shed its bureaucratic and interfering image by passing on some of its welfare functions to the family, i.e. the traditional nuclear family in which women are central to discipline and careful management. Women claiming benefits are seen to subvert this ideal and

---

3   Cook, 'Women On Welfare', 1987.

to be individually responsible for problematic family behaviour and mismanagement, they are seen as feckless, idle and irresponsible. Prisoners' families fit uneasily into this notion. They are expected to uphold current expectations of familism but within a set of circumstances which renders this an almost impossible task. Caught involuntarily in the welfare trap, they find themselves in the unenviable position of being forced into dependence upon the State even though this heightens their already deviant status. They contravene every notion of the ideal family, but not through choice. They do not have the option of conforming to dependence and yet the State shrinks back from supporting their independence. In short, they are controlled into dependence, and this is reinforced in conditions of independence.

Since imprisonment is still largely imprisonment of the poor, many families and relationships are already under stress and the impact of imprisonment serves to heighten this stress and add to the cycle of deprivation. It is crucial for the families of prisoners that such a cycle be broken, and also if any hopes for the rehabilitation of the prisoner are ever to be realised. It is surely obvious that the maintaining of marital relationships and the family unit must also be to the advantage of the prisoner, and therefore the prison authorities as well (although this should not be the only reason). A large percentage of escapees give family worries as the reason for absconding. If these were to be mitigated the prisoner is less resentful, less agitated, and less of a problem in terms of control during sentence, and less of a threat in terms of re-offending subsequent to sentence. At present, any notions of rehabilitation are subverted by the lack of constructive family policy within prisons.

Paradoxically, there is a widespread acceptance of the family as a potential source of rehabilitation, but without any real assessment of the hidden costs to the families, and especially to the women. There is a very real dichotomy between the underlying assumptions regarding the families as being guilty by association and therefore undeserving, and the expectation that they, the supposedly guilty and undeserving, are also a source of rehabilitation. The two notions appear irreconcilable. If prisoners' families are indeed a vital treatment agent, then this function should be acknowledged and the former notion, with all its bigotry and discrimination, should be discarded. It might also be prudent to ascertain whether the families already perceive themselves as treatment agents, and if they do not, do they want to become such? If, on the other hand, it is accepted that the families are guilty and undeserving, then they should not be burdened with the additional responsibility of rehabilitation. It is not possible to 'have your cake and eat it'.

If, in a supposedly civilised society, custodial sentences should involve the minimum of personal social damage to all concerned, and the prisoner should remain integrated with his family and wider society, then there must be some means by which relationships can be sustained. There are no such means over and above scanty visits and letters. Why not? This can be put down to a lack of political will, opposition from prison staff who generally regard prisoners' families as guilty by association and not worthy of humane treatment, and pure short-sightedness on the part of the Home Office.

Whilst the prisoner has the rules and boundaries of the prison world explained to him, either by prison officers or other inmates, the family left outside do not, and are left to grapple with an uncertain and often unknown situation in which exists no statutory body possessing the responsibility for outlining the rules and boundaries of their own situation or that of their imprisoned partner. They lack the minimum information necessary to assess their situation in a realistic light. Events occur which will profoundly affect their lives and yet they do not receive the facts to interpret these events or to allow them to reach an effective or reasonable response, they do not have the basic civil right of freedom of information. Hence the family are increasingly vulnerable to transgressing unknown limitations to the possible detriment of themselves and their imprisoned partner. The workings of the penal and welfare systems are never explained to them.

Why not? Again the 'hoarding' of life-long significance can be seen as an element in the control of prisoners' families.

There are many different levels of control, and different levels of perception of control. It need not be obvious to be effective. In the case of prisoners' families, it is far from obvious but extremely effective. The more overt levels of their control include, the lack of available information, the mystification of the prison system, and bureaucratic neglect, whilst the more covert levels of control include the deliberate inculcating into prisoners' families a fear of transgressing unknown boundaries, and the harnessing of women's unpaid domestic activities to underpin imprisonment policies. The effect of these interacting levels of control is to inhibit the female dependents of prisoners, subtly, but with their compliance. They feel luckier than their partners because they at least are 'free'. But this freedom is illusory. They are prisoners and victims. The prison is sometimes of their own making, since they lack the knowledge and self-esteem to walk out from the limitations imposed upon them. Their docility and compliance is both cause and effect of their own and the State's social control, and their isolation, silence, and invisibility is highly functional to the State. Thus, their behaviour is controlled in private and public, by themselves and the State.

This outline illustrates the no-man's land which prisoners' families inhabit. Their persistent omission from both penal and welfare policy is informative and indicative of a process too concerned to be accidental indifference. The question regarding their neglect, the 'why not', in turn becomes the 'why?'

The answer lies in the neat fit between prisoners' families and the implementation of imprisonment policies. Women are the traditional buffers to all sorts of family crises and as such provide an invisible support infrastructure imprisonment, but one which is recognised by the State. Far from being socially obsolete, as their neglect initially suggests, prisoners' families in reality perform a crucial role in the imprisonment process. They provide an invaluable free resource which the State does not hesitate to use.

I would argue then, that the neglect of prisoners' families forms a particularly punitive element of a wider network of social control policies, both of women and of men through women, and further, that it is a deliberate strategy aimed also at reinforcing the principle of deterrence. I would further argue that into the isolated and minimal existence of prisoners families should be slotted some form of timely and sensitive statutory intervention as of right, and not as a discretionary and uncertain privilege dependent upon some ill-defined criteria.

It may appear contradictory to argue for an increase in State intervention particularly if Foucault's classification knowledge/power spiral is accepted as valid. The short-term benefits of intervention may be outweighed in the long term by increased surveillance and control. If prisoners' families were to be drawn into the knowledge/power process, then State control over them could intensify and they could be burdened with additional responsibilities, especially if alternatives to imprisonment were implemented. An appearance of liberal reform could mask an increased exploitation of such families. So what is the answer? One possibility is that any degree of demystification of the penal and welfare systems stemming from State intervention must increase the families' knowledge base; thus they will gain power from knowledge. To do what? To analyse their own function to the State? Then what? But at least they would possess a basis of knowledge from which to negotiate, and a basis of power from which to form a political constituency and so challenge the State's control. What is certain amongst all this hypothesis is that the neglect of prisoners' families, and their control, is more than an abstract principle. It is an issue which affects approximately 25,000 families[4] each year and one which can loosely be termed a 'political bogeyman'.

The dilemma posed to any open recognition of the problems facing these families is complex and linked to the premise

---

4    In England and Wales in 1986.

upon which society in general and penal policy in particular rests. Such an acknowledgement would illustrate the actual fragility of many other wider and seemingly deep-rooted assumptions, not necessarily directly connected with prisoners or their families, but through which much of our existence is ordered. To recognise, acknowledge, offer and thereby accept responsibility for the devastation of families caused by imprisonment would open up to question the entire issue of crime causation, the purpose of imprisonment, its effectiveness as a deterrent and the whole package of penal policy, inevitably giving rise to a questioning of prevailing social, economic and political structures. If crime and its disparate effects are seen to be due to societal dysfunctions, then the State must be seen as responsible for predicating those conditions in which crime occurs, and therefore for alleviating such conditions. Only a drastic restructuring of society could achieve this end, but such restructuring does not seem to be a politically viable proposition at present, especially in a Tory climate of a retrenchment of attitudes toward law and order and all its ramifications.

Any help or support granted to the families of prisoners would indicate a guilt or responsibility on the part of the State for that particular group within society, and so for other disadvantaged groups. This would threaten the traditional assumptions regarding the causes of crime, family roles and the strength of the family as a stable and educative unit. A government under pressure from public disillusionment, economic crisis, increasing unemployment and a rising crime rate and prison population is unlikely to accept such a responsibility and must rely therefore upon bolstering blanket ideologies concerning crime and criminals. Many of the preconceptions held by the public and perhaps the judiciary also, and carefully nurtured by the media, would be shattered if they were to see the reality of the situation – a situation in which there are no minimum standards within our ambiguous penal system for the prisoner or his family. The specificity of punishment is truly being violated. In order to distance the possibility of such an enlightenment, the media stress the avaricious, vicious, violent and inarticulate criminal to ensure that the public see the penal system in terms of its punishing the evil, the cruel, the undesirable, those who threaten social order. The prisoner's family is portrayed as being vulgar and socially responsible, being at least partially guilty of the offence.

For the public then to see State aid over and above the financial aid available to prisoner's families through the provisions of the Welfare State would be interpreted as a volte face and a contradiction of both penal and welfare policy. It would not suit State purposes to reveal that 80% of the prison population are petty offenders, far removed from implanted perceptions of the infamous mega-criminal, nor would it suit such purpose to reveal that many of this 80% are socially inadequate and should not be in prison in the first place. Nor would it serve the ultimate purpose of control and deterrence for the State to reveal that, contrary to public opinion, very few families live lavishly from the proceeds of crime during the period of sentence, although a small minority undoubtedly do.

It would be political suicide to build up one picture of crime and criminals to the voting public, instilling fear and prejudice into them, and presenting a law and order platform, and then contravene it by aiding prisoners' families. It would be similarly inept to over-emphasise the conditions of severe financial and emotional hardship in which most of these families live. This would not serve the purpose of sustaining the myth of a caring and benevolent system which punishes only the guilty and protects society from injustice. Rather, the State relies on the non-vocality of prisoners' wives and families, aware that in their heightened vulnerability, isolation, and turmoil, they will present no cohesive and cogent demands for support and reform. Their perceptions of self are coloured by their own internalisation of media visions of crime and criminals, and by their acceptance of their social position and role in society. By presenting images of crime, and the dire consequences of any deviance, particularly in women, the State has managed with the help of the media to control the behaviour and attitudes of prisoners' wives and so ensure their conformity even when entangled in a completely contradictory situation. The women lack the confidence and cohesion necessary to become an effective force for change, and their isolation renders them both silent and invisible. There is no-one to champion their rights in parliament and no community agency to offer support. There is a need to stimulate these victims of the penal system away from individual apathy and towards a recognition and expression of their own unique strength and importance, and to enable them to deny their existing structural position and so discard their isolation and control.

It is becoming increasingly apparent that for society and penal policy to recognise the existence of the problems inherent in the shadow of imprisonment would involve a major shift in philosophy. Such a mammoth task is unlikely to attract a favourable response from the present government and it is, therefore, within societal attitudes and community networks that change must be sought if prisoners' families are ever to gain a political voice and public credibility.

## Bibliography

Beccaria, C. *On Crime and Punishments*, translated by Henry Paolucci. (USA: Bobbs-Merrill Co Inc) 1963.

Cook, D. 'Women On Welfare: In Crime or Injustice'. In *Gender, Crime and Justice*, edited by P. Carlen and A. Worral. (Milton Keynes: Open University Press) 1987.

Jones, M. *Justice and Journalism*. (Barry Rose) 1974.

Jones, M. *Crime, Punishment and the Press*. (London: NACRO) 1980.

# THE DECADE FOR RAPE

**Karen Leander**

*This is an abridged version of a chapter originally published in 'Brott i välfärden Om brottslighet, utsatthet och kriminalpolitik' edited by Henrik Tham, Chapter 10*

To paraphrase the English researcher Liz Kelly[1], if the 1990s signified a turning point in the efforts to counteract domestic violence, this must be the decade for rape. While rape and other forms of sexual violence have never been explicitly excluded from academic or activist work against gendered violence, there are many examples of where rape has nonetheless been relegated to the background.

It has long been maintained that distinctions are formally and informally made between 'jump-from-the-bushes rape' ('real rapes') and more suspect rapes where a prior relationship may exist between victim and offender, where there is a lack of force and resistance, and where there is an 'absence of evidence corroborating the victim's account'.[2]

[1] Conference on *Criminalizing Gendered Violence, Local, National and International Perspectives*, 14-15 September 2005, University of Bristol, School of Policy Studies.

[2] Estrich, *Real Rape. How the Legal System Victimizes Women Who Say No.* 1987, p.18.

Against the background of the multiplicity of actions that are included in the concept of rape, the response of society to rape has been widely analyzed and found wanting.

# REGULATION RATHER THAN PROHIBITION

The purpose of this chapter is to examine how the application of the criminal law in cases of rape has contributed to a delegitimization of the criminal justice system (CJS), as indicated by the CJS's inability to protect due process rights with regard to accused persons at the same as serving the interests of the accusers.

Criticism of contemporary society's treatment of rape as a criminal offence mirrors general criticisms of the CJS. In 1990, in their overview of the critical perspective of deviance and social control, Davis and Stasz discussed the emphasis in radical criminology, for example, on race, class, ethnicity, age, gender and other significant social differences in the 'deviantizing process'. They go on to discuss what has been called 'overcriminalization', how policing and punishment focuses on minorities, and on children of the poor and of single mothers. Further, they highlight the inconsistency in the fact that great harms to individuals and society caused by corporate (and environment) crime are often the least controlled.[3] Other central aspects of the critical perspective are the role of power as well as the role of the State in creating crime, in which the CJS becomes an 'after-the-fact and futile response to the very conditions which government policy creates in the first place'.[4]

No area has been more criticized than the way in which the CJS has dealt with crimes such as woman battering and rape. There has been considerable movement within the CJS in Sweden to correct some of these deficiencies. For example, rape within marriage was criminalized with the new Criminal

---

[3]   Davis and Stasz, *Social Control of Deviance: A Critical Perspective* 1990, p. 63.
[4]   *Ibid.*, p. 296.

Code of 1965, and most sexual crimes and all assault within the home were transformed from complainant crimes to public prosecution crimes in the early 1980s.

These reforms can be viewed against the background of legal developments over a period of centuries. It has been shown that early rape laws under the 'kvinnofrid' protections of the 1200s- and 1300s in Sweden were aimed at protecting men's interests in women's sexual integrity. For example, the rape of another man's betrothed or wife was seen as more deserving of the law's protection than the rape of women not falling into these categories. Researchers have concluded that it was the husband's (material) interest in his wife not becoming impregnated by another man more than the violation itself that was the interest receiving protection from the law. The focus from men's interests in women as their property was gradually shifted to a focus on the violation itself in latter day Sweden. Subsequently, legislators struggled in the 1970s and 1980s to modernize the sexual crime laws to achieve two goals at the same time, to recognize changing sexual mores not least with regard to women's sexuality at the same time as not lessening women's right to sexual self-determination by weakening protections against non-consensual sexuality.

## WHERE DOES THE CRIMINAL JUSTICE SYSTEM FAIL US?

Following from general criticisms of the CJS, criminal law, and criminology from critical and feminist criminologists, gender researchers have identified three areas in which rape survivors often report feeling that their legal needs are not met by the criminal justice responses: (1) attrition of rape cases from police report to conviction; (2) retraumatization; and (3) the disparate implementation along gender, class, and ethnic lines.[5] The discussion here will focus on attrition

---

[5]    Koss, "Restoring Rape Survivors: Justice, Advocacy and a Call to Action". 2006, p.206-234.

and the issues of consent and intent. Finally, some alternatives to the present use of the criminal justice system will be discussed.

# ATTRITION

Attrition refers to the process by which rape cases drop out of the legal process, and thus do not result in a criminal conviction.[6] In a report submitted to the UK Home Office in 2005, Liz Kelly and other researchers from the London Metropolitan University make it clear that most cases that fall out of the criminal justice system do so early in the process. There it is maintained that, at the most, 25 percent of rapes are reported; in Sweden, this figure has been set at 5-10 percent for sexual abuse.[7] Further, it is decisions made during the investigative phase that are responsible for the high attrition rate.

In this report, Kelly and the other researchers use the term 'victim withdrawal' to refer to a victim's decision for various reasons to cease cooperating with the investigation, most often leading to the case being dropped. Since the amendments in Sweden in 1984 that brought rape under public prosecution, there are no longer any formal grounds on which a victim can withdraw her complaint to the police ('återta sin angivelse'). Nevertheless, these reforms led to an accelerated rate of increase in police-reported rapes, following a gradual rise throughout the post-war period, but not to a corresponding increase in convictions, which remained at a relatively constant level during the same period.

With the subsequent rising rate of reported rapes, but a continuing stable level of convictions, the percentage of rape cases reported to the police that end in a conviction under the crime caption of rape is decreasing. In a report prepared for the kick-off conference for a nation-wide multi-agency initiative in 1992, Leander traced the flow of

---

[6]   Kelly et al *A Gap or a Chasm? Attrition in Reported Rape Cases.* 2005, p.7.

[7]   SOU, *Sexualbrotten – Ett ökat skydd för den sexuella integriteten och angränsande frågor.* 2001, p. 83.

reported rapes through the criminal justice system, based on criminal statistics available from Statistics Sweden. She found that three-quarters of reported rapes were dropped during the police and prosecutorial investigative stages in both 1985 and 1991, with 12 percent leading to conviction in 1991.[8] Applying the same categorization to figures for 2006, the following is found (the percentages of the number of reported rapes):

| Rapes reported to the police | Prosecutions for rape | Convictions for rape |
|---|---|---|
| 4,208 | 740 (18%) | 226 (5%) |

The statistics[9] from 2006 show that about 28 percent of the cases were dropped due to the perpetrator remaining unidentified; about 12 percent due to under-aged or deceased perpetrators, and other reasons; further, almost one-third were dropped by prosecutors under the decision of 'crime cannot be proven'. The remaining category of about 11 percent may be accounted for by the re-captioned of offences reported as rapes but prosecuted as 'sexual force', 'sexual exploitation' or assault, or various statistical effects such as one convicted offender having been reported for several rapes. In sum, the overall rate of convictions for rape has decreased by more than half since the early 1990s.

In their report, Kelly and others maintain that attrition research has identified an international paradox in that conviction rates have decreased during the very same period as broad changes have been made in statutory definitions of rape and in procedural rules. Kelly and the other authors conclude that making incremental improvements at each stage of the criminal justice process will be more likely to lead to improvements than trying to bridge all the gaps in one leap. To accomplish this, their recommendations are

---

8    Leander, "Kvinnomisshandel och våldtäkt i kriminalstatistiken". 1992.
9    www.bra.se.

based on the notion of implementing a shift within the criminal justice system from a focus on discrediting rape victims to one of improving evidence gathering and case-building, including inter-agency cooperation at the investigative stage and improving recording practices and statistical routines.

While I agree that the implementation of these recommendations would lead to improvements, what would still be evading us is how to apply the law to facts of concrete cases, not least of all with regard to the issues of consent and intent. I do not believe that it is merely a paradox that Kelly and others have identified but rather a glass ceiling delineating the extent to which we can use the blunt instrument of criminal justice in individual cases of rape.

## APPLYING THE LAW TO FACTS

Most rape laws contain wording that includes coercion on the part of perpetrators leading to the commission of sexual acts against the wishes of the victim. In that these same sexual actions would be legitimate if engaged in consensually, what needs to be proven is that the actions took place against the wishes of the victim, that the victim did not 'consent'.

Over the past decade, several high profile rape cases in Sweden have addressed some aspects of the issues of consent and intent. The most recent case concerns a young woman who accompanied two men whom she knew well – and had engaged in sex with previously – to one of their apartments after a night of partying in Stureplan in Stockholm. While the initial sexual activities were apparently engaged in consensually by all three, the woman reported the men to the police for rape a short while after leaving the apartment in the early morning hours. She claimed that the events had turned coercive and that despite her protests, the men continued with their sexual actions until they had spent themselves and fell asleep.

The trial court acquitted the defendants and now the case is under appeal. The court in essence acknowledged that at some point during her stay in one of the men's apartments, she had been coerced into intercourse and other equivalent activities. Nevertheless, the court ruled that reasonable doubt still existed as to whether the men had understood the woman's change in status from a consenting participant to a non-consenting victim.

Two facts were found to favour the men's argument that they had no intent to rape. First, the three individuals had engaged in similar sexual activities on prior occasions, with violence and degradation as part of the sexual activity. Even though it is likely, according to the court, that there was probably more violence used on the night in question than had previously been the case, it is clear that the occurrence of violence could not be interpreted exclusively as a means of coercion. Second, the victim was the most intoxicated of the three and her extreme state of intoxication may imply that her efforts to resist any further sexual activities were feeble.

## CONSENT 4-EVER

Space does not allow more than a few comments about both of these facts that were interpreted in the defendants' favour. It is clear that prior consent no longer officially is to be seen as a presumption of present consent. Indeed, rape within marriage was criminalized in Sweden with the adoption of the Criminal Code in 1962. Although the general legal rule seems to be that consent is assumed unless explicitly withdrawn, the principle is simpler to apply to incidents that occur at different points in time. At what point consent dissolves into non-consent during one and the same incident is difficult to establish. Even more difficult is to establish this during one and the same sex act.

The second aspect of the case that was used to support the men's argument that they lacked intent to rape, that the woman's protests might have been enfeebled due to her intoxication, has received considerable commentary. It has been asserted that the court could have interpreted the fact of the woman's extreme intoxication as an indication that she was in a helpless state or condition, regardless of how she got into that state and regardless of how long the condition lasted. Instead, the court maintained that the woman's intoxication might have contributed to the men's obliviousness to her desire for them to stop.

In any case, the Stureplan defendants were acquitted despite the admission by the court that the victim had been coerced into sexual activities. It was decided in 2005 not to eliminate the prerequisite of violence or threat of violence to be able to call an action rape against an adult. What makes this difficult is that violence in and of itself is not a sufficient criterion for deeming an encounter to be non-consensual. Physicality in sex ('rough sex') that takes forms totally acceptable for some could be interpreted or experienced as abusive or violent by others.

So the issue does not concern whether certain acts may be seen as violent in and of themselves, such as hitting, spanking, anal penetration, or any number of activities. The issue is whether the activity was fully, freely, willingly entered into by all parties involved.[10] Perhaps it is reasonable to accept that the victim of the Stureplan rape consented to 'rough sex' but it strains credibility to accept that she consented to the violence that caused wounds, left her torn and bleeding in her vagina and anus, or, for that matter, to anything that occurred after her self-reported vocal, loud, and physical protests. She claimed that one of the men encouraged the other to rape her, and the police who met her soon after she left the apartment testified that her whole body was shaking and had difficulty walking due to soreness. Again, the men confessed to all the sexual activities, underplaying the violent features according to the court, but claimed that the woman never used 'stop words', so that nothing appeared out of the ordinary to them.

---

[10]   According to Chapter 24 of the Swedish Criminal Code, not consent, nor even explicit consent, is sufficient to avoid an incident being rape. According to this chapter, consent must be freely and voluntarily given, such that it cannot be given under the influence of physical or psychological coercion. This should be seen as the difference between "submission" ("giving in" rather than "giving up") and consent.

# CRIMINALIZATION OF WHAT?

There is an old adage that the charge of rape is easy to make, hard to prove, and harder still for the accused to defend himself against, regardless of innocence.[11] The adoption of such thinking into the legal system is centuries old and led to the definition of evidentiary rules that have required corroboration of the victim's account, a quick complaint to the police, historically, proof of a woman's prior chastity. But this adage has never had a basis in real-life. As a rule, raped women have never found it 'easy' to repeatedly and in explicit detail describe for strangers – or anyone - what has transcribed in the intimate sphere and risk being humiliated, discredited, disbelieved, and even reviled for their efforts.

The issue of false allegations of rape is important to address. In the early 1980s, Swedish criminologist Leif GW Persson set the proportion of reported rapes that were deliberately falsely made at around two percent.[12] The 2005 Kelly study discussed above found the highest rates at nine percent, but set the overall rate for their study material at three percent. Further there has been little evidence of systematic abuse of due process in the form of untoward convictions of innocent men for rape. Against the background of an estimated 85-90 percent of committed rapes that are never reported to the police, the apprehensions about miscarriages of justice seem to be aimed in the wrong direction.

In light of these discussions, the question must be asked whether changes in the law would actually help in assessing whether a woman has consented and whether a man believed that she had and thus lacked the necessary intent in cases as the one discussed above.

---

[11]  Estrich, *Real Rape. How the Legal System Victimizes Women Who Say No.* 1987, p.5.

[12]  Persson, *Våldtäkt – en kriminologisk kartläggning av våldtäktsbrotten.* 1981, p.39.

# CAN ONE EVEN DISCUSS ALTERNATIVES TO CRIMINAL SANCTIONS?

If one accepts that the criminal law on rape and its application actually cause harm in many cases, what are there for
alternatives?

Alternatives within the criminal law could be considered
first. In the public climate in Sweden today, however, if a rape
case is taken as far as to court, but that the finding of guilt is
for 'a lesser crime' or the sanction meted out is 'light' in public
opinion – the outcry is that there has been no justice. This is
the first step where a new discourse should be introduced.
While deterrence and punishment are two functions of the
criminal law, others may be of equal importance over a long
perspective. Rehabilitation, norm-building, and the interrup-
tion of destructive life choices by individuals may serve the
society better than the full impact of convictions for rape with
potential ensuing long imprisonment sentences.

In a speech given in Stockholm in 2006, Australian
criminologist John Braithwaite applied the theory of re-inte-
grative shaming to the issue of rape, in particular concepts
of shame displacement and narcissistic price to rape as a
weapon of war and conflict.[13] Braithwaite identified part of
the problem of contemporary warfare as a crime problem
arguing that war 'interrupts the unthinkableness of rape'
in many contexts. He argues that 'restorative justice can
be designed to bring [the perpetrators] to experience the
shame they should feel for rape'.

While I do not believe that rapes or domestic violence
should be handled in Sweden by mediation where an emphasis
on forgiveness or reconciliation may be unduly taxing for the
victims of these crimes, there are aspects of the 'reintegrative
shaming' that ought to be relevant in any search for alternatives to the criminal justice system.

---

[13]    Braithwaite, *Rape, Shame and Pride*. 2006.

In their article concerning a so-called 'integrative feminist model' for counteracting intimate partner violence, McPhail and others discussed alternatives to the criminal justice system. One example was legal scholar Linda Mills' proposed Intimacy Abuse Circles (IACs) consisting of 'groups made up of family, friends, and appropriate community members working within a restorative justice model to hold the perpetrator accountable'.[14] It was emphasized here that frontline workers within the violence against women's movement were critical of the criminal justice system both for over- and under-reacting, even in cases of serious abuse.

The criminal law appears incapable – at least on its own – to weigh simultaneously issues of consent, intent, and the facts of events that occur without no outside witnesses and within intimate spheres. Legal principles and the due process rights of accused are stringently protected in light of the seriousness with which rape is seen in the criminal law. Thus, even the 'regulation' of rape, let alone its prohibition, simply seems beyond the capacity of the criminal justice system.

## FROM CRIMINALIZATION TO CIVILIZATION : WHAT COULD VICTIMS GAIN?

So if not lesser crimes or restorative justice, then what? Perhaps we could reach even further afield for other alternatives. In the late 1980s, lawyers at The Clara Wichman Institute in Amsterdam revealed their practice of encouraging lawyers for raped and battered women to use the civil rather than the criminal law to gain redress. It was their contention that even victims whose rapists are convicted often feel like losers at the end of the process, after having their credibility – and worth as persons – questioned and/or attacked throughout the process. Nor did the legal response seem ever to match the seriousness of the abuse.

---

[14]  McPhail et al, "An Integrative Feminist Model: The Evolving Feminist Perspective on Intimate Partner Violence." 2007,: pp. 817-841, 824.

Further, the burden of proof in the civil law is lower in civil cases (informally described as 51% of the evidence, in the US 'a preponderance of the evidence'), and thus a higher probability of a ruling that a wrong has been done, and that someone has to be held responsible. The civil law offered victims a greater chance to participate in the process, increasing their sense of empowerment, in contrast to criminal trials where the victim often feels swept aside by various other actors and considerations. What are the possible sanctions for these wrong doers? Obviously, they would be less harsh than those offered in the criminal justice system. Economic compensation or being banned from certain towns or areas of cities or even various types of service was possible under Dutch law at that time.

There are many objections that could be levelled at the proposal to use civil law instead of criminal law, the main one being that it could be seen as a form of 'decriminalization' of rape and sexual violence, and that resignation or capitulation in the face of a clear wrong compounds the wrong. Students of criminology have remarked that civil sanctions involving monetary compensation could be interpreted as 'payment for services rendered' or that the procedures would attract 'victims' who were in it for the money.

In addition, sanctions such as far-reaching and long-lasting 'banishment' from certain geographical areas would be difficult to enforce. None of these potential limitations however seem as damaging as the manner in which the justice system works today. Further, criminal sanctions could be triggered upon further abusive behaviour and/or upon failure to comply with the court's civil sanctions.

## CONCLUSION

Nearly 20 years have lapsed since I first heard the ideas of civil law from the lawyers at the Clara Wichman Institute, and nearly 25 years have passed since rape became a public prosecution crime in Sweden. It does not seem far-fetched to maintain that women's and victims' interests have not been well served during this period. I think the time has come to consider complements to the criminal law – rather than substitutes – that would serve to turn more power of legal redress to the victims of sexual violence, to empower them here as women have been in other fields, until worthy alternatives within the State's apparatus emerge.

While rape will always be considered a criminal act, the criminal justice system must re-examine what rape is. Moreover, we all must also re-examine what justice means in this multifaceted context. If using civil law would lead to the greater reporting of cases of sexual coercion, to more clarity over what can and should be expected of the criminal justice system, and of a strengthened sense of empowerment, redress, and equality/emancipation, then it is time we tried it.

## Bibliography

Braithwaite, J. *Rape, Shame and Pride.* Address to Stockholm Criminology Symposium, 6 June, (Canberra: Australian National University) 2006

Davis, N. and Stasz, C. *Social Control of Deviance: A Critical Perspective.* (New York: McGraw-Hill) 1990.

Estrich, S. *Real Rape. How the Legal System Victimizes Women Who Say No.* (Cambridge, MA: Harvard University Press) 1987.

Kelly, L., Lovett, J. and Regan, L. *A Gap or a Chasm? Attrition in Reported Rape Cases.*, Home Office Research Study 293. (London: Home Office) 2005.

Koss, M. 'Restoring Rape Survivors: Justice, Advocacy and a Call to Action'. *Annals of the New York Academy of Science,* 2006

Leander, K., 'Kvinnomisshandel och våldtäkt i kriminalstatistiken'. Conference presentation 'Att möta våld mot kvinnor', Arlanda Hotell, 12-13 Oktober 1992 (unpublished).

McPhail, B., Busch, N., Kulkarni, S. and Rice, G. 'An Integrative Feminist Model: The Evolving Feminist Perspective on Intimate Partner Violence.' *Violence Against Women* 13(8) 2007

Persson, L. *Våldtäkt – en kriminologisk kartläggning av våldtäktsbrotten.* (Stockholm: LiberFörlag) 1981.

SOU, *Sexualbrotten – Ett ökat skydd för den sexuella integriteten och angränsande frågor.* Betänkande av 1998 års sexualbrottskommitté. Stockholm: Justitiedepartementet, 2001.

# APPENDIX I

## 41 CONFERENCES OF THE EUROPEAN GROUP FOR THE STUDY OF DEVIANCE AND SOCIAL CONTROL

## 1973-2013

1.  1973  **Impruneta ,Florence, Italy**
    *Social Control in Europe: Scope and Prospects for a Radical Criminology*
    13-16 September 1973

2.  1974  **Colchester, England**
    *The Development of Social Control and Possible Alternatives*
    13-16 September 1974

3.  1975  **Amsterdam, Netherlands**
    *Crimes of the Powerful*
    9-12 September 1975

4.  1976  **Vienna, Austria**
    *Economic Change and Legal Control*
    10-13 September 1976

5.  1977  **Barcelona, Spain**
    *The State and Social Control*
    9-12 September 1977

6.  1978  **Bremen, Federal Republic of Germany**
    *Law and Order: Terrorism and State Violence*
    7-10 September 1978

7.   1979   **Copenhagen, Denmark**
*Deviance and Discipline*
6-9 September 1979

8.   1980   **Leuven, Belgium**
*State Control on Information in the Field of Deviance and Social Control: Resource, Analysis, Counter Strategies*
4-7 September 1980

9.   1981   **Derry, Northern Ireland**
*Securing the State: The Politics of Internal Security in Europe*
3-6 September 1981

10.   1982   **Bologna, Italy**
*Youth and the Economic Crisis: New Forms of Social Control and Counter Strategies*
31 August-3 September 1982

11.   1983   **Hyytiälä, Finland**
*Social Movements, the State and Problems of Action*
9-12 September 1983

12.   1984   **Cardiff, Wales**
*The State of Information in 1984: Social Conflict, Social Control and the New Technology*
6-9 September 1984

13.   1985   **Hamburg, Germany**
*The Expansion of European Prison Systems*
12-15 September 1985

14.   1986   **Madrid, Spain**
*Civil Rights, Public Opinion and the State*
10-14 September 1986

15.   1987   **Vienna, Austria**
*Justice and Ideology: Definitions and Strategies for the 1990's'*
10-13 September 1987

16.   1988   **Synnseter fjellstue, Norway**
*Gender, Sexuality and Social Control*
1-4 September 1988

17.   1989   **Ormskirk, Lancashire, England**
*Beyond Domination*
31 August-3 September 1989

18.    1990    **Haarlem, Netherlands**
             *Criminal Justice in a European Legal Order: Migration and Penal*
             *Reform*
             4-7 September 1990

19.    1991    **Potsdam, Germany**
             *Social Justice and European Transformations: Processes of Mar-*
             *ginalisation and Integration. Changes in Social Policies*
             4-8 September 1991

20.    1992    **Padova, Italy**
             *Citizenship, Human Rights, And Minorities: Rethinking Social*
             *Control in the New Europe*
             3-6 September 1992

21.    1993    **Prague, Czech Republic**
             *Control as Enterprise: East and West*
             29 August 29-1 September 1993

22.    1994    **Komitini, Greece**
             *The Use and Abuse of Power: Beyond Control*
             25-28 August 1994

23.    1995    **Crossmaglen, Northern Ireland**
             *Confronting Control: Theories and Practices of Resistance*
             31 August- 4 September 1995

24.    1996    **Bangor, Wales**
             *State Crime and Human Rights*
             12-16 September 1996

25.    1997    **Kazimierz Dolny, Poland**
             *Europe in Transition: Past Trends and Future*
             *Perspectives*
             11-14 September 1997

26.    1998    **Spetses, Greece**
             *Controlling the Movement of People: Critical Perspectives on*
             *Practices, Policies and Consequences*
             27-30 August 1998

27.    1999    **Palanga, Lithuania**
             *Criminal Injustices and the Production of Harm*
             2-5 September 1999

28.  2000  **Nyneshamn, Sweden**
*Punishment enough?*
31 August-3 September 2000

29.  2001  **Venice, Italy**
*The Ambivalence of Conflicts and Social Change*
6-9 September 2001

30.  2002  **Krakow, Poland**
*Social Control and Violence: Breaking the Cycle*
29 September- 1 August 2002

31.  2003  **Helsinki, Finland**
*Critical Perspectives on Crime Prevention*
30 August- 2 September 2003

32.  2004  **Bristol, England**
*Critical Perspectives on the Discipline of Criminology And International Criminal Justice Policies*
16-19 September 2004

33.  2005  **Belfast, Northern Ireland**
*Crime, Justice and Transition*
1-4 September 2005

34.  2006  **Corinth, Peloponnese, Greece**
*The Regulation of Migration, Asylum and Movement in the 'New Europe'*
31 August-3 September 2006

35.  2007  **Utrecht, Netherlands**
*Exploring Relations of Power*
30 August-3 September 2007

36.  2008  **Padova, Italy**
*Conflict, Penal Policies and Prison Systems*
4-7 September 2008

37.  2009  **Preston, Lancashire, England**
*'Crime', Justice, and Control: The Challenge of Recession*
26-29 August 2009

38.  2010  **Lesvos, Greece**
*The Politics of Criminology*
1-5 September 2010

39.   2011   **Chambéry, France**
*No borders? Exclusion, Justice and the Politics of Fear*
3-7 September 2011

40.   2012   **Nicosia, Cyprus**
*'Beyond the Wire': Regulating Division, Conflict and Resistance*
5-9 September 2012

41.   2013   **Oslo, Norway**
*Critical Criminology in a Changing World: Tradition and Innovation*
29 August-1 September 2013

# APPENDIX 2
## PREVIOUSLY PUBLISHED BOOKS OF EUROPEAN GROUP CONFERENCE PAPERS

**Bianchi, H, Simondi, M & Taylor, I. (eds) Deviance and Control in Europe: Papers from the European Group for the Study of Deviance and Social Control, (London John Wiley & Sons) 1975**

1. Bianchi, H, Simondi, M & Taylor, I.
'Introduction by the Editors

PART 1: NATIONAL REPORTS ON THE STATE OF
CRIMINOLOGY AND DEVIANCY CONTROL

2. Cohen, S. & Taylor, L. 'From psychopaths to outsiders: British Criminology and the National Deviancy conference'
3. Seppilli. T. & Abbozzo, G.G. 'The state of research into social control and deviance in Italy'
4. Bianchi, H. 'Social control and deviance in the Netherlands'
5. Schumann, K. 'Approaching crime and deviance: a Note on the contributions by Scientists, Officials of Social Control and Social Activists During the Last Five Years in West Germany'
6. Dahl, T.S. 'The state of criminology in Norway: A Short Report'

PART 2: PRESENTATIONS ON THE PRISON MOVEMENT IN EUROPE
7. Mathiesen, T. & Roine, W 'The prison movement in Scandinavia'
8. Fitzgerald, M. 'The British Prisoners' Movement: Its Aims and Methods'
9. Donzelot, J. 'The Prison Movement in France'
10. Rauty, R. 'Introductory Note to the Prison Revolts in Italy in 1973'
11. Modona, G.N. 'Reform of the Italian Prison: A Left Perspective'
12. Invernizzi, I. 'Class Struggle in the Prisons: Practical and Theoretical Problems'
13. Dejours, C., Margara, A. & Cohen, S. 'Discussion on Medicine in Prison'
14. Donzelot, J., Ivernizzi, I, McIntosh, M. & Mathieson, T. 'Discussion on Women in Prison

PART 3: SELECTED CONFERENCE PAPERS
15. McIntosh, M. 'New Directions in the Study of Criminal Organization'
16. Makela, K. 'The Societal Tasks of the System of Criminal Law'
17. Ciacci, M. 'Psychiatric Control: A Report on the Italian Situation'
18. Hepworth, M. 'The Criminalisation of Blackmail'

**The European Group for the Study of Deviance and Social Control (eds.) Terrorism and the Violence of the State: Working Papers in European Criminology No. 1. (Hamburg: EGSDSC) 1980**

1. de Sousa Santos, B. 'Some notes on "Terrorism" and State Violence'
2. Scheerer, S. "Law Making in a State of Siege: Some regularities in the legislative response to political violence'
3. Schwinghammer, T. 'Theory and Practice: "The Comments of the Commandos"'

4. Muckenberger, U. 'The "Mescalero Affair" has become a Legal Scandal'
5. de Wit, J. & Ponsaers, P 'The Mescalero Case'
6. Bruckner, P. 'Principils obsta. or: Incitement to Discord'
7. EGSDSC, 'Declaration of the European Group'
8. EGSDSC, 'Advertisement placed in the Weser Kurier published 14.9.1978'

**Brusten, M & Ponsaers, P. (eds.) State Control on Information in the Field of Deviance and Social Control: Working Papers in European Criminology No. 2. (Leuven: EGSDSC) 1981**

Brusten, M & Ponsaers, P. 'Introductory Note'
General Overview of the subject
1. Brusten, M. & Van Outrive, L. 'The relationship between State institutions and the social sciences in the field of deviance and social control'
2. Baratta, A. & Smaus, G 'Comments on the paper of M. Brusten and L. Van Outrive'

NATIONAL REPORTS
3. Brusten, M. 'Social control of criminology and criminologists'.
4. Schumann, K. 'On proper and deviant criminology - Varieties in the production of legitimation for penal law'.
5. Behr, C-P., Gipsen, D., Klien-Sconnefeld S., Naffin, K. & Zillmer, H. 'The use of scientific discoveries for the maintenance and extension of State control - On the effect of legitimation and the utilization of science'.
6. Jepsen, J. 'Control of criminologists - state and science and the state of science in the State of Denmark'.
7. Faugeron, C. 'Les conditions de la recherche en sociologie de la déviance et du contrôle sociale en France'. (With English Summary)

8. Stangl, W. 'Considerations about the process of everyday control over science'.
9. Lapis, T. 'The political economy of the development of Italian Criminology'.
10. Squires, P. 'The policing of knowledge: Criminal statistics and criminal categories'.

CONTRIBUTIONS ON SPECIFIC THEMES
11. Van Kerckvoorde, J. & Kerstemont , F. 'La position des citoyens devant l'automatisation croissante de l'information'. (With English Summary)
12. Young, J. 'The manufacture of news: a critique of the present convergence in mass media theory.'

**Hillyard, P. & Squires, P. (eds.) Securing the State: Politics of Internal Security in Europe: Working Papers in European Criminology No. 3. (Bristol: EGSDSC) 1982**

Hillyard, P. & Squires, P. 'Introductory Note'

I. PRODUCTION OF INSECURITY
1. Dalstra, K. 'The Immanent Structure of Crime Control'.
2. Wright, S. 'The International Trade in the Technology of Repression'.

II ADMINISTERING INSECURITY
3. Brusten, M. 'Police and Politics: Analytical Aspects and Empirical Data Against the Ideology of a 'politically neutral police force'.
4. Jorgensen, B. 'Defending the terrorists: Queen's Counsel before the Diplock Courts'.
5. Hualde, G. & Lezana, J. 'Police action in the Basque Country: the development of repressive measures'.

III SOCIAL INSECURITY
 6.  Squires, P. 'Internal security and Social Insecurity'.
 7.  Miralles, T. & Munagorri, I. 'State Control
     and the Internal Security in Spain'.
 8.  Mosconi, G. & Pisapia, G. 'The stereotype of the
     repentant terrorist: his nature and functions'.
 9.  Smith, P. 'Emergency legislation: the
     Prevention of Terrorism Acts'.

IV CARCERAL INSECURITY
 10.  Heatley, P. & Tomlinson, M. 'The Politics of
      Imprisonment in Ireland: some historic notes'.
 11.  Caldarone, R. & Valeriani, P. 'Prison Politics
      and Prisoners Struggles in Italy'.

**Squires, P. & Hillyard, P. (eds.) Disputing Deviance:
Experience of Youth in the 80s: Working Papers in
European Criminology No. 4. (Bristol: EGSDSC) 1983**

Mosconi, G. & Pavarini, M. 'Introductory Note'

I. THEORETICAL CONTROVERSIES
 1.  Pitch T. 'Adequacy or Obsolescence
     of the Notion of Deviance'.
 2.  Stangl, W. 'The Effect of Penal Control on Society'.
 3.  De Leo, G. 'Decline or Eclipse of
     Juvenile Delinquency'.

II YOUTH AND SOCIAL CONTROL
 4.  Ella, N. 'Transition from Youth
     Protection to Youth Control'.
 5.  Ambroset, S., Carrer, F., Capolucci, A. &
     Gazzola, A. 'Juvenile Delinquency in Italy'.
 6.  Herriger, N 'The Prevention of Juvenile Delinquency
     and the Widening net of Social Control'.
 7.  Loney, M. 'The Youth Opportunities
     Programme: Requiem and Rebirth'

8. Malinowski, P. 'Youth is it a Social Problem'.
9. Ericsson, K. & Stangeland, P. 'Is the Social Control of Youth Really Tightening'.

III SOCIAL MOVEMENTS AND SOCIAL CONTROL

10. Lodi, G. 'The Collective Mobilisation of Youth in the 1970s and 80s'.
11. Uusitalo, P. 'Policing Environmental Conflicts in Finland and Norway'.
12. Gisper, D., Klein-Schonnefeld, S., Naffin, K. & Zillmer, H. 'Analyses on Terrorism'.

**Hillyard, P., Rolston, B. & Tomlinson, M. (eds.) Social movements and Social conflicts: Working Papers in European Criminology No. 5. (EGSDSC) 1984**

Hillyard, P., Rolston, B. & Tomlinson, M. 'Introductory Note'

1. Alapuro, R. 'On Collective Action and the State in Finland, 1900-1930'.
2. Bjornshauge, L. 'Youth riots - Marginal Deviance or Fundamental and Concrete Criticism of Society?'
3. Lezana, J. & Miralles, T. 'Youth in the Basque Country: A Social Movement or a Marginal minority?'
4. Stalstrom, O. 'Profiles in Courage: Problems of Action of the Finnish Gay movement in crisis'.
5. Haukaa, R. 'The Women's Liberation Movement in Norway'.
6. Moerings, M. 'Protest in the Netherlands: Developments in a Pillarised Society'.
7. McCartney, J. 'The Falls Road Taxi Association: A Case Study in the Management of Political Stigma'.
8. Rolston, B. 'The Republican Movement and Elections: An Historical Account'
9. Hillyard, P. 'Popular Justice in Northern Ireland'.

## Rolston, B. (ed.) The State of Information in 1984: Conflict, Social Control and New Technology: Working Papers in European Criminology No. 6. (Jordanstown: EGSDSC) 1985

Rolston, B. 'Introduction'

I. WALES – SOCIETY, ECONOMY AND POLITICS
1. Welsh Campaign for Civil and Political Liberties, 'Women and the Strike: It's a whole way of life'.
2. Evans, J. 'The Peace Movement in Wales'.
3. Rees, T. 'Youth Unemployment, Migration and the Employment of Men and Women in Wales'.
4. Mainwaring, L. 'The South Wales Economy in the Post-War Period'.

II NEW TECHNOLOGY AND ITS CONTRADICTIONS
5. Pounder, C. 'The British Police and Computers: Recent Trends and Developments'.
6. Beaulieu, M. 'The Use of Computers by the Correctional Service of Canada to Registers and Disclose information on Federal Inmates: Comments on the Practices and Principles"
7. Bevere, A. 'Coercive Apparatus and the Use of Computers in Italian Legislation'.
8. Brieske, R. 'New Technology and the deskilling of female Employees'.
9. Scanagatta, S. 'Young People's Use of Microelectronics in Italy'.
10. Stodolsky, D. 'Personal Computers in Educational and Democratic Processes: the American Experience and the Danish Context'.
11. Mathiasen, K. 'The People's Data Project: An Alternative Use for Computers'.

III IDEOLOGY AND THE CONTROL OF INFORMATION

12. Mathiesen, T. 'Criminal Policy at the Crossroads: Report at 'Anhorung zur Situation des Strafvolluges in hessen', Hessichen Lantag, 6 September 1984'.
13. Gronfors, M. & Stalstrom, O. 'Ethical Aspects of the Production of Information on AIDS'.
14. Powell, C. 'Control of Criminology and Legal Policy: the case of Finnish 'Neo-Classicism''.
15. Lloyd, C. & Scola, J. 'Policing Two Nations: Community Crime Prevention and Public Order Policing'.
16. Ward, T. 'Coroners, Police and Deaths in Custody in England: a Historical Perspective'.

**Rolston, B. & Tomlinson, M. (eds.) The Expansion of European Prison Systems: Working Papers in European Criminology No. 7. (Belfast: EGSDSC) 1986**

de Haan, W. & Tomlinson, M. 'Introduction'

A. EXPANSION OF PRISON SYSTEMS

1. de Haan, W. 'Explaining Expansion: The Dutch case'.
2. Scheerer, S. 'Dissolution and Expansion'.
3. Mosconi, B. 'References for a Real Alternative to Prison'
4. Sim, J. 'Working for the Clampdown: Prisons and Politics in England and Wales'.
5. Miralles, T. 'The Spanish Prison Situation in 1985'.
6. Moerings, M. 'Prison Overcrowding in the United States'.
7. Fox, J. 'Conservative Social policy, Social control and Racism: the Politics of New York State Prison expansion, 1975-1985.'

B. PRISON REGIME

8.   Boock, J.B. 'Conditions for Remand prisoners'.
9.   Koch, I. 'Mental and Social Sequelae of Isolation'.
10.  Siegmeirer, U. 'Women in Prison'
11.  Pecic, D. 'Imprisonment of Mothers,
     Punishment for Children: the situation in
     the Federal Republic of Germany'.
12.  Schick, H. 'Everyday Life of Male Prisoners'.
13.  Scraton, P. & Chadwick, K. 'The Experiment
     that went Wrong: the crisis of deaths in
     Custody at the Glenochil Youth Complex'.

C. SPECIAL CATEGORIES

14.  Rolston, B. & Tomlinson, M. 'Long-
     Term Imprisonment in northern ireland:
     Psychological or Political Survival'.
15.  Schubert, M. 'Political Prisoners in West
     Germany: their situation and some consequences
     concerning their rights in respect of the treat-
     ment of political prisoners in international law'.
16.  Janssen, H. 'Political Prisoners: some thoughts on the
     status of politically motivated offenders in Europe'.
17.  Tengeler, S. 'Political justice in Stammheim:
     the case of Peter Jørgen Boock'.
18.  Klaus, M with Prison Justice Group, 'Life
     Imprisonment in the Federal Republic of Germany'.

D. IDEOLOGICAL 'ALTERNATIVES' AND NET-WIDENING

19.  Stålstrom, O. & Gronfors, M. 'Internment
     or Information? On Different Strategies
     for Containing the AIDS Crisis'.
20.  Schwenkle-Omar, I. 'An Outline
     Of Division in Hamburg'.
21.  Powell, C. 'Televising Penal Policy for
     Young Men: a view from Wales'.

**Rolston, B. & Tomlinson, M. (eds.) Civil Rights Public**

## Opinion and the State: Working Papers in European Criminology No. 8. (Belfast: EGSDSC) 1987

Rolston, B. & Tomlinson, M. 'Introduction'

PART ONE
1. de Haan, W. 'Fuzzy Morals and Flakey Politics: the Coming Out of Critical Criminology'.
2. McMahon, M. 'The State of Policing Reform in Toronto'.
3. Durieux, H. 'The Rotterdam Junkie Union and Affiliates'.
4. Smith, S. 'Neglect as Control: Prisoners' Families'.
5. Levi, M. 'Public Opinion, the State and the Control of Business Crime'.
6. Jepsen, J. 'Moral Panics and the Spread of Control Models in Europe'.
7. Wright, S. 'Public Order Technology: 'Less-Lethal Weapons''.
8. van Swaaningen, R. 'The Image of Power: Abolitionism, Emancipation, Authoritarian Idolatry and the Ability of Unbelief'.
9. van Kerckvoorde, J. 'Statistics, Official Statements and Public Rumour'.
10. Campbell, D. & Lee, B. 'Policing Contemporary Britain: Re-Addressing the Balance'.

PART TWO
11. Folguera, P. 'Women: Protagonists of Social Change in Spain, 1975-1986'.
12. Bennun, M. 'The Judiciary in Franco's Spain and in South Africa'.
13. Pastor, S. 'Liberty Versus security: Should Drugs be Illegal?'
14. Carrion, J.S. 'Drugs and the Mass Media: The Social Construction of a Reality'.

**Rolston, B. & Tomlinson, M. (eds.) Justice & Ideology: Strategies for the 1990s. Working Papers in European Criminology No. 9. (Belfast: EGSDSC) 1989**

1. de Celis, J. B. 'Whither Abolitionism?'
2. Chambliss, W.J. 'State Organized Crime'.
3. de Haan, W. 'The Necessity of Punishment in a Just Social Order: A critical Appraisal'.
4. Fijnaut, C. 'The Contemporary Evolution of Criminology in the Netherlands'.
5. Hirvonen, A. 'Forget Criminology: The Radical Strategies of Abolition and Deconstruction'.
6. Knauder, S. 'Justice and Imprisonment in the Light of their Effects on the Ex-Convicts in Two Cultural Settings'.
7. Lacombe, D. 'The Demand for the Criminalisation of Pornography: A State-Made Ideological Construction or a Demand Articulated in Civil Society?'
8. Minkkinen, P. 'The Criminal Myth and Ideology: An Outline for an Exercise in the Semiotics of Criminology'.
9. Mosconi, B. 'The Gozzini Law: Conflict in Reform'.
10. Nielsen, B.G. 'Criminal Justice and Social Service: Conflict or Cooperation in Incest Cases?'
11. Pilgram, A. 'The Politics of Crime Control in Austria: History and Theory'.
12. Platek, M. 'Ideology and Justice: Some Practical Polish Connotations'.
13. Ruggiero, V. 'An Encounter with Realist Criminology'.
14. Ryan, M. & Ward, T. 'Left Realism Against the Rest Revisited: Or Some Particularities of the British'.

15. Stangl, W. 'Who Has the Right to Prosecute? The Reform of Criminal Procedure in the Nineteenth century and the Abolitionist Trend in Contemporary Criminology'.
16. Steinert, H. 'Marxian Theory and Abolitionism: Introduction to a Discussion'.
17. Powell, C. 'Contemporary Criminology: Whatever Happened to the Anarchic Impulse'.
18. Gronfors, M. 'Mediation: An Experiment in Finland'.
19. van Ransbeek, H. 'Reflections on Abolitionist Practice: Some Results of Abolitionist Research on "Petty Crime" in Two Social contexts'.
20. van Swaaningen, R. 'Strategies of Reform: Some Historical Examples'.
21. Wantula, H. 'Deviance and Social Control in Western Europe and Poland'.
22. Weber, H-M. & Wilson, C. 'What is to be Done about Marginalisation and Criminalisation? Some Thoughts on a Comparison between England and Wales and the Federal Republic of Germany'.
23. Van Kerckvoorde, J. 'Criminal Statistics. Crime and the Administration of Criminal Justice'.
24. Hes, J. 'Suppressed Minorities and the Need for Protection and Moral Disapproval'.

**Rolston, B. & Tomlinson, M. (eds.) Gender Sexuality & Social Control: Working Papers in European Criminology No. 10. (Belfast: EGSDSC) 1990**

1. Widerberg, K. 'Female Sexualisation - Learning Subordination through the Body: A New Method and a New Knowledge?'
2. Durieux, H. 'Metaphors on Order and Deviance from the Work of Julia Kristeva'.
3. Kellough, G. 'The 'Ideological Ceiling' of Male Culture'.
4. Eggert, A., & Rolston, B. 'Exporting the

Problem: Abortion and the Law in Ireland'.
5. O'Malley, S. & Hall, G. 'I Have No Past'.
6. Wiemann, B. 'The Rise and Decline of the Care System for Unmarried Mothers and Changing Forms of Social Control'.
7. Ryan, J., Ryan, M. & Ward, T. 'Feminism, Philanthropy and Social Control: The The Origins of Women's Policing in England'.
8. Skidmore, P. 'Genderising Deviance: News Media Constructions of Women and Crime'.
9. Prieur, A. 'The Male Role and Sexual Assault'.
10. Berge, A. 'Sexual Violence: The Gender Question as a Challenge to Progressive Criminology and Social Theory'.
11. Smyth, M. 'Kincora: Towards an Analysis'.
12. Finstad, L. 'Sexual Offenders out of Prison: Principles for a Realistic Utopia'.
13. van Swaaningen, R. 'Feminism, Criminology and Criminal Law: Troublesome Relationship'.
14. Meima, M. 'Sexual Violence, Criminal Law and Abolitionism'.
15. Berjerse, J. & Kool, R. 'The Traitorous Temptation of Criminal Justice: Deceptive Appearances? The Dutch Women's Movement, Violence against Women and the Criminal Justice System'
16. de Jongste, W. 'The Protection of Women by the Criminal Justice System? Reflections on Feminism, Abolitionism and Power'.

**Ruggiero, V. (ed) Citizenship, Human Rights and Minorities: Rethinking Social Control in the New Europe [XX Conference of The European Group for the Study of Deviance and Social Control, Padova 3-6 September 1992] (Athens: Ant. N. Sakkoulas Publishers). 1996**

1. Ruggerio, V. 'Introduction'.
2. Melossi, D. 'Weak Leviathan and strong democracy: two styles of social control as they apply to the construction of a European Community'.
3. Van Outrive, L. 'Legislation and decision making in Europe. International police cooperation and human rights'.
4. Van Outrive, L. 'European Parliament Committee on civil liberties and internal affairs working document on police cooperation'.
5. Pastore, M. ''Boundary' conflicts around and inside the European Community'.
6. Krarup, O. 'The democratic 'no' and its legal meaning'.
7. Klovedal Reich, E. 'A utopia for a living people'.
8. Dahlerup, D. 'More women than men said 'no' to Maastricht'.
9. Wilson. C. ''Going to Europe': Prisoners' right and the effectiveness of European standards'.
10. Yeates, N. 'Appeals to citizenship in the unification of Europe: the political and social context of the EC's third programme to combat poverty'.
11. Calamti, S. 'The violation of human rights in Northern Ireland'.
12. Ruggiero, V. 'The Italian political refugees in Paris'.
13. Edwards, J. 'Group rights v. individual rights – The case of race conscious policies'
14. Scholter, M. & Trenx, H-Z. 'The social construction of the 'asylum abuses' in the Federal Republic of Germany'.

## Georgoulas, S. (ed) The Politics of Criminology: Critical studies on deviance and social control [38th Annual Conference of European Group] (Zurich: LIT). 2012

Georgoulas, S. 'Introduction'.

PART 1 CRITICAL CRIMINOLOGY: FROM THE PAST TO THE FUTURE

1. Georgoulas, S. 'Radix of radical criminology – Hesiod'.
2. Malloch, M. & Munro, B. 'Crime, Critique and Utopia'.
3. Bell, E. 'Neoliberal crime policy: Who profits?'.
4. Ruggiero, V. 'Criminal enterprise, identity and repertoires of action'.

Part 2 Contemporary Critical Criminology Case Studies

5. Orr, D. 'Lehman brothers, Obama and the case for corporate regulation'.
6. Norris, P. 'Public order policing in the UK: From paramilitary policing to neighbourhood policing?'.
7. Hayes, M. 'The imposition of internment without trial in Northern Ireland, August 1971: Causes, consequences and lessons'.
8. Delimitsos, K. 'Restructuring government's expertise on violence and delinquency in France'.
9. Karamalidou, A. 'The educative and emancipatory potential of human rights in prisons: Lessons from English and Dutch prisons'.
10. Sorvatzioti, D. 'Poor criminals in prison: violation of their fundamental human rights'.
11. Nikolopoulos, G. 'The criminalisation of the migration policy and the new European territorialities of social control'.
12. Ericson, C. 'Programmes for abusive men – results from a Swedish evaluation study'.
13. Peroni, C. 'Gender, violence and law in the post-feminist and queer debate in Italy'.
14. Harris, J. ''Little innocents no more': criminalising

childhood and sexuality in the UK'.

PART 3 INTRODUCING CRITICAL CRIMINOLOGICAL
RESEARCH – UNIVERSITY OF THE AEGEAN

15. Sotiris, P. 'Revolt or deviance? Greek intellectuals
    and the December 2008 revolt of the Greek youth'.
16. Voulvouli, A. 'LGBT movements, biopolitics
    and new criminology: a preliminary research
    in Eastern Mediterranean Region'.
17. Demeli, T. 'Going through the gates: Prison
    and motherhood, adjustment and solidarity'.
18. Kitsiou, A. 'Focus group, a research
    method to analyse free software move-
    ment and social construction of crime'.
19. Sarantdis, D. 'A participant observa-
    tion of police culture in Greece'.
20. Rinis, N. 'Cinema codes and crime: qualita-
    tive analysis of the movie 'Hoodwinked''.
21. Kouroutzas, C. 'Forensic science and criminology: the
    role of medical coroners: a pilot qualitative research'.

**Bell, E. (ed) No Borders: Immigration and the Politic
of Fear (Chambery: Universite' de Savoie). 2012**

Scott, D. 'Foreword: The European Group
for the Study of Deviance and Social Control'.
1. Bell, E. 'Introduction'.
2. Blanchard, E., Clochard, O. & Rodier, C. 'The
   new frontiers of immigration policy'.
3. Kaczmarek-Firth, A. 'An examination of the
   effects of contradictions in Globalisation
   on Europe's Migration laws'.
4. Fischer, N. 'Policing and the rule of law: a critique of
   the French deportation of unauthorised immigrants'.
5. Santorso, S. 'Migration and deten-
   tion: changes in Italian legislation'.
6. Crocitti, S. 'Do immigration policies

work? The case of Italy'.
7.  Bracci, F. 'The 'Chinese deviant': Building the perfect enemy in a local area'.
8.  Fabini, G. 'Buongiorno, documenti'. Police identity checks in Italy: Stories from migrants and local police officers'.
9.  Parra, C. 'Latinos by nationality and illegal by ethnicity: otherness and the condition of fear in the US'.'
10. Michalowski, R. 'Re-bordering social space in Arizona's war on the immigrant 'other''.
11. Hoenig, R. 'Monsters on the borderscape of detention: Some Australian print media depictions of residents of Woomera Village and asylum seekers in immigration detention'.

# APPENDIX 3
## COORDINATORS OF THE EUROPEAN GROUP 1973-2013

Mario Simondi (1973 – 1977)
Didi Gipser (1977 – 1983)
Sabine Klein-Schonnefeld (1983 – 1985)
Karen Leander (1985 – 2009)
David Scott (2009 – 2012)
Emma Bell (2012 – current)

European Group for the Study of
Deviance and Social Control

email: europeangroupcoordinator@gmail.com
website: www.europeangroup.org